WALLENBERG IS HERE!

The True Story About How Raoul Wallenberg Faced Down the Nazi War Machine & the Infamous Eichmann & Saved Tens of Thousands of Budapest Jews

By

Carl L. Steinhouse

© 2002 by Carl L. Steinhouse. All rights reserved.

No part of this book may be reproduced, stored in a retrieval system, or transmitted by means, electronic, mechanical, photocopying, recording, or otherwise, without written consent from the author.

ISBN: 1-4033-4558-9 (e-book)
ISBN: 1-4033-4559-7 (Paperback)

Library of Congress Control Number: 2002108220

This book is printed on acid free paper.

Printed in the United States of America
Bloomington, IN

1st Books - rev. 11/11/02

Dedication

In memory of Martha Levi and Georgina Faludi, friends who were victims of Nazism

Hundreds of people, packed into this airless room and sitting in their own waste, seemed beyond caring. Shocked, even with his experience, by this new demonstration of Nazi depravity and brutality, he stood there silent and appalled. Then, some stirring caught his attention—it buzzed through the room. He caught the whisper, "Wallenberg is here!"

PREFACE AND ACKNOWLEDGEMENTS

For the most part, this story was driven by the facts I amassed from interviews, a visit to Budapest and volumes of written materials. For the continuity and flow of the story, certain events are not in exact chronological order and some are combined; some characters are amalgamations of more than one real person, but based on my research of what the Nazis actually did in Budapest and elsewhere. For example, the roundup scenes in the Hungarian provincial town of Mukachevo occurred. However, the ballerina, Teca Zöldi, SS Lieutenant Hans Kröner and the Jewish underground leader Solomon, are not real people. What happened to the ballerina, however, was not atypical because it was common for the Nazis to use Jewish entertainers for their own enjoyment before murdering them. The crimes committed by Kröner were representative of the conduct of the SS not only in Mukachevo, but also throughout Hungary, and there were many Solomons in the Jewish underground, but too lightly armed and insufficient in number to do anything but harass the Germans. József and Roza Friedman, Keleman and Gitta Kaplun, and Izsak and Viktoria Kamya, Darda Swartse and Samulka are fictional but the events involving them were taken from actual incidents that happened to far too many Jews.

Hungarian names begin with the family name and then the personal name. I have reversed that order for the convenience of the English-speaking readers.

I am grateful to Dr. Peter Siegler, Dr. Georgina Faludi and George Sebok, victims who shared with me their painful memories of Budapest in 1944 and 1945. The published books of those who worked with Wallenberg in Budapest, such as Per Anger and Lars Berg, or those who were saved by him, such as Agnes Adachi, were important to my research, as were numerous other books on Wallenberg. I am also grateful to the Anti-Defamation League of B'nai B'rith and to Rachel Oestreicher Bernheim of the Raoul Wallenberg Committee of the United States for the materials they provided to me.

The story, of course, is almost as much about Adolph Eichmann and Nazism as it is about Raoul Wallenberg. Transcripts from the trial of Eichmann in Jerusalem were invaluable as were the many books written about him.

Many authors provided valuable information on Nazi leaders and insights into Nazism: William L. Shirer, Hannah Arendt, Ronald Lewin, Jeno Lévi, Lucy Davidowicz, Saul Friedlander, Richard Breitman, Ronald Lewin, Hannah Vogt, Sebastian Haffner, Joachim Remak, Leni Yahl, Dr. Michael Berenbaum, among others. My thanks to Professor Stephen M. Berk of Union College (Schenectady, N.Y.) for providing me with tapes of his lectures on the Holocaust and Nazism.

I am indebted to Fred and Allyne Schwartz, Joe Bondi, Ray Carlson, Dr. Peter Siegler and my children for their valuable insights and comments after reading part or all of my manuscript and to author Hollis Alpert and Janine Warsaw for the valuable criticisms of my early works. I appreciated the encouragement of Professor Nancy Shuster, who made me believe I really was an author and not merely a writer. I am in everlasting debt to my editor, Susan C. Winslow and her tough love approach to the manuscript. Any flaws in the manuscript are from my own failure to follow advice.

I owe more than I can express to my wife, Diana, who put up with my long hours and grouchiness at interruptions. She also suffered through reading my first and second drafts with grace and provided significant insights.

Carl Steinhouse

PROLOGUE

Two men of the same generation, dedicated to their respective tasks, but with widely disparate backgrounds, nurturing, environment and education, arrived in Budapest in 1944, fated to be locked in a great historical battle for human lives. The German, Adolph Eichmann, was determined to exterminate the Jews; the Swede, Raoul Wallenberg, was committed to frustrating that goal. The casual observer might reasonably conclude the contest to be one-sided, the German backed by the determined leaders, military might and ruthlessness of the Third Reich, and the Swede supported only by the certainty of his moral position, his ingenuity, wits, nerve and diplomatic standing, and American funds. Such a casual observer, however, couldn't have been more wrong.

***

His father, Raoul Wallenberg, a Swedish naval officer, had already died of cancer by the time Raoul Gustav Wallenberg was born in his maternal grandparents' summer home in Kapptsta, Sweden, on August 4, 1912. His mother, Maj Wising, daughter of Sweden's first neurosurgeon, Dr. Per Wising, raised Raoul, helped by her mother and her father-in-law, the diplomat Gustav Oskar Wallenberg. When Raoul was six, Maj married Frederik von Dardel, who treated the boy as his own son. Maj and Frederik gave Raoul two siblings, Guy and Nina.

The famous Swedish Wallenbergs were divided into two branches. One branch dedicated itself to increasing its fortune from the Wallenberg industrial and financial empire, while the other branch devoted itself to public service as advisers to kings and prime ministers of Sweden, and as diplomats. Raoul belonged to this second branch of the family.

As a child, Raoul read voraciously, including all thirty-five volumes of a Swedish encyclopedia. He had a passion for battleships, planes and all forms of construction. Indifferent to competitive sports, he enjoyed hiking, running and bicycling. A top student in school, he excelled in languages and debating. He mastered English, French, German and Russian. Though he had talents as a painter, color blindness dashed any hopes of painting as a career. On graduation from high school, he served a tour of duty in the Swedish military.

Grandfather Wallenberg, whom Raoul called "Farfar," took the young man under his wing and guided his education, training and experiences, hoping to mold a citizen of the world, prepared for a career in international banking. With Farfar's encouragement Raoul enrolled in the University of Michigan. His classmates described him as fearless, unassuming, with a great sense of humor, often self-deprecating, with an uncanny ability to imitate and mimic both people and animals. His professors called him unusually bright, an impassioned and effective debater and someone who showed great insight in finding simple solutions to complex problems. He also had a wanderlust that propelled him to hitchhike throughout the United States and Mexico. He graduated in 1935, the top student in his class of eleven hundred, with a degree in architecture.

Farfar arranged for Raoul to work in South Africa in order to obtain commercial business experience and then sent him to Palestine in early 1936 to work in a friend's bank in Haifa. There he first learned about Nazi atrocities against the Jews.

Wallenberg returned to Stockholm in late 1936, deciding that banking wasn't for him. As far as working for the Wallenberg organization, his cousins, who controlled it, were not too keen on that, so he secured a position with a Hungarian Jew, Kálmán Lauer, who had a food export business in Stockholm. As a Jew, Lauer was no longer able to travel throughout Europe, even to visit his home and family in Budapest, so Wallenberg took on the task of marketing Lauer's food products in German-occupied Europe. In dealing with the Nazis, he gained valuable knowledge about them, coming to understand how authority and official-looking documents impressed them and won their respect. He observed also, firsthand, Nazi harassment of Jews in all the occupied territories.

***

Karl "Adolph" Eichmann was born on March 19, 1906, in the German Rhineland city of Solingen, but he was raised in the Austrian city of Linz-on-the-Danube. His mother died when he was ten. His father, an office manager in public transportation, created an austere and loveless home for his children. Both he and his second wife were strict disciplinarians, giving Adolph nowhere to turn for nurturing.

As a rebellious teenager, Adolph joined a gang that dedicated itself to beating up Jewish youths. He did not complete high school and later dropped out of technical school, blaming his school problems on his authoritarian father. Adolph so resented his father that he renounced the elder Eichmann's religion, eventually declaring himself to be a *Gottgläubiger*, the Nazi term for those who had broken with Christianity.

He joined the Nazi Party, accepting Nazi dogma that the Germans had lost World War I solely because of the traitorous leaders of the civilian government, Bolsheviks and the greedy Jews. He adopted, without critical analysis, the wildly disparate Nazi claims that the Jews were, at once, both greedy capitalists and Marxist Communists. But he never really knew or understood the Nazi program or its bible, *Mein Kampf*.

After Eichmann lost his job in 1932 as a traveling salesman for an Austrian oil company, Ernst Kaltenbrunner, a leader in the *Schutzstaffen* (SS), recruited him for that elite unit of state security and Hitler's bodyguards, even though he considered Eichmann his physical, social and mental inferior. In 1934, Eichmann joined an SS brigade in Germany, where he took his training. Bored with his assigned desk job as a file clerk, he applied for, and was hired by, Heinrich Himmler's Security Service, the SD. Eventually, he was put in charge of the Gestapo's newly established Jewish Department.

Eichmann impressed his superiors with his diligence. He learned everything he could about the Jews and showed himself to be a stickler for organization and detail. His colleagues did not particularly like him. They described him as a colorless officer: pedantic, punctilious, obsessed with neatness and order and ingratiatingly subservient to his superiors, snapping to attention whenever one was in the vicinity. A subordinate characterized him as a person with lower-class habits and mentality–boorish, crude and cowardly, one who avoided, where possible, encounters with the affluent. Flying terrified him and he lived in constant fear of being assassinated.

As head of the Jewish Department, Eichmann studied Zionism, reading Theodor Herzl's *The Jewish State*, *The Encyclopedia Judaica* and Adolph Bohm's *History of Zionism*. Ultimately, he prepared an SS orientation pamphlet on the subject. He spent a short time in Palestine before the British threw him out. He picked up a few Hebrew words and liked to brag to superiors, and later, warn Jews, that he was fluent in the language. The task of implementing the Final Solution–the extermination of the Jews of Europe-fell on Eichmann, given his organizational abilities, his skill with minute details and his own trumpeted knowledge of Judaism. With great efficiency he directed the rounding up and transporting of Jews in the various countries of Europe to the death camps.

CHAPTER 1

Stockholm, Bromma Airport, July 6, 1944

With a light breeze and only a few high clouds drifting lazily across the sky, Raoul Wallenberg, standing on the tarmac waiting to board the German passenger plane, felt at least one small sense of relief—a predicted smooth flight to his first stop, Berlin. Everything else about this trip to Budapest was fraught with pitfalls and danger—the Germans wouldn't be beyond killing him if they found out his mission was being funded and directed by the Americans, or that his contact in Stockholm was the American, Ivar Olsen, reputedly connected with the American spy agency, the OSS.

Wallenberg had spent two full days at the Swedish Foreign Ministry reading dispatches from the legation in Budapest. What Colonel Adolph Eichmann, the chief of the Gestapo's Jewish Department, had done and was now doing to the Jews in Hungary chilled his blood. The last surviving Jewish community in Europe gave Wallenberg's mission both a sense of urgency and destiny—the saving of European Jewry. Every day counted so he'd moved up his planned departure from August to July because Eichmann was shipping out ten to twelve thousand Jews a day to Auschwitz and certain death.

The enormity of Wallenberg's mission had him questioning his own abilities. *A half million lives hang in the balance,* he thought, *and I'm supposed to save them. What have I taken on? What qualifications do I have? I must be out of my mind!*

Wallenberg had deposited the first installment of $100,000 from the American Jewish Joint Distribution Committee, which funded his efforts, to his special Swedish bank account in Stockholm. Prominent Hungarian exiles had given him a crash course in Hungarian politics, a picture of the general conditions prevailing in Hungary, and the names of political figures who could be helpful. His friend and former employer, Kálmán Lauer, a Hungarian Jew whose family was trapped in Budapest, had given him a similar list of the names of business and professional people. Others had added to the store of information on resources, clandestine and open, that might be available to him. Wallenberg also had some personal knowledge of Budapest through his business trips there representing Lauer's food export business.

The Auschwitz Protocols, a report from Jews who escaped that death camp, detailed the horrors of the extermination camps, giving substance to rumors too horrible to be believed.

A small group had come to the airport to see him off—Lauer, Fritz Hollander, a businessman and leader in the Jewish community and the World Jewish Congress, and the Stockholm Rabbi, Marcus Ehrenpreis. Wallenberg smiled inwardly, recalling the rabbi's initial strong opposition to his appointment to the mission–a young privileged protestant boy, too immature and brash, and too ready to talk about payoffs and bribes to save lives.

Ehrenpreis hadn't spared the harsh words at their first meeting. "If I may be blunt, you're too mediocre for the mission. Even the Germans approve of you." But the persistent Wallenberg had brought the rabbi around to his way of thinking that any course of action, if it saved lives, was appropriate. Eventually, the rabbi had become one of his staunchest supporters.

Looking at his visitors, Wallenberg shook his head in feigned umbrage. "I see that no one from the Foreign Ministry is here to see me off."

"Are you really surprised?" laughed Lauer. "You ran roughshod over them."

Wallenberg knew exactly what Lauer meant. Wallenberg had insisted that he not be hindered by rules of diplomacy and bureaucratic red tape, that he not answer to any bosses, that he prepare reports only when he felt it necessary and that to save lives, he must have the freedom to do whatever he wanted, whenever he wanted. Over the objections of the Foreign Ministry, King Gustav had agreed to Wallenberg's terms.

Hollander chuckled. "The Foreign Office almost choked on your pièce de résistance, your proposed use of bribes and payoffs. How undiplomatic! How un-Swedish! Our politicians and diplomats are timid to a fault and absolutely horrified at the possibility of scandal."

"Living for years in the shadow of the Russian and German giants has made cowards of our leaders," Ehrenpreis added. He turned his gaze on Wallenberg. "My friend, you're terrifying the Foreign Ministry. I just hope you don't have to call on them for help."

Wallenberg pursed his lips. "I know. We can thank the king, who overruled the cringing diplomats and appointed me first secretary of the Budapest Legation and his personal representative. The key to success is my diplomatic status. The king even agreed to request a personal audience for me with Regent Horthy."

"Oh, that must have really sat well with the Foreign Minister," Hollander remarked sarcastically.

Wallenberg laughed. "I recall the Foreign Minister's very last words to me." Hooking his thumbs in his windbreaker as if he had suspenders, Wallenberg puffed out his chest and strutted around the tarmac. He lowered his voice an octave. "Harump, Mr. Wallenberg, just remember that you are now a Swedish diplomat. You must carry on the fine tradition of the Foreign Service, harump, harump. Do not embarrass Sweden or your legation in Budapest, harump."

The three visitors roared at his imitation of the pompous foreign minister. Lauer wasn't surprised; he was used to Wallenberg's antics. Wallenberg would come back from selling trips, imitating, in caricature, this pompous German ambassador, or that German field marshal, or even Hitler himself.

Nodding his head toward the two knapsacks that constituted Wallenberg's luggage, Lauer asked, "What are you going to do with that old secondhand revolver you packed? You could have bought a better weapon than that."

Wallenberg shrugged, "I didn't want to waste money I could use to bribe Nazis. Besides, the gun is only to give me courage. I don't ever plan to use it."

The rabbi looked Wallenberg over—hiking boots and windbreaker, with two stuffed knapsacks slung over his shoulder and laughed. "You look more like a Boy Scout than a high-ranking Swedish diplomat. But that very well may be your saving grace."

Wallenberg held up the long trench coat draped over his arm. "I'll change to this when I reach Budapest. That, and my Anthony Eden homburg should fool the Nazis into thinking I'm a diplomat."

The engines of the waiting prop plane sputtered to a start. "Gentlemen, it's time to take my leave."

The rabbi, overcome by emotion, raised his arms for a traditional Hebrew benediction. "May God bless thee and preserve thee. May the Lord make His face to shine upon thee and be gracious unto thee. May the Lord lift up his countenance unto thee and grant thee peace."

"Thank you, Rabbi, that means a lot. You have placed high expectations on me." He looked into the Ehrenpreis's moist eyes. "With the Wallenberg tradition behind me, there is no limit to what can be accomplished."

The rabbi nodded. "There's a Talmudic saying, 'Those who set off on a mission of humanity can be assured of God's special protection.'" He took Wallenberg's hands in his, cleared his throat and said huskily, "You are in his hands, I am sure."

Wallenberg checked his pockets—for the fourth time. He'd stuffed them with the letters from Hungarians in Sweden to their relatives in Budapest and with his lists of corrupt Hungarian passport officials and underground anti-Nazis who could prove helpful. All the papers were still there. With a wave, he turned, climbed the steps to the airplane and disappeared into the cabin.

***

The three Jews watched the German plane taxi down the runway. Ehrenpreis turned to Lauer, putting his arm around his shoulder. "A very courageous young man, this Wallenberg of yours."

Lauer sighed. "True, and he'll need all the bravery he can muster."

Tempelhof Airfield, Berlin, Several Hours Later

His sister, Nina, and her husband, Gunnar Lagergren, waved to Wallenberg from the tarmac as he stepped off the plane. His lanky sister, with sharp, strong, facial features not unlike Wallenberg himself, but with lively, wide blue eyes, threw her arms around him.

Gunnar took one of Wallenberg's knapsacks and led him to the waiting car. They climbed in.

Nina took his hand. "You will come home with us, Raoul. We have reserved nice accommodations tomorrow for you on the train to Budapest." There were no flights to Budapest so Wallenberg would have to take the Budapest Express train from Berlin's Anhalter Bahnhof station.

He kissed her tenderly on the cheek. "My dear Nina, forgive me, but I must leave on the first available train. We'll get together soon and catch up on old times. The war can't last much longer."

"But Raoul, there are no seats on the train to Budapest until tomorrow. There is nothing that can't wait one day, is there?"

Before he could answer, the air raid sirens wailed. Gunnar turned around. "I'm sorry, but we'll have to pull over and go down into the air raid shelter. It's the Allied bombers again."

They joined others on the street scurrying for the shelters. Seated on a bench in the murky shelter, Wallenberg clasped and unclasped his hands continually. He winced at the muffled roar of explosions and the swaying of the overhead light fixtures. The color drained from his face. He looked at his sister, smiling sheepishly. "I've never been under a bombing attack before."

She squeezed his shoulder. "I can't say I'm used to it, but I have become more stoic about it. They say it's the bombs you don't hear that get you."

He nodded.

Nina's face brightened. "I have some good news for you. I'm pregnant."

That seemed to get Wallenberg's mind off the air raid and he began chatting excitedly. "I'm going to be an uncle! What do you think about that? This is great news. You must let me know as soon as the baby is born."

The all clear sounded. While they walked back to the car, Nina frowned and seized his hand. "Tell me, Raoul, will you be in danger in Budapest?"

"Don't be silly," he said reassuringly. "I'll have an administrative job in the legation. Besides, as a diplomat from a neutral, nonbelligerent country, I'm fully protected. How dangerous can that be? But it is I who should be worried, not you. With the Allies bombing Berlin daily, you are in far more danger."

They climbed into the car. Wallenberg looked directly at his sister. "Now please, take me to the railway station immediately. I must catch the next train out."

"Without a seat?" She protested. "Raoul, you are mad."

He half smiled and shrugged. "You're not the first to tell me that. But trust me, dear sister, it's important."

Carl L. Steinhouse

The Budapest Express, Late Afternoon

Once in the rail terminal, Wallenberg donned his long trench coat and set the homburg on his head. His reflection in a glass pane told him that he looked a little more official than when he'd debarked the plane.

As his sister had warned, the Budapest Express was packed with German troops returning to the Eastern Front. There were no seats. Wallenberg squeezed through the corridor, avoiding the chatting and sleeping bodies overflowing the compartments until he finally found a small unoccupied space on the floor. He dropped his knapsacks and sat on them. The odor of men in close contact assaulted his nostrils. It would be a long night, but he didn't mind. He'd use the time memorizing the lists stuffed in his pocket; then he'd tear them up and toss them out the train window, a few shredded pieces at a time.

He caught snippets of excited conversation by the soldiers that things were getting desperate on the Eastern Front and all leaves had been canceled. Occasionally, he'd get up and look out the window at the scenery rushing by. The effects of the Allied carpet-bombing were readily apparent in the skeletons of yesterday's towns, some still smoldering.

As darkness descended, he could see his reflection in the glass, riding silently alongside him. He stared at his trench coat, the collar pulled up so that it touched the back of his hat. He fell into a contemplative silence, then smiled, *I look more like a saboteur than a Swedish diplomat—and I'm probably a little of both.*

The smile faded when he thought again about the task facing him. From the Foreign Ministry dispatches, he knew that from May to the end of June Eichmann had shipped to the death camps, more than 400,000 Hungarian Jews—that was virtually all the Jews in the provinces. He shook his head—*400,000!* Any day now, Eichmann would be turning his attention to Budapest, if he has not already done so.

A freight train, going in the opposite direction, suddenly whooshed by, giving Wallenberg a start. He shuddered. It didn't take long to figure out why. That train might be carrying thousands of Jews to their death in Auschwitz or some other concentration camp.

Wallenberg thought about Eichmann, whom the Jews called *Der Bluthund*, the Bloodhound. What kind of a man could commit such atrocities? If only this mission had been started in March when Eichmann had stormed into Hungary. Three precious months and nearly a half million lives wasted.

His mouth clamped tight, he tried again to grapple with the enormity of the crime. How had the Nazis led the German nation into the grotesque "Final Solution," the extermination of all European Jewry? Wallenberg couldn't still his mind as the train raced relentlessly forward to his confrontation with Eichmann's killing machine.

How had the Nazis imparted that monstrous, merciless program to German officialdom and the German people? Why did so many accept it and participate? What had happened two years ago?

CHAPTER 2

Over Two Years Before, Berlin, Reich Security headquarters in Wannsee, January 20, 1942

On this brisk winter morning, Lieutenant Colonel Adolph Eichmann rose at dawn, hardly able to contain his excitement. Three months ago, *Reichsführer* Heinrich Himmler had personally promoted him to *Obersturmbannführer*, lieutenant colonel, and assigned him an important role in carrying out the Final Solution to the Jewish question, a term Eichmann took credit for coining. He had spent weeks preparing the agenda for this meeting at 56 AM-Grosseu, an imposing three-story villa nestled in the park–like setting at Wannsee, a fashionable neighborhood in southwestern Berlin. Formerly the home of a Prussian aristocrat, it was now headquarters of General Reinhard Heydrich, head of Reich Security and administrator of concentration camps, and one of Eichmann's bosses.

He dressed with his usual scrupulous precision, gulped down a hasty breakfast and hurried to the ballroom. On the long conference table he neatly laid out sixteen copies of the necessary papers, one set for each participant at the conference. Then, almost reverently, he placed before each chair, sixteen brass nameplates representing the elite of the Schutzstaffen, the SS, and selected undersecretaries in the civilian government of the Third Reich. Never before had he been in the company of so many important men.

With two hours to go before the meeting, Eichmann bundled himself up against the cold in his gray SS greatcoat and cap and set out for a walk in the garden. As he strolled slowly along the path overlooking the lake, Grosser Wannsee, he left boot prints in the light snow covering. The morning sun peeked over the horizon through broken cloud cover, its splintered orange rays reflecting off the mirror-like lake, the villa and the bare trees.

Taking in the peaceful setting and the fact that this villa was also the German headquarters of the world's best known crime fighting agency, Interpol, he smiled thinly. He appreciated the ironic contrast to the purpose of the conference—to plan and initiate the mass extermination of a people on a scale never before attempted by modern man. He knew the enemies of the Third Reich would call it the world's greatest crime. But he and his colleagues were convinced that the biological base of European Jewry had to be destroyed in order to ensure the survival of the German people and the Thousand-year Reich prophesied by the Führer. As the acknowledged expert specialist on the Jewish Question, he would soon be sharing the limelight with the top leaders of the SS and the government. Quite an achievement for a school dropout his father said would never amount to anything. Well, the old bastard could rot in hell.

Eichmann's self-congratulatory musings were interrupted by footsteps. His immediate superior, General Heinrich Müller, strolled toward him from the other direction. Eichmann disliked him. With Müller, Eichmann thought, you never knew where you stood.

The short, stocky, block-headed Müller, with the expressionless face, looked like a peasant masquerading in an SS uniform. Stubborn and opinionated, he wasn't even a member of the Nazi Party, yet he had the respect of Himmler and Heydrich for his blind obedience and willingness to take on any dirty task. Müller was a man of few words. His subordinates called him "the great Sphinx"—but never to his face.

Müller nodded. Eichmann saluted smartly and clicked his heels. "*Heil* Hitler! Everything is ready for the conference, General, though I admit to being a little nervous about how the Reich Civil Service will react to our well thought-out program."

Eichmann wasn't worried about the SS attendees at the conference—they would wholeheartedly support the annihilation of the Jews. But the Civil Service politicians? They were a big question mark. This would be their first exposure to the plan and their initial involvement in its implementation. Without their full cooperation, the SS alone could not carry out the operation on such a massive scale.

Müller half scowled, half grunted, not bothering to return the salute. "Don't worry, those civilian toadies will come around, especially now that we are at war with the Americans." He paused and smiled. "Besides we'll shoot those who don't agree. Yes?" The general strode away without further comment or any farewell.

Eichmann nodded at Müller's retreating back. Eichmann considered war with America as a gift dropped in his lap. For years, the Führer had striven to avoid such a war, at least until he could dispose of Europe–it was certainly no secret in the SS and the Abwehr, the German counterintelligence.

Eichmann folded his arms across his chest. The craven *Abwehr* operatives, he thought, currying favor with the Führer, fed Hitler what he wanted to hear, playing up the importance of the American isolationist movement and the growth of the German-American Bund as evidence of the lack of will of the American people to wage war. The illusion of continued American non-involvement had been shattered by the Japanese attack on Hawaii. The Führer, acting bravely and against the advice of some of his cowardly generals, decided to join Germany's Japanese ally and declare war on the United States. Eichmann couldn't believe those generals would risk their careers with cowardly sniveling at taking on what they called "the sleeping giant."

Eichmann did not share those views. On the contrary, he was delighted with the developments. His career would be advanced because the widening of the war would free the Führer from worries of how Germany looked in the eyes of the world, particularly the Americans. Now, the Führer will have no inhibitions about exterminating the Jews. Eichmann would be given the opportunity to establish his competency in the eyes of the Führer himself.

The conference, postponed once after the Japanese attack on Hawaii, had taken on a new vitality, giving even greater breadth to the Final Solution. As a result, Eichmann's role in it had increased exponentially. Smiling, he addressed the mute, leafless trees. "Nothing can stay my hand now, nothing."

Eichmann took out a small nail file and carefully cleaned and smoothed the nails on each finger. He would look his best for all those important representatives of the Third Reich. He glanced at his watch. It was time. He headed back to the villa.

The conference had been arranged in the strictest secrecy. Given the magnitude of the operation, Eichmann had no illusions that the Final Solution could be kept under wraps for very long. That was fine with him since it would propel his ascent to fame and fortune. He looked down at his jackboots and grimaced at the accumulated snow and mud covering the high polish. That would never do. He couldn't abide sloppiness and filth. He'd have to clean his boots before the conference convened.

Wallenberg is here!

Climbing the broad white stone steps to the balustraded veranda that girded the back of the mansion's main floor, Eichmann pushed open one of the large, arched double doors. His heels clicked loudly as he crossed the polished Carrara marble floor.

When he reached the imposing curved staircase, he put one foot on the third step, bent over and wiped off his boot with his handkerchief; he repeated the process for the other boot. Satisfied, he smoothed his form-fitting jacket. His ascendancy in the ranks of the SS was about to begin.

Some of the early arrivals, assembled in the wood paneled reception hall, were engaged in animated conversation spurred on, undoubtedly, by the free flow of liquor served by the butler and his staff. Eichmann, who never felt comfortable in social situations involving the upper class, accepted a glass of schnapps and immediately took refuge in the large, empty conference hall.

The lowest ranking SS officer at the conference, Eichmann represented the Berlin Center for Jewish Emigration, also known as *Dienststelle Eichmann*, the Eichmann Authority. He sat at the table arranging and re-arranging his papers in neat, exact piles. He looked around at the arched windows heavily draped with dark curtains. The intricately contoured wooden moldings on the walls framed finely grained mahogany paneling bearing light sconces. But for the Final Solution, he thought, he would never have had the opportunity to be in such a grand aristocratic room.

As the assemblage, still immersed in conversation, started to drift into the conference hall, Eichmann rose and stood stiffly behind his chair, trying to hide his nervousness. He recognized at least two of the undersecretaries of the Third Reich, Dr. Gerhart Klopfer of the Party Chancellery and Wilhelm Stuckart of the Interior Ministry. Two of his superiors in the SS, Generals Heinrich Müller and Otto Hofmann, strolled in engrossed in conversation, paying Eichmann no heed. Nevertheless, he snapped to attention, almost as a reflex action.

Fifteen attendees and a woman stenographer took their assigned seats. The room fell silent, all eyes turning toward the door as the sixteenth attendee, Lieutenant General Reinhard Heydrich, entered the room with three armed bodyguards. The officials all stood. Shucking his cap and greatcoat into the arms of a bodyguard, Heydrich took his seat in the middle of the long conference table. He raised his right hand and lowered it, palm down, motioning the group to resume their seats.

Heydrich pulled a document from his leather folder. He cleared his throat loudly. "Under orders from our Führer, *Reichsmarschall* Goering has prepared this directive to me." He held up the paper. "I quote, 'I hereby commission you to make all necessary preparation, in the organizational, material and financial sense, to bring about a total solution of the Jewish problem in the German sphere of influence in Europe. Other government agencies are instructed to cooperate whenever called upon.'"

Heydrich glanced around the room before continuing. "The operative words of Goering's directive are 'total solution.' We in the SS have termed it the 'Final Solution.'"

Heydrich's hand, the one with the death's head ring on the fourth finger, punctuated the air. "*Reichsführer* Himmler has been given the overall responsibility for the Final Solution, regardless of geographic boundaries."

Eichmann wondered about all those oral orders of Hitler, magically passed down to his apostles, Himmler, Goering or Goebbels. He'd never seen a written order by Hitler. Hitler would say something and the triumvirate would set about issuing orders, rules and regulations. Eichmann dropped the thought and returned his attention to Heydrich.

"Today, here in this room, I will be very blunt—I have to be. But what I say next must stay among us. The Final Solution means the total eradication of the Jewish vermin."

Heydrich paused, looking at each face in the room, many of them wide-eyed. "You heard correctly—there will be no more emigration. When we are finished, European Jewry will no longer exist. The Final Solution will be applied to 11 million people distributed among thirty-four countries, many under German control, some yet to be conquered. This, gentlemen, will be our sacred crusade and duty."

Not a soul stirred–like they were holding their collective breath.

"Be very clear—we are not here to debate whether to implement the Final Solution—that decision, gentlemen, has been made and communicated to *Reichsmarschall* Goering and *Reichsführer* Himmler by our beloved Führer. Your job today, as indicated in the directive, is to work out the details. That is why you, from a broad spectrum of the government, have been invited to this conference, selected because you have the skills to make it happen."

Eichmann, at Heydrich's immediate right, responsible for the minutes of the conference, wrote furiously, notwithstanding the presence of a stenographer. He would see to the small details himself, as he always did.

He looked with a mixture of admiration and jealousy at the tall, blond, athletic Heydrich, whose outward appearance portrayed the very model of an Aryan superman of Nordic myth so popularized by Nazi ideologists. Heydrich was an accomplished fencer, musician and pilot. Eichmann had heard fellow SS officers, on more than one occasion, comment privately that Heydrich had the talents and looks that Himmler could only envy. Himmler was a short man, slim, with close-set eyes framed by a pince-nez, thin lips as pale as his complexion and virtually no chin. He had small, slender hands, seemingly almost translucent, and dark hair cut as if he'd been barbered with a soup bowl on his head. Himmler looked like a prissy elementary school teacher—in short, a mousy, little man.

Eichmann could empathize with Himmler. Similar aspersions had been cast at him for being so un-Aryan in appearance and so totally lacking in athletic ability. The SS required its members to be proficient in sports, and it was only a fortuitous leg injury that enabled Eichmann to beg off from participating in athletics. He was sure that injury saved his SS career. Short and dark skinned, Eichmann didn't look much different from the Jews he'll be deporting. As a youngster, some schoolmates had taunted him with the sobriquet *Der Kleine Jude*, the Little Jew. In frustration, he'd taken to assaulting younger Jewish boys, beating one so severely that he almost died. Fortunately for Eichmann, assaults on Jews in Austria, even in those days, were treated with great leniency.

The taunts of Eichmann had persisted. In his early days in the SS, they had called him "Ziggie," and sometimes, *Revolverschnauze*, revolver nose. Eichmann frowned. *They wouldn't dare say that now,* he thought.

Heydrich paused, scanning the assembled group. He had their full attention. "I appreciate your taking the time from your busy schedules to attend this meeting." He then introduced each of the representatives but held off on Eichmann. Eichmann knew that would come later.

"The *Reichsführer* has told me the Jewish question in Europe will be given top priority, more important than prosecuting the war against our other enemies."

Murmurs raced through the room, dying just as quickly.

"You will recall that first we forced the Jews out of the various sectors of German life and then we removed the Jews from Germany, many by emigration. But emigration, the Führer has decided, is no longer an option. Instead, gentlemen, we will comb Europe from east to west, country by country, city by city, and hamlet by hamlet, to find the Jews." He raised his voice, pounding the table with his fist. Some in the audience flinched. "We will solve the Jewish problem once and for all."

Heydrich's eyes moved from face to face, searching out their emotions and reactions. Each of them must have felt the searing visual examination by the head of the Gestapo. They stirred nervously in their seats. Eichmann also scanned the room but couldn't yet read the reaction of the civil servants.

Heydrich shouted, "Finally, gentlemen, Europe will be Jew free! *Heil* Hitler!"

First one, then another, stood. Soon all the attendees were on their feet, breaking into wild applause. Eichmann, smiling, sighed with relief and joined the clapping. The program has the support of the Civil Service.

Heydrich raised both hands for quiet. The audience settled back. Heydrich reviewed the statistics: Jews already deported and remaining Jews, country by country. Eichmann's mind wandered—he already knew the figures since he'd put them together for Heydrich's speech. His thoughts turned to last August when Heydrich had called him into his office to inform him of the Führer's plan.

Heydrich had hemmed and hawed concerning Hitler's orders about Jewish emigration. Eichmann had wondered what his point was, since emigration had all but ceased at that time. Finally, he came out with it. "The Jews are the eternal enemies of the German people and must be extirpated. While the war is still on, all Jews we can reach must be exterminated, without exception. If we don't succeed now in eliminating the biological basis of Jewry, they will come back later to destroy the German people. In other words, Eichmann, the Führer has ordered the physical extermination of the Jews."

Wallenberg is here!

Heydrich had sat back and silently watched Eichmann's reaction. Eichmann had shrugged. "Fine, General. What are my orders?" Heydrich had broken into a big grin, stood, walked over to Eichmann and slapped him on the back. "You will be my man, Adolph."

Later, Himmler himself had called Eichmann into his office. Eichmann had sat down about ten feet from the desk, having been warned that the *Reichsführer* was obsessed about catching other people's germs—any closer and Himmler would have a fit.

"I am extremely pleased with your hard work on the Jewish question," Himmler said. "Keep it up and after the glorious victory of our Third Reich, you will be granted an estate in Bohemia and the title of World Commissar for Jewish Affairs." Eichmann had thanked the *Reichsführer* profusely, as if victory was just around the corner. He knew it could be many years away but that thought, of course, he kept to himself.

Heydrich raised his voice, intruding on Eichmann's reminiscing. Eichmann returned his attention to the SS general, watching him move over to a large, color-coded map of Europe sitting on a pine wood easel.

"We face an ambitious program. We have to find and trace millions of people throughout this entire region." His arm swept over most of Europe. "We must catalogue the Jews, assemble them and then—well, you know what—I don't have to spell it out, do I?" He chuckled. "E-L-I-M-I-N-A-T-E."

The audience tittered. The minutes of the meeting, of course, would not be so blunt, substituting instead to the euphemisms of "deportation" and "resettlement."

Heydrich waited for the audience to quiet down. "We in this room have the abilities to accomplish this operation. We must accomplish it! Our work will be momentous—this is an historic occasion, and, I assure you, our role in it will be remembered long after we're gone. You, my dear friends, will be heroes of the Third Reich for a millennium!"

Cheering erupted. He waited until it died away, then resumed speaking.

"Able-bodied Jews will be moved eastward and used for labor. The rest will be summarily executed. A large part of the labor force will not survive the rigors of work. Those that do must then be eradicated or else the natural selection of the fittest will form the germ cell from which the Jews can build themselves up again, recreating Jewry. This is a lesson from history. We shall learn from it.

"Gentlemen, I invite discussion of the Final Solution."

Undersecretary Wilhelm Stuckart of the Reich Ministry of the Interior stood. A jurist, he had co-authored the Nuremberg anti-Jewish racial laws in the mid-thirties. He was a loyal supporter of the SS. Eichmann expected that he would support the Final Solution with enthusiasm.

Stuckart cleared his throat. "You will have the wholehearted cooperation of the Ministry of Interior in the Final Solution. As you know, I have been a strong proponent of sterilizing non-Aryans and dissolving mixed marriages. This approach would solve both problems."

Heydrich frowned impatiently. "Yes, yes, Minister, just what is your point?"

"No point, General, just a question. The Jewish children, are they to be eliminated also?"

Heydrich's eyes bored into Stuckart. "Especially the children." Then he softened his tone. "We must kill the children or else they will grow up to become avengers."

Stuckart nodded. "That is fine with me." He sat down.

Undersecretary of State Martin Luther moved his chair back and slowly came to his feet, his hands hooked into his lapels. Luther, a former furniture mover, portly, with thick glasses, had risen rapidly within the ranks of the Foreign Office despite his having been indicted for embezzlement of party funds—an indictment that was eventually thrown out, thanks to Himmler. Luther, the propagandist for the Foreign Office, became Himmler and Heydrich's agent within the ministry, gradually undermining Foreign Minister Joachim von Ribbentrop, whom Himmler detested. Eichmann did not expect Luther to present a problem.

"I support the concept of the Final Solution, but on behalf of the Foreign Office, I must protest that mass Jewish evacuation would create grave difficulties in such countries as Denmark and Norway. I suggest limiting deportations to the Balkans and Western Europe, for the time being."

Heydrich assured Luther that the SS would work closely with the Foreign Ministry to solve the problems in Scandinavia and elsewhere. "We are in the process of dealing with the problem of the Jews in

Hungary, who are being protected by their government. But we will solve it, and those of the Norway and Denmark, as well."

Gauleiter Dr. Alfred Meyer, Reich minister for the Occupied Eastern Territories, shouted out a question from his seat. "How will you accomplish the, uh, Solution, once the Jews are in custody?"

Heydrich turned to Eichmann. "Colonel, will you address that question?" Heydrich introduced Eichmann as the Jewish specialist, responsible for implementing the bureaucratic procedures for the Final Solution.

Eichmann stood, bowed and looked over his audience. He'd prepared well for this moment. "Gentlemen, in the numbers we are contemplating, shooting all the Jews is impossible. It is highly inefficient, wastes precious ammunition and takes its toll on our SS heroes, who would have to shoot women and children. Instead, we are building enormous facilities at our concentration camps to exterminate the Jews by gassing." Eichmann heard the audience stir and murmur.

"We have developed a gas called Zyklon B that will do the job quickly and efficiently. Technicians from the manufacturers of this agricultural pesticide assure me that, with some tinkering and fine-tuning, the program is feasible. We anticipate each facility will be able to handle ten thousand people a day."

Meyer shook his head. "But so many bodies?"

Eichmann smiled. "We are taking care of that with expanded crematoria facilities in all camps."

Dr. Erich Neumann, representing Hermann Goering, spoke up. "We cannot evacuate the Jews working in the arms factories until there are non-Jews to replace them."

Eichmann frowned. "The Final Solution has the same priority as the war effort. Such a large exception cannot be tolerated and..."

Heydrich interrupted. "Dr. Neumann, we will certainly take your needs into account." Heydrich focused his stare on Eichmann, shaking his head almost imperceptibly. "Now, let's move on."

Heydrich motioned to Eichmann to bend over. The general whispered in his ear, "If I were you, I'd be a little more diplomatic with Goering's man. Believe me, Adolph, you don't want to make an enemy of the *Reichsmarschall.*" Eichmann nodded glumly.

Dr. Rudolph Lange, commander of security police for Latvia, rose to his feet. Eichmann envied Lange's record, one he hoped some day to exceed by a wide margin. Lange's *Einsatzkommando* 2 group had killed more than 35,000 Jews and thousands of others in Latvia during the six months of German occupation there. "Tell me, Colonel Eichmann, does that mean my men in the Eastern Territories should stop shooting Jews?"

Eichmann paused to consider the question. "As I understand it, in Eastern territories where Jews are already being killed as they are found by the Einsatzgruppen, the procedure will continue that way for the time being."

"That is acceptable," Lange said. He began to ask another question, thought the better of it, and sat down.

Eichmann continued. "There is a reason for the attendance of the leaders of the Civil Service at this conference. We will need the help of your departments for logistical reasons. The seizure and deportation of millions of Jews to the East is no simple police measure. Civil authorities will have to collect and funnel Jewish property. Legislation is needed for making the victims stateless so that we can confiscate their property and make it impossible for any country to inquire into their fate. Disposal of Jewish property will require financial arrangements and transfer of funds—the Ministry of Finance of the Reichsbank must prepare facilities to receive the huge amounts of Jewish property collected from all over Europe and be able to sort out the gold and jewelry and send it to the Prussian State Mint. The Ministry of Transportation must provide the necessary freight cars, routings and priorities and see to it the other trains do not conflict with the deportation rail schedules." Eichmann sat down.

Heydrich resumed control of the meeting.

Dr. Roland Freisler of the Justice Ministry rose slowly and deliberately, taking off his reading glasses. Eichmann liked Freisler, even though he was a lawyer. Freisler had changed the Berlin People's Court from a wimpy coddler of crooks and traitors into a no-nonsense tribunal, dispatching quickly and firmly criminals and dissidents, making short shrift of their legalisms and delaying maneuvers. He was known as the "hanging judge." More power to him for his ruthless application of Nazi and anti-Jewish laws, and for putting away or executing Bolsheviks, Jew-lovers, liberals and traitors. We need more hard men like him, thought Eichmann.

Freisler smiled slightly, waving his glasses at Heydrich. "General, we are ahead of you. As you know, the laws governing Jewish privileges and property are already in place. My ministry is well on its way to removing all the remaining rights the Jews and Gypsies have. We've drafted the necessary laws to confiscate legally all Jew-property, which will become assets of the Third Reich."

Heydrich nodded. "Thank you, Dr. Freisler. We are indebted to you for your prompt action."

Eichmann watched Dr. Josef Bühler, representing Hans Frank's General Government in eastern Poland, raise his hand. In Eichmann's eyes, he was a pompous ass from the Civil Service, stuffed into his three-piece striped suit, chains dangling from his vest pocket. His boss, Frank, was another blowhard who was starving and shooting Poles while living an extravagant life of luxury in some royal castle. The Gestapo was well aware of his excesses but chose, for its own reasons, to overlook them, especially his ransacking of Polish art treasures for his own, not the Reich's, benefit—ordinarily a capital offense.

Heydrich nodded to Bühler, who spoke from his seat.

"I have one favor to ask. Implement the Final Solution first in Eastern Poland, and as soon as possible. We have, in our area of administration, 2.5 million Jews, most of whom are not fit for work and take up both space and scarce resources, not to mention the fact that they are also bearers of disease and operators of the black markets. They constitute a great danger to us. Oh yes, and please, don't ship us any more of them."

A brief look of annoyance crossed Heydrich's face and disappeared. He assured Bühler that he was well aware of the situation in the General Government and it would be considered a priority area for the Final Solution. As far as shipping more Jews into Eastern Poland, that was unavoidable and Governor Frank would have to put up with some inconveniences while the program was in its initial stages.

A delighted Eichmann watched in fascination as the German Civil Service representatives enthusiastically discussed problem-solving topics in such a spirited manner. They were really into it. Who would have believed it?

A debate ensued on the question of half-breeds—the *Mischling*—and exceptions to the Final Solution for mixed marriages of Aryans and Jews. Neumann suggested that if the half-breeds were sterilized, the problem would solve itself in a generation or two.

Stuckart agreed with the suggestion for sterilization but objected to any exceptions for mixed marriages. "Keeping track of them would be an administrative nightmare for my ministry and a never-ending amount of work."

Eichmann caught Heydrich's eye. "Yes, Colonel Eichmann?"

Eichmann rose from his chair. "If we are to effectuate the Final Solution, which by its very terms means a total solution, there should be no exceptions for anyone with Jewish blood, no mixed-marriage exceptions and no patchwork solutions like sterilization. Anyone with any Jewish blood is a full Jew and should be treated accordingly."

Heydrich cut off debate. "I have heard enough on this issue. A decision will be made later and communicated to you. We have a fine lunch waiting to be served, so let us adjourn this conference and enjoy ourselves."

As Eichmann gathered up his papers, the enormity of their accomplishment struck him. It had taken a dozen politicians and generals, plus a few colonels, a little less than an hour and a half to formulate and, it was hoped, seal the fate of 11 million Jews. Half of the attendees held doctoral degrees and they adopted *his* program, that of a high school dropout.

Waiters served a sumptuous lunch in the palatial dining room and then solicitously poured brandies. The participants, satisfied with the morning's work, proposed toast after toast to the Führer, to Germany, and to one another.

After lunch was concluded, the participants were still chatting excitedly. Eichmann picked up his briefcase and prepared to leave to return to his office, but Heydrich pulled him aside, whispering, "Stay a bit. Join General Müller and me for drinks in the adjoining study as soon as everyone leaves."

Delighted, Eichmann clicked his heels and bowed. "Thank you, General." Never before had he felt part of the inner circle of the Gestapo, and now he was invited to a private party with the head of Reich Security and the Gestapo chief. Things didn't get much better than this!

When the gathering finally took the gentle hints to leave, the three Gestapo men moved into the paneled study. Heydrich motioned them to sit around the large table in front of the hot crackling blaze in the fireplace. A waiter served more brandy. Heydrich pulled out a box of large, expensive cigars, and they lit up, one by one, until a pungent haze enveloped the room. Eichmann sat back in his chair, blowing smoke at the ceiling while they toasted each other and the Final Solution. They continued to smoke, drink and toast. Eichmann had never before seen Heydrich smoke anything. Now he puffed away furiously on the giant cigar.

Sitting in front of the large fire, Eichmann started to perspire. Heydrich saw it and laughed.

"Colonel, for once, relax. Unbutton that jacket of yours and loosen your tie. You'll be in good company."

Heydrich put down the cigar and threw off his own jacket. Suddenly, he let out a whoop and jumped up on his chair, startling the staid Eichmann. With athletic prowess, Heydrich leaped effortlessly onto the heavy wooden table and began to dance. His heels clicked loudly on the oak top. Even the Sphinx, Müller, laughed, threw off his jacket and tie and joined Heydrich on the table.

Unaccustomed to such uninhibited conduct, the embarrassed Eichmann shifted nervously in his chair, wishing he'd left earlier. Heydrich motioned him onto the table. Eichmann sighed. Abandoning his customary restraint, he shucked his jacket and tie and climbed on the table, but with a lot more difficulty than the lithe Heydrich. Soon all three were dancing on the table, throwing and smashing brandy glasses into the fireplace with great flourish and abandon.

Three hours later, Eichmann, happy, drunk and exhausted, flopped back into a chair. He was elated for two reasons. First, he was now one of the "in" group. Second, and just as important, the old boys' club of the Reich Civil Service had actually fought for the honor of taking the lead in annihilating 11 million people.

If the cream of the Third Reich government is so enthusiastic about the Final Solution, who am I to judge or have my own thoughts on this matter? he mused. I only carry out the laws of the land as prescribed by the Führer himself and the orders of my superiors. That is my sworn duty.

He took another swallow of brandy and looked through the empty glass at the refracted image of the chandelier. He smiled. "Like Pontius Pilate," he murmured, "I feel free from all guilt."

Auschwitz, One Week Later

Eichmann's staff car entered the town of Oswiecim in southern Poland early in the day. The morning fog from the nearby marshes still hung over the streets, as it did on most mornings. Eichmann wondered how people could voluntarily live in such a place. As a large rail center surrounded by marshes, it was a natural site for a concentration camp, but it had no redeeming virtues he could discern as a place to live.

The staff car crossed the town and approached the huge main gate of Auschwitz I Concentration Camp. The large metal letters on top of the gate proclaimed, ARBEIT MACHT FREI, work makes you free. The gate guard looked into the car and immediately waved it through. The car passed a series of electrified barbed wire fences supported by posts that looked like inverted letter Js.

Bordering on German-occupied Czechoslovakia, the huge camp, its barracks in neat rows as far as the eye could see, was a depressing sight, especially in the dead of winter. Eichmann passed row upon row of inmates, mostly Jews, trying to stand still out in the cold, most with no coats, wearing only jackets and pants with large, vertical stripes. Their heads were shaven and they shifted from foot to foot, trying to keep warm. All eyes were cast down, no one wanting to call attention to himself, while the SS camp guards and the *kapos*, the prisoner guards, took roll calls and body counts. The inmates would probably stand out there for over an hour. Some had fallen in their places, but no heads turned to glance at them, and no one moved to assist them.

Auschwitz, a railroad hub and former Austrian cavalry barracks, had been appropriated by Himmler originally as a quarantine camp and then expanded into a concentration camp for "dangerous" enemies of the Reich. The original camp, called Auschwitz I, was simply a slave labor camp. Now though, Eichmann did not see how, under current conditions, the inmates could possibly toil for more than a few weeks before succumbing. They labored at Auschwitz I and died in droves, but the true killing camp was at Auschwitz II—otherwise known as Birkenau, a quarter of a kilometer to the west. Both camps shared Auschwitz's extensive rail facilities. At an earlier visit, the commandant had briefed Eichmann on camp procedures. When Jews and other enemies of the Reich were shipped in, they were separated at the railhead. The fit-for-labor group marched into Auschwitz I, and all others—the old, the infirm, the children and the women with infants—marched in the other direction to Auschwitz II, Birkenau, for extermination.

The staff car pulled up at a nondescript, two-story brick building on the perimeter of the barracks. Hopping out of the car, Eichmann climbed the steps to the office of Major Rudolph Höss, the commandant of both camps. He'd visited Höss here late last summer, alerting him to the plans to ship Jews from all over Europe to Auschwitz and other camps. Now it was official.

Eichmann shook hands with Höss, then strolled over to the small gauze-curtained window to the right of Höss's desk. He could see the vast expanse of barracks immediately below the office. Further out, he could see the construction of a large brick building with long, slim vents every few feet around the entire edifice. Eichmann knew this was a partially completed gas chamber.

Eichmann sat in front of the desk in the spare office, crossing his legs and, with his handkerchief, dusting off his highly polished jackboots. He looked at Höss closely. "Commandant, the Final Solution is no longer a proposal—it has been made the official policy of the government, under orders from the Führer."

Höss nodded. "So I heard, but I have no details."

Eichmann brought Höss up to date on the events of the Wannsee Conference and the outpouring of support from the Civil Service.

Höss pursed his lips. "I'm surprised, Colonel. They haven't lived with this the way we in the SS have."

Eichmann smiled. "From their reaction, you would think they'd been trained by the Gestapo. But enough about them. How are the trials going on the Zyklon B gas?"

Höss picked up a small sample canister of the experimental gas with the logo of Degesch of Hamburg on the lower half of the label. "The conversion of the cyanide crystal pesticide into Zyklon B has been quite successful." He waved it in front of Eichmann.

Instinctively, Eichmann leaned back in his chair away from the canister, frowning. "Is it safe to handle the canister like that?"

Höss laughed. "Quite safe, Colonel, I assure you. The canister must be opened with a special tool to release the gas. There will be no accidents with this product." He put the canister down and glanced out of the window. "*Reichsführer* Himmler is due any minute. Then, I will give a demonstration of the effectiveness of this Zyklon B. You will be quite impressed."

Eichmann stared at the canister. "Good, because a lot depends on this gas."

Höss nodded. "I hear you were just in Minsk. What did you think of the *Einsatzgruppen* methods?"

Eichmann fell into a brief speculative silence, rubbing his chin and unfolding his legs. "Quite illuminating, seeing firsthand, the *Einsatzgruppen* at work. I watched the Jews being rounded up." He chuckled. "The fools were told they were merely to be transported elsewhere. They climbed into trucks without resistance and were taken to a remote forest clearing where huge tank trenches had been dug. The Jews obediently lined up, ten at a time, at the edge of the trench and then were shot in the back of the head at point blank range. They fell conveniently into the ditch."

Eichmann paused, shaking his head at the memory. "Except for one mother standing near me. She held her infant tightly and refused to move to the ditch. The SS officer simply shot her and the baby where they stood with one bullet. The baby's brains splattered all over, including on my leather coat. It was quite messy." He sighed, "I had to have the coat specially cleaned. The leather will never be the same."

Höss's eyes wandered over to Eichmann's leather overcoat hanging on a hook by the entrance to the office.

Eichmann leaned forward in his chair, looking at the canister. "Personally, I'm glad we'll be using the gas. I hear that all that shooting of women and children has had a negative effect on the morale of the SS troops. Himmler has no stomach for the *Einsatzgruppen* methods either. He also got spattered with blood and brains and was so repulsed by it, he nearly fainted."

Höss smiled.

Eichmann touched the gas canister gingerly. "The *Reichsführer* will support the use of Zyklon B, I know it."

Eichmann heard a car pull up. He looked out the window. Himmler had arrived.

Höss stood up. "Come, Colonel. Himmler won't climb the stairs and doesn't like to be kept waiting."

The two officers descended from the office and joined Himmler in his limousine. Höss, sitting in front with the driver, directed him to the Auschwitz II-Birkenau. On the way, he summarized for the *Reichsführer* the advantages of Zyklon B. Pointing to a small red brick building, he ordered the driver, "Pull over here."

Eichmann looked at the structure. Its heavy door was closed. Tall link fences, topped with barbed wire and created a long corridor, like a horse corral. Off to one side was a footbridge over a canal that was an open channel for sewage. Emerging from the car, Eichmann wrinkled his nose at the foul odor.

Höss signaled and a guard pushed open the large, well-lined door to the gas chamber. Höss disappeared inside and clicked on the switch for the one bare light bulb dangling from the ceiling. Eichmann and Himmler followed him into the building.

Höss's arm swept around the room. "This is, of course, only a small test facility for trying out Zyklon B. We are building much larger units now, each of which will be able to hold seven hundred to one thousand individuals at a time."

Nodding, Himmler looked up at the sprinkler-like heads protruding out of the ceiling in neat rows, covering the entire room. "It looks like a shower room. Are we going to clean the Jews before exterminating them?"

Höss laughed. "That's exactly the idea, *Reichsführer*, to leave them thinking they are about to take communal showers. We create this elaborate charade to keep them from panicking and causing delays and injuries to our guards."

Himmler wiped his glasses. "A good plan. And how are you preserving the valuables of these Jews, the gold in their teeth, their eyeglasses, jewelry, money and watches?"

With another grim smile, Höss assured him, "As you will see, we have in place a routine for all that."

Himmler folded his arms on his chest, his eyes boring into Höss. "You must make sure that your SS people understand that all the property confiscated goes into the Reich Treasury, no exceptions. SS personnel appropriating Jewish property for themselves will be executed, summarily."

"I understand clearly, *Reichsführer*, and so will they."

Eichmann wondered silently how Hans Frank, head of the General Government in Eastern Poland, could get away with stealing millions in Jewish loot for his own benefit.

The three stepped outside the brick building and moved off to one side. One hundred women, children and older men were led into the barbed wire enclosure, lined with wooden benches.

The chief guard shouted at the pathetic group. "You will strip off all your clothing, eyeglasses and artificial limbs. Put them in one neat pile and your money and valuables in another. Note the number on the bench. You will pick up your belongings exactly at this spot after being cleansed in the shower and delousing room."

Some of the women and children were crying, but the crowd was largely compliant. Eichmann marveled at that. Ukrainian guards with leather whips encouraged those who were slow undressing. Stark naked men, women and children were marched past the three SS officers, resplendent in their form-fitting uniforms and highly polished jackboots. A guard flung open the door to the chamber. The Jews hesitated. The beefy guard shouted, "Nothing is going to hurt you! You will shower and be disinfected. It's a way to prevent contagious diseases. You will be handed a towel on your way out."

Höss whispered to Himmler and Eichmann, "Most of them will grasp at this straw in a last desperate hope, but many of them already know what awaits them and have simply lost the will to resist."

Eichmann noticed Himmler studying the SS people supervising the process.

Himmler bent his head toward Eichmann. In a low voice, he declared, "Thanks to the strong, hard men we have trained for this job, these are battles that the coming generation will not have to fight."

The guards pushed and shoved all the Jews into the chamber until it was packed so tight the prisoners could neither sit nor slide to the floor. They would remain standing, even in death, like cigarettes in a freshly opened pack.

Höss led his guests to the rear of the building. "Gassing them and then clearing out the gas so that the workers can safely pull out the bodies will take about a half hour."

Höss pointed to the large double doors. "The corpses will be shoved out there. Then, a dozen workers will check the mouths, opening them with iron hooks. Dentists with hammers will knock out gold teeth, bridges and crowns. The gold will be separated out from the rest of the material."

"And who does this ghoulish work?" asked Himmler.

Wallenberg is here!

"Other prisoners. We call them the Jewish *Kommandos*. They have been promised their lives in return for doing this terrible work, plus a small percentage of the money and valuables collected."

Himmler looked troubled. Höss caught it. "Don't worry, it's just part of the big lie. They last only about three weeks and then join the others in the 'shower rooms.'"

The door to the chamber was shut and locked. The sergeant shouted to the orderlies to pour the cyanide crystals down through the narrow vertical vents.

Höss pointed to the small, round windows. "You can watch them die through the viewing portholes."

Himmler shook his head. "No thanks, I've seen enough. I'm satisfied that you have this well under control."

Over a lunch of Wiener schnitzel and spaetzle, washed down with a hearty German beer, Himmler, in his school master style, began lecturing Höss. "Commandant, the Führer is most anxious to get started exterminating the Jews, so you'll have to live with overcrowding and other difficulties for now. We simply won't delay implementation of the Final Solution. Your Birkenau will be a major killing center of Jews and Gypsies."

"I understand, *Reichsführer.*"

"Good." Then Himmler grinned. "Oh yes, you will be pleased to know that as of today you are promoted to *Obersturmbannführer*. Congratulations Lieutenant Colonel Höss."

Höss flashed a brief smile.

Himmler turned serious, giving Höss a sharp look. "I have imposed a code of silence on all SS officers concerning the Final Solution. Breaking it will constitute a capital offense. You will advise all those under your command."

"Yes, *Reichsführer.*"

Himmler got up from the lunch table. "The morning has been very illuminating. I must get back to Berlin. The Führer awaits my report."

Höss and Eichmann clicked their heels, snapped *Heil* Hitler salutes and watched Himmler disappear into the waiting car.

As the car pulled away, Höss looked pensive for a minute, then shook his head. "What will happen in Auschwitz will be so terrible that no one in the world will believe it to be possible. Even if someone should succeed in escaping from Auschwitz and try to tell the world what goes on here, it would brand him as a fantastic liar."

"And by the time they do believe, it will be too late, Europe will be Jew-free."

Höss shook his head. "I hope the Führer knows what he's doing, taking on these Americans. I have a feeling about not letting sleeping dogs lie. Have we embarked upon the Final Solution as a glorious crusade for the Reich or out of bewilderment and fear of possible defeat?"

"Höss," said Eichmann, his eyes narrowing, "you'd be wise to keep such thoughts to yourself."

Berlin, Eichmann's Headquarters, February 1942

Eichmann had summoned the top officers in his Gestapo Section IV B4. Included were his principal deputies, Majors Hermann Krumey and Dieter Wisliceny. "Gentlemen," he began, "I have news that should warm your hearts on this otherwise dreary February day. The Führer has decided to exterminate all of Europe's Jews and will use the gas chambers that this section had a hand in developing. For this, we should all be very proud. Our section has been given the responsibility for implementing this Final Solution. All our written records should continue to use the time-honored euphemisms of 'resettlement' and 'deportation.' We are not to use 'extermination,' 'killing,' or similar terms."

Eichmann paused to see the impact of his statement. Wisliceny looked down at his hands, then spoke up. "I assume, Sir, you have written orders for such an undertaking."

Eichmann, annoyed, reached back to his safe and withdrew a thin file. He waved it at Wisliceny. "Of course I have an order. It was signed by Himmler himself and given to me at Reich Security headquarters. The *Reichsführer* told me to my face that I'm personally charged with carrying it out. Is that good enough for you or do you want your own personal copy of the written order?" Eichmann's tone had a threatening edge to it.

Wisliceny shook his head. "No, Colonel, your word is sufficient, of course."

"Good. Victory will soon be ours. However, before the war ends, we must hasten to make Europe free of Jews. This may be our last chance, because with the coming of peace, we shall not be able as easily to apply such methods."

Wallenberg is here!

Eichmann looked over his assembled staff. "We face a cunning and resourceful enemy. I expect you to carry out your duties without mercy."

They all nodded.

"Major Krumey will be giving you your assignments."

Wisliceny leaned over and whispered to Major Krumey, who nodded. Eichmann caught it and compressed his lips in anger. "Dieter, do you want to share your thoughts with the rest of us."

Wisliceny shrugged. "It was nothing important."

With that, the meeting ended. Eichmann motioned Krumey to follow him. Krumey walked fast to catch up.

Eichmann looked at him with piercing eyes. "Share Wisliceny's insights with me, also, if you don't mind."

Krumey hesitated, then mumbled, "All he said was 'God grant that our enemies never get an opportunity to do the same to the German people.'"

"That type of sentiment can get him—and you—in serious trouble," Eichmann growled. "Both of you should just concentrate on carrying out your assignments. It is, after all, the Führer's order and there is no room for flippancy or waffling, especially from *my* senior officers."

CHAPTER 3

Washington, D.C., Office of the President, January 1944

Grace Tully, the President's secretary, busied herself at a file cabinet behind her desk while the visitor sat nearby, just outside the Oval Office. Secretary of the Treasury Henry Morgenthau, Jr., quietly lost in thought, perused the document in his lap. Suddenly he began fidgeting. He fanned the pages of the *Report to the Secretary on the Acquiescence of This Government in the Murder of the Jews*. For reasons he could only guess involved a mixture of some anti-alien, anti-immigration and anti-Semitic attitudes combined with bureaucratic inefficiency, the State Department had suppressed information on the murder of European Jewry–murder on a scale unheard of in modern civilization.

Morgenthau had been reluctant at first to push the President, even in the face of what one of his own undersecretaries aptly described as the State Department's "underground movement to let the Jews be killed."

Looking at the eighteen-page report that had changed his mind, he adjusted his thin, wire-frame glasses, pinched tightly on the bridge of his nose. The paper was the product of three subordinates—Protestants—in his own Treasury Department. He'd condensed it to nine pages—it was this version that was being read by FDR as Morgenthau waited. The President would learn about the State Department's indifference to the fate of European Jewry; how it withheld information about atrocities; and how it sabotaged the rescue efforts of Jewish-American agencies and others.

Morgenthau, a Jew of German extraction, came from a family steeped in public-service tradition. His father had been an adviser to Woodrow Wilson. He himself had helped FDR effectuate New Deal programs and had later devised brilliant monetary policies to facilitate America's war effort. He was one of a few in the Cabinet to have the President's ear.

Morgenthau recalled his recent conversation with Rabbi Stephen Wise, a notable figure in the American Jewish Reform movement,

Wallenberg is here!

active Zionist and spiritual leader of a large Reform congregation, the Free Synagogue of New York City. Rabbi Wise's relationship with Roosevelt stretched back even further than his own–to the late twenties, when Wise had supported Roosevelt's successful run for governor of New York. While on an intimate "Boss-Steve" basis with the president, the rabbi was not optimistic that Roosevelt would do anything. The December 1942 meeting still rankled. After a "Dear Boss" appeal by Wise, Morgenthau had arranged the only conference a group of Jewish leaders had ever had with FDR. However, after an emotional meeting in which the President had promised action, nothing had ever happened. Wise considered it a great personal failure and a blow to his prestige. But the rabbi encouraged Morgenthau to see the president. It was too important not to try.

"I know Roosevelt's no anti-Semite despite what some of our *landsmen* say," the rabbi had told Morgenthau. "Maybe he'll act after reading the report."

Morgenthau frowned. "I wish I had your confidence but this is a presidential election year. "Look what happened to the *St. Louis*. FDR didn't lift a damn finger to help, even at the strong urging of the First Lady."

The *St. Louis*, a ship full of Jews fleeing Germany, had been turned back by every country at every port in the Western Hemisphere where it attempted entry, including the United States.

Tully looked up when Morgenthau pounded the report angrily with his fist. *Why weren't they able to land somewhere in North America?* he thought. *Because it wasn't politically expedient to permit a bunch of Jews to enter this country, even if meant saving their lives, that's why.* FDR, ever the politician, feared the anti-alien sentiment, so prevalent in this country. So the ship and its passengers had to sail back to Hamburg to face the prospect of extermination.

He sighed. *He'd been in politics too many years to harbor any thoughts that politicians will make the moral choice over the politically expedient one—especially when it involves Jews. For too long,* he thought, *the administration has employed the State Department's bureaucracy as a convenient laundry chute to get rid of bothersome issues like refugees.*

The noise from the buzzer on Tully's desk startled him out of his musings. She rose, opened the door to the Oval Office and motioned him in. Morgenthau took a deep breath and slowly walked into the great office, not sure what he'd do if the President failed to act now. Resign? That certainly was an option, but not a particularly appealing one.

Morgenthau had been in the Oval Office more times than he could count, yet the room never failed to awe him, not so much by its size, furnishings and grandeur, which were imposing enough, but by the sheer history that had unfolded here under the leadership of the likes of Lincoln, Teddy Roosevelt, and Wilson, not to mention the political greats who had served under them.

Franklin Delano Roosevelt, behind the large presidential desk, puffed away on the cigarette in the long Bakelite holder held at a rakish 45-degree angle upwards from his lips—classic Roosevelt. The President, engrossed in signing papers, did not acknowledge him at first, so Morgenthau stood in front of his desk, waiting.

Roosevelt finally finished and looked up at his visitor. "Mr. Secretary, please–sit down. I didn't mean to be such a poor host and leave you standing. I apologize."

Morgenthau smiled. How Roosevelt could enunciate so clearly without that damn cigarette holder moving so much as an inch in his mouth never failed to amaze him.

Roosevelt leaned back. "Henry, thanks for coming in." He slowly shook his head, "That report, it's horrible, just horrible. I mean to do something right away to save the remaining Jews."

Morgenthau took a deep breath. He'd heard that before.

Roosevelt picked up the papers on his desk and waved them at his visitor. "I have, Henry, just signed Executive Order 9417, forming the WRB, the War Refugee Board. It will be charged with carrying out the efforts to rescue the Jewish refugees."

Morgenthau exhaled. "And who'll head the board, Mr. President?"

Roosevelt adjusted his pince-nez and looked directly at Morgenthau, smiling. "John Pehle. And the effort will be funded, of that I assure you."

Roosevelt raising his hand, looked at Morgenthau. "I know what you're thinking—he's not Jewish. I felt that a reputable, well-respected non-Jew would be more effective in dealing with the government bureaucracy. But you know Pehle better than I do. He's a career member of the your Treasury Department. Those guys at State won't be able to ride roughshod over or finesse him. Don't you agree?"

Morgenthau nodded. "He's a good man, not one of the anti-Jewish clique, and quite energetic. He'll do an outstanding job."

Roosevelt grunted his approval.

Morgenthau did not bring up that he'd already urged the President to appoint the internationally known and respected Wendell Wilkie for any such effort. Roosevelt rejected the suggestion out of hand because he did not want to give that particular Republican—his opponent in the last election—any more of a buildup than necessary. Pehle, however, was high up on Morgenthau's list, so the choice satisfied him.

Morgenthau thanked the President. FDR spoke soothingly, his familiar American upper-class accent resonating throughout the room. "Thank me, Henry, when they're saved. The WRB has a lot of work to do with little time left. Please tell your people that I'm sorry I waited so long."

"Your people!" thought Morgenthau, looking into his lap, keeping his mouth shut. The Establishment, even those not anti-Semitic, couldn't help looking on the Jews as different—another species. The President wouldn't tell a priest that Catholics were "your people." *Our people are your people, too, Mr. President,* he lectured silently.

Roosevelt looked into the Secretary of the Treasury's eyes. Morgenthau had the eerie feeling that Roosevelt always knew exactly what his Secretary was thinking.

FDR leaned forward. "Cheer up, Henry. You'll be pleased to know that I have also been active on the diplomatic front. I sent a note to Regent Horthy in Hungary to the effect that if he did not protect his Jews from the Nazis or if he allowed the Nazis to deport Hungary's Jews, I would see that he was subject to retribution as a war criminal. The Brits—Anthony Eden—have also warned Horthy. We've spoken to the Vatican, all the neutral nations and the International Red Cross and I'm confident at least some of them will weigh in with efforts to save the Jews."

Roosevelt finally took the cigarette holder out of his mouth. He sighed audibly. "Of course, the reality is that Germany is more of a threat to Horthy than far-off America. So who knows? Perhaps we can work in Budapest through a neutral diplomat. I've asked Pehle to look into it. I promise you this, we'll apply all the pressure we can muster."

Grace Tully popped her head in the office and nodded.

"Henry, I have Secretary of State Hull cooling his heels in the other room. Thank you for coming in."

The President, crippled by polio, did not rise to see him out. Morgenthau nodded curtly to the next entrant to the Oval Office, Cordell Hull. There was no love lost between the Treasury Secretary and the State Department.

Later, Morgenthau would look back on this meeting as the one that set in motion perhaps the greatest sustained rescue efforts in history—and much of it would occur in, of all places, Budapest, the birthplace of Rabbi Wise.

Berlin, Office of the Chief of the Gestapo, March 1944

The secretary disappeared into the office of General Müller, chief of the Gestapo, so Eichmann waited—and wondered. Müller rarely called for him, leaving Eichmann to run his Jewish Department as he saw fit. Now, either he was in trouble or something big was coming up. Being summoned by the chief of the Gestapo would give anyone pause and Eichmann was no exception—it was not uncommon for the Gestapo to arrest its own. He dismissed such musings as ludicrous paranoia. Nevertheless, he fidgeted, twirling the silver ring on his finger, examining its *Totenkopfverbände*, the SS death's head symbol, and slipping it off to read the inscription, "To My Dear Adolph, Heinrich Himmler." His eyes settled on another *Totenkopfverbände* attached to the peaked cap sitting in his lap. He smiled ruefully. The *Totenkopfverbände* could be a double-edged sword for those who wore it.

Presently, he stood up and moved over to a wall mirror, adjusting his SS jacket's lapels with the silver-embroidered twin *Sig Rune*, the double lightening flashes of the SS, on one side and his lieutenant colonel's insignia, four diamonds and a silver stripe, on the other. Satisfied that everything looked in place, he didn't hear the secretary come out of Müller's office; her voice gave him a start. "You may go in now, Colonel."

Müller was speaking on the telephone, his back to Eichmann. He was framed by the large tasseled banner hanging behind the desk, the black swastika in a white circle on a red field. The Nazis had appropriated the archaic good-luck *Hakenkreuz* symbol of many peoples from the ancient Egyptians to the American Indian.

Eichmann snapped to attention behind Müller's back, as he always did in the presence of a superior officer. He stood there, ramrod straight, until Müller swiveled around and motioned him to a chair. Putting his hand over the receiver, he said softly, "Relax, Colonel, you're not on the parade ground now."

Müller frowned. He knew that admonitions wouldn't help because Eichmann was the ultimate bootlicker towards his superiors but a hell on wheels to his underlings.

Müller finally hung up. Studying the officer who finally seated himself stiffly in a high backed-chair, he wondered how this humorless little man managed always to have the pressed, polished look of a clothes mannequin, no matter what the time of day. By midmorning, the thick-necked Müller had already removed his high-collared jacket and loosened his bothersome tie.

The general shook his head and broke eye contact while he searched through a pile of papers on his desk. Holding aloft what he was looking for, he returned Eichmann's gaze. "The *Reichsführer* has personally ordered that you leave for Hungary as head of the Security Police there to take charge of shipping all Jews to the camps." Müller tapped the paper with his index finger. "His phrasing may be of interest to you: 'Send down to Hungary, the master in person.'"

Eichmann's frozen expression loosened a bit. "Himmler said that?"

"Those were his exact words. He also said, 'Eichmann will assume personal control of the Hungary situation in Budapest.'" As Muller paused, Eichmann leaned forward, waiting for more. Müller let him hang there for a minute, then continued. "His orders are very clear: 'Comb the country from east to west for Jews and send them all to Auschwitz as quickly as possible. Begin with the eastern provinces, where the Russians are closest.'"

Müller's eyes narrowed as he slapped the document on the desktop. "The *Reichsführer* was quite emphatic: nothing like the Warsaw Ghetto revolt must be repeated in any way. You will be well-advised to heed that admonition."

"I understand."

"Make sure you do because I will hold you personally responsible for any failure to maintain control in Hungary."

Eichmann knitted his brow. "I must point out two conflicting facts, General. One, Hungary is an ally and a sovereign nation. This is not the situation of an occupied country like Yugoslavia or France. Two, the Hungarians have a history of not being cooperative in solving their Jewish question. I'm not clear on how much latitude "I'll have to proceed if Regent Horthy continues to oppose our program."

"That's changing, even as we speak. The Führer is sick of coddling the cowardly Hungarians and their strutting leader, Horthy, who protects his Jews, making them the only untouched Jewish community in Europe. The Führer believes that Hungarian Prime Minister Miklós Kállay, encouraged by the Jews and the Hungarian aristocracy, has been in secret negotiations with the Allies. The Führer has issued secret orders to occupy Hungary. The Wehrmacht is, at this moment, preparing to invade."

Eichmann's eyes widened.

Müller nodded. "You've heard correctly, the German Army will arrive in Hungary within a week and you must go in with them. So, assemble your team and be prepared to move out fast. We may not have that much time to clear all the Jews out of Europe."

Müller looked down at his papers, adjusting the piles. His gestures told Eichmann the meeting was over. Eichmann stood, clicked his heels and saluted.

Müller, waving him away, growled. "Remember, I'm depending on you."

Eichmann did a smart about-face and marched out of his superior's office, ramrod stiff.

Berlin, Eichmann's Office, a Half Hour Later

In March 1944, Colonel Eichmann commanded a considerable force at his Gestapo headquarters at Kurfuerstenstrasse 116. Since Wannsee, proud of his efforts at implementing the Final Solution, he had honed to a fine bureaucratic art the procedures for rounding up and transporting the Jews to the killing camps. Commended publicly by the *Reichsführer* for his organizing abilities, Eichmann's stock had risen considerably in the eyes of the SS.

Wallenberg is here!

Sitting back in his chair, about to meet with his staff on the greatest project of his career, he enjoyed a cigarette and let his mind wander. When he was finished in Budapest, he will have surpassed everyone in the number of Jews exterminated. Perhaps he'd even receive an Iron Cross from the Führer personally. He smiled. *Not bad for the stupid boy who couldn't make it through high school, eh, Father?*

But Eichmann also knew that he might not have much time to accomplish his mission. Despite the propaganda, he knew the war was not going well for Germany though he was careful to keep those views to himself.

Eichmann reviewed in his mind the modus operandi, not that he needed any refresher course. If he had to define his job, he would say it involved the bankrupting, detaining, concentrating, loading, convoying and transporting the Jews to the camps. *Judenrein*, Jew-clearing, started with the imposition of degrading anti-Jewish regulations. Jews would be forced to wear yellow Star of David patches or armbands, not only for easy identification for the Gestapo but also to single them out to the Gentile community as lepers and pariahs.

The next step would be to eject them from the economy, bar them from the professions and turn their businesses over to non-Jews. Eichmann thought this latter step a very clever bit of innovation on his part because those new non-Jew business owners would have a vested interest in never permitting the Jews' return.

A seemingly innocuous "registration" process would initiate the property confiscation phase and progress rapidly to total and permanent seizure. Another of his brainstorms: sharing a portion of the looted Jewish property with the local governments—that made them enthusiastic partners in the effort.

Eichmann inhaled deeply on his cigarette and, with satisfaction, recalled how he had had to use all his powers of persuasion to convince Himmler, who was loath to surrender a *pfennig* of looted wealth, to share with local governments. Confronting Himmler was risky. One had carefully to pick the issues on which to argue with the *Reichsführer*, who tolerated dissent very badly with sometimes disastrous results for the dissenter.

The formation of a *Judenrat*, a Jewish council, in the area of occupation was crucial to *Judenrein*. Eichmann would appoint rabbis, community leaders, businessmen and other Jews of influence, charging them with overall responsibility for accurately and promptly executing all of his orders. Every order would be enforced with a carefully planned program of terror whereby *Judenrat* members were, alternatively, taken hostage, arrested or sent to labor camps. Sometimes they were shot or hanged as punishment for actual, perceived or trumped-up violations.

At his initial meeting with the *Judenrat*, Eichmann typically would warn council members that sabotaging the execution of Gestapo orders would result in grave steps being taken against them and their families. Shooting a few was always an effective example.

His outbursts against the Jews could be attributed partly to a calculated effort to make them terrified of him and keep them wondering what he'd do next, and partly to letting his hatred of them get the better of him, resulting in the slaughter of some council members.

To lay the groundwork for the *Judenrein* program, Eichmann would require the *Judenrat* to take a census of the Jewish population, classifying it by sex and age. This would be used later to force the council to identify, locate and gather those Jews.

Progressively, the Jews would be concentrated in the city. Then he'd order them crammed in the ghettos and would execute those who tried to leave. Upon deportation of a Jew to a killing camp, the council was charged with handing over, in good order, the assets of the deportee for the final confiscation.

Fit Jews were usually not deported immediately. The *Judenrat* had the additional responsibility of supplying workers for forced-labor battalions. It wasn't much better than deportation. Many died from overwork, malnutrition and beatings. The burden of such labor often fell on the poorest Jews, those who could not afford to pay for substitutes. Others hid to avoid assignments to labor camps. But as more and more workers were required and the supply of fit workers dwindled, buying one's way out of labor battalions became less of an option. The *Judenrat* became stricter, knowing that the ghetto would suffer an even worse fate if the quota of workers could not be filled. In this way, Eichmann placed Jewish authorities in conflict with other Jews.

To fill the trains bound for the death camps, the council was told how many Jews were required on a particular day and ordered to prepare lists of people to be deported. Some council members, up to now carrying out Nazi directives, balked. They could not bring themselves to finger their fellows for death, so they simply refused. Such recalcitrants were shot; other council members committed suicide before they could be arrested. Eichmann recalled that one, before being executed, had explained that, as a Jew, he would not be guilty of complicity in such crimes, quoting a rabbinical saying, "Let them kill you but don't cross the line."

Of course, there were always the Jews who hid to escape deportation. The Jewish Police rounded them up. Eichmann liked that particular innovation. Some Jews joined the police voluntarily, liking the military-style life and assuming they would be used to protect the Jewish community and enforce traffic laws. They quickly discovered otherwise. Terrorized by the Germans, most of the Jewish Police followed Nazi orders. The SS wasted no time eliminating all the soft-hearted among the Jewish Police, leaving mostly the ruthless and the scum, willing to use clubs and rubber hoses to force fellow Jews to obey the Germans. This they did in return for their own immunity from deportation—or so they thought. Thus, instead of protecting the ghetto, the Jewish Police became its mortal enemy—and that served Eichmann just fine. The last to be shipped to the camps would be the council members and the Jewish Police. Their assistance only bought them time, not survival.

While Eichmann did not expect Jews to share a general enthusiasm over their destruction, their cooperation was the cornerstone to achieving *Judenrein*. Without Jewish help in the administrative details and police work, there would either be chaos or an impossibly severe drain on German manpower. Hence, the establishment of Quisling puppet governments in the occupied territories was always accompanied by the organization of a local *Judenrat*.

Eichmann lit another cigarette. Taking a deep drag, the smoke filled his lungs. Without the cooperation of the victims it would hardly have been possible for a few thousand people in the SS, mostly office workers, to liquidate hundreds of thousands of other people. He smiled. End of story for the Jews.

Berlin, Eichmann's Conference Room, a Few Minutes Later

Eichmann called in his Jew-clearing experts, Dieter Wisliceny, who had cleared out Greece and Slovakia; Hermann Krumey, who had done the same in Vienna, Warsaw and Amsterdam; and Theodor Dannecker, who had cleared Paris and Bulgaria.

"Gentlemen, Operation Margarethe will commence in seven days." Eichmann saw looks of incomprehension. "The SS will occupy Hungary and we will clear out the last big pocket of Jews." Smiling at the expressions of surprise on their faces, he continued, "The Führer has placed upon our shoulders the task of finishing this life and death struggle of the Third Reich, the extermination of the last of European Jewry."

Eichmann stood and strutted around the room, jabbing his forefinger in the air for emphasis. "In less than six months, I fully intend to announce proudly to the Führer that the Jewish vermin of Hungary have been wiped out. It will be the fruition of our efforts, the crowning of three years' hard work and thought, marking another glorious page in the history of the Third Reich." He paused, his eyes boring into them. "And you *will* make it happen."

***

As Eichmann continued his harangue, Krumey saw Wisliceny roll his eyes. Their gazes met. He knew what Wisliceny was thinking— they'd had the conversation many times before wondering how the ragtag, mostly unarmed Jews, the weaklings of the world, could possibly pose a threat to the mighty Third Reich.

Krumey broke eye contact, disturbed. It was not the sort of conversation one should be suspected of even thinking about, much less having with anyone else. He fingered a short linked chain, attached to which was his small oval metal Gestapo warrant disk, stamped with *Geheime Staatspolizei* and his Gestapo number. The warrant disk identified him as a Gestapo officer with unlimited powers of access and arrest. Clause 7 of Hitler's Constitution provided that power. There could be no appeal by anyone arrested by the Gestapo; even the highest court was forbidden to reexamine any Gestapo decision. It put the Gestapo above the law of the land.

Wallenberg is here!

Krumey put his disk away. True, he mused, it was a lot of power, but no protection against fellow Gestapo, especially if one were suspected of harboring seditious thoughts. Unfortunately, seeing one Gestapo officer arresting another was not a rare occurrence.

Wisliceny asked a question, breaking Krumey's train of thought. "We have the whole country to cover. Where do we start?"

Eichmann stretched, reaching high behind himself to roll down a large map of Hungary. "Hungary will be divided into six zones; the last, Zone VI, is Budapest."

He tapped the map with a long wooden pointer. "We will start here, in Zone I, Carpatho-Ruthenia, clear it of Jews and then proceed to Zone II, and so on. Budapest will be cleared last. Preparations have been made at ten concentration camps to receive the Hungarian Jews. The concentration, ghettoization and transportation of Jews will be accomplished with the assistance of the Hungarian Provincial Gendarmes under the command of Colonel László Ferenczy."

Krumey nodded. "Good, we need a hoodlum like him to do the dirty work. Some of those Hungarian peasant police act like the direct offsprings of the Huns."

The Hungarian Gendarmes, mostly lacking even elementary education, were the survivors of a merciless system of selection by Colonel Ferenczy, a cadre of hardened, brutal men of unquestioning obedience. They let their easily identifiable uniforms and black hats decorated with tall, black cock feathers, speak for them. On duty, they had the right to detain, search and interrogate anyone who aroused their suspicions.

Eichmann sat down again. "Some of Ferenczy's investigators and detectives will be attached to our unit and at our disposal."

"And when does our unit leave for Hungary?" asked Wisliceny.

"You and Krumey will leave first, accompanying the advance Wehrmacht force. Act quickly to commandeer part of the five-star Majestic Hotel on Schwab Hill in Buda for our offices, before the army takes over the entire hotel. Then you will find me a suitable personal residence. I prefer one of those villas on Roses Hill. See to it."

"Which of us will head the effort?" Krumey asked. Both he and Wisliceny held the same rank.

"This time, neither of you. I have been ordered by the *Reichsführer* to take personal charge and that, gentlemen, is precisely what I intend to do. To accomplish this in months, rather than years, I will require all of you to accompany me to Budapest"

Eichmann stood again to roll up the map and then turned to Krumey. "Set up a staff meeting for the entire *Dienststelle Eichmann* for this afternoon. I will instruct them on our sacred mission."

Wisliceny and Krumey gathered their papers. Eichmann smiled. "One more item, Gentlemen. I have given the group of us going to Hungary the name Eichmann *Kommando*. I rather like that. It will strike fear in the hearts of the Hungarians and Jews. The Eichmann *Kommando* will follow the main invasion force into Budapest."

Wisliceny rolled his eyes again without commenting.

Krumey knew what his colleague was thinking. First he called them *Dienststelle Eichmann*, now this. Eichmann, the expert in self-aggrandizement, was doing it again. That's how the toady, the uneducated little bastard, and former subordinate, leapfrogged them and was now their superior. *What was the damn Gestapo coming to?*

Wallenberg is here!

HUNGARY IN 1944

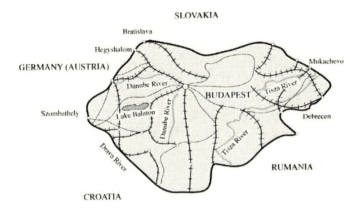

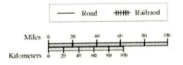

Salzburg, Germany (Formerly Austria), Schloss Klessheim Castle, March 19, 1944

The heavy maroon plush curtains were drawn shut. The only illumination emanated from the flickering light of the movie projector in the great room of the Baroque castle that was Hitler's Salzburg retreat. Hitler, joined by Foreign Minister Joachim von Ribbentrop and Edmund Veesenmayer of the German Foreign Ministry, watched a slapstick comedy, one of his favorite activities. In his leather club chair, Hitler roared with laughter and slapped his thigh while a bored Veesenmayer crossed and uncrossed his legs, not even remembering what he was watching.

It amazed Veesenmayer how these stupid movies preoccupied the Führer when there was crucial work to be done. Veesenmayer, of course, would not dare express that thought to anyone, much less to the Führer himself. Just thinking it was dangerous. Veesenmayer smirked. In the Reich, a nation of informers, thanks to the feared and efficient Gestapo, he had learned the skills to survive. Neighbors were expected to inform on neighbors, children on parents, workers on co-workers, employers on employees, pupils on teachers. He would keep his thoughts to himself, thank you, he had long ago decided.

Veesenmayer looked up as he heard a chair scrape on the floor. Von Ribbentrop excused himself to check on Miklós Horthy, former admiral in the Austrian Imperial Navy, and now long-time regent of Hungary, whom Hitler had kept waiting in another room for almost a day. *That lucky bastard von Ribbentrop, he doesn't have to suffer through the rest of this garbage,* thought Veesenmayer.

Hitler's loud guffaws at some pratfall interrupted Veesenmayer's musings. The Führer continually looked over at Veesenmayer, checking for his reaction. Veesenmayer forced a laugh, but Hitler wasn't fooled. He shook his head. "You must learn to relax, Veesenmayer. Everything will be accomplished in due time. You will have a lot on your plate as Reich plenipotentiary of Hungary, but right now, you will enjoy the movie with me."

"Of course, *Mein* Führer."

Mercifully, the movie ended. The lights went on. Hitler looked at Veesenmayer. "It's time to call in Horthy, that dung admiral who has no navy, ruling over a kingdom that has no king." Hitler laughed harshly, brushing the hair out of his eyes. "We have kept that pathetic mouse waiting long enough, let's deliver the bad news."

As they had discussed earlier, Hitler planned to tell Horthy that the Hungarians could no longer be trusted to protect Germany's southern flank from the Soviets or to solve its own Jewish problems.

Hitler folded himself into the chair behind his large ornate desk. He straightened his jacket and tightened his tie. "Veesenmayer, tell von Ribbentrop to fetch the admiral."

Wallenberg is here!

Admiral Miklós Horthy, regent of Hungary since 1920, had brought calm to that country after thwarting the attempted overthrow of the government by the Red Terror of Béla Kun. Horthy's distrust of Western democracies and hatred of the Soviet Union had led, eventually, to his pact with Germany. Thus, up to now at least, Hitler had left Hungary alone. The regent, tall, ramrod straight, with sharp, Roman features and a full head of graying hair combed straight back, had regal bearing. Physically, he was the antithesis of the Führer. Horthy's experience of long years as head of state gave him, at least in Hitler's mind, an air of condescension. For those reasons alone, Veesenmayer knew, Hitler resented the man.

Horthy greeted Hitler with a slight bow. "Herr Chancellor."

Hitler simply glared at Horthy, saying nothing for at least minute. He liked to use silence as a means of making people he disliked feel uncomfortable. This scene had been played out many times before in Hitler's confrontations, particularly with the heads of smaller countries. Veesenmayer leaned forward to hear the explosion he knew was coming.

Hitler, pulling on his small, square mustache, growled in a low voice, "Do you think you can act like a traitor without being found out?"

The regent blinked. "Excuse me, Chancellor?"

Hitler rose. Leaning on the desk with his fists, he thundered, "You think I don't know you are trying to make secret deals with the Allies? I won't have it. It's treason! You are betraying the Third Reich just as Italy did." Working himself up, he screamed, "You must reinforce your cowardly troops, who will continue to fight side by side with the Wehrmacht against the Slavic hordes. Either that, or we will destroy you." Hitler paused to take a deep breath. Horthy stood still, clenching and unclenching his fists.

Hitler's voice dropped to a growl. "I will see Hungary occupied by Slovak and Rumanian troops, if you don't cooperate."

"I don't understand," protested Horthy. "We've always been your loyal ally."

Hitler waved away the statement. "Worse, you're protecting the Jews, and I won't stand for that! You hear me?"

Horthy continued to stand straight, the color returning to his shocked features. Veesenmayer smiled. Vintage Hitler, he thought. As head of a sovereign state, the regent obviously had never experienced from another head of state a dressing-down like this. But Horthy was in good company—the same thing had happened to the aging and bewildered Czech president, Emil Hácha, before Germany invaded his country.

Hitler wasn't through. He worked himself up again, froth collecting in the corners of his mouth, his face reddening. He bellowed, "There are even two Jews still in the upper house of the Hungarian Parliament!" Spittle flew in all directions.

Having regained some measure of composure, Horthy explained, "The Jews were an important industrial force in my country. Even today, Jewish companies still survive and operate because the Wehrmacht war machine needs their products. Shall I close them down, too? Perhaps in Germany, it's different, but in Hungary, it's extremely difficult to eliminate totally the Jews from our economy; they are too important a part of it. Nevertheless, as you demanded, I destroyed their businesses, took their property, forced them out of most professions and prohibited them from owning land. What more do you want? I can't just murder them, can I?"

Hitler looked at Horthy through hooded eyes. He stopped shouting, but his voice was just as menacing. "No, Regent, I simply expect you to help us place them in concentration camps as was done to the Slovakian Jews. We'll take care of the rest."

Horthy, who hadn't been invited to sit, continued to stand stiffly. From his full height of over six feet his face flushed, he responded in a deep, firm voice. "I find your conduct and language offensive and unacceptable, Chancellor. You are talking to the regent of Hungary, not one of your lackeys. Your attempt to bully is an insult to the sovereignty of Hungary. I'm returning to Budapest—now."

As the regent turned to leave, Hitler hit the buzzer twice, then raced around the desk to chase Horthy. "Come back here," he screamed, "or you won't have any sovereignty left to insult. How dare you leave my presence without permission?"

The air raid sirens, wailing their high pitched, undulating cry, drowned out Hitler's words. His aide burst in. "*Mein* Führer, English bombers are coming in. We must take shelter, immediately."

Hitler took the lead leaving the room and going down the stairs into the well-stocked cellar. Horthy, ignoring Hitler, stood his ground and turned to the foreign minister. "If you would be so kind, please put a call through to my train. I must prepare to leave immediately after the air raid is over."

Von Ribbentrop shrugged. "Regent, telephone communications have been disrupted. All the lines are dead. I apologize for the inconvenience." Horthy scowled but followed him into the shelter in the cellar.

Several uncomfortable hours passed. There was little conversation, and none with Hitler. The Führer sat, arms folded, in a trancelike state. He seemed fixated on the *Hakenkreuz* banner hanging on the thick stone wall of the shelter.

Finally, the sirens emitted several short wails. Von Ribbentrop smiled, "The all-clear has sounded." Hitler shook off the trance and he turned to his aide. "We will have dinner in the main dining room. See to it."

Horthy shook his head. "I must leave, I have no time for dinner."

Hitler walked past Horthy, ignoring him, but at the top of the cellar stairs, von Ribbentrop blocked the regent's way. "Sorry, Regent. A very heavy fog has set in and it's not possible to negotiate these mountain roads by car at this time."

Horthy pushed the foreign minister aside, climbing the stairs to the first floor and striding to the nearest window. He could see nothing, the fog as thick as goulash.

Hitler had already disappeared down the corridor. Horthy faced von Ribbentrop, his features reflecting rage and fear. "I am in the castle of a madman. I may not leave it alive."

Von Ribbentrop pretended to look shocked. "Regent, we are not the barbarians! Your fears should be reserved for the Soviets. I assure you, you are as safe here as you would be in your own Budapest castle."

Horthy grunted, following the foreign minister into the dining room where Hitler was already seated and eating. An uncomfortable quiet pervaded the room. Hitler didn't once acknowledge Horthy's presence. Horthy, sipping a glass of Liebfraumilch, glared at his host. Hitler drank his usual–several glasses of mineral water. Dinner was served, slowly.

As the waiter removed the dinner plates, Horthy turned to von Ribbentrop. "This is the thanks Hungary gets after it lost a large part of its army fighting the Soviets at the Don River. The whole scene is ridiculous, I demand to leave—now."

Von Ribbentrop looked at Hitler. The Führer nodded.

"Yes, I suppose it's time," von Ribbentrop said. "You may leave now, Regent. Your train is ready and waiting. By the way, we have coupled another car onto your train for Reich Plenipotentiary Edmund Veesenmayer and his staff of political and propaganda experts. They will accompany you."

"Plenipotentiary Veesenmayer? Political experts?"

Von Ribbentrop smiled. "Oh, did I neglect to tell you? At this moment German SS troops are entering your country. The Führer has decided that the unrestricted presence of some one million Jews is a definite menace to the safety of the German army in the Balkan Peninsula. We are, temporarily, of course, occupying your country for your own safety. As long as you cooperate, you may continue as regent."

"Cooperate?"

"Yes. You must fire that traitorous, Jew-loving, Prime Minister Kállay. I have prepared a joint communiqué stating that the entry of German troops into Hungary was by mutual consent."

Horthy snorted. "You may as well have added that I begged Hitler to have Hungary occupied by Slovak and Rumanian troops, which was another of his threats. No, my dear von Ribbentrop, I can't stop you from occupying my country, but I won't issue a joint communiqué that I invited the Germans in."

Von Ribbentrop shrugged. "As you wish."

Horthy's eyes narrowed to slits. "This was all a ruse to keep me here incommunicado, wasn't it? There was no air raid and the telephones weren't out of order, were they?"

Von Ribbentrop spread his arms in a mea culpa gesture. "I'm afraid they weren't, Regent."

"And how did you arrange the fog?"

"It wasn't difficult. A few smoke screen machines, courtesy of the Waffen SS, can be very effective, don't you agree?"

"I feel as if I've spent a night at the opera, with me playing the fool. It's time to leave this farce."

CHAPTER 4

Budapest, Kitchen of József Friedman in Pest, March 19, 1944

József Friedman, a sugar cube held firmly between his teeth, sipped some hot tea. Invigorated by the cold but sunny morning, he gazed out the open window. Earlier, he'd listened on the wireless to a clandestine BBC report that Hungarian Prime Minister Miklós Kállay would soon go on the air to announce that Hungary had broken with Germany and was joining with the Allies.

Friedman finished the tea and rinsed the cup. He took a chilled bottle of champagne from the icebox. He opened it with a flourish, the cork caroming off the ceiling.

"You shouldn't be celebrating yet," his wife, Roza, admonished, shaking her head over her own tea. "Cork the champagne, or you'll give us a *kineahora*."

Friedman dismissed her protests of a jinx with a wave of the hand. "Ah, that's so typical of women, superstitious and pessimistic. You just don't understand politics. Come listen and learn. Kállay should be on any minute now." He switched on the radio and turned up the volume. He looked out again. It was Sunday and the street was quiet.

The Hungarian national anthem blared, then the prime minister was introduced. The radio crackled with static. "My fellow Hungarians, I am pleased to announce momentous news about the war…"

Friedman raised his glass and smiled at his wife.

"…We have concluded a…"

Silence.

Friedman fiddled with the tuning dial. He smacked the radio with his hand. Suddenly, the "Horst Wessel Song," sung by a lusty German male chorus, burst forth like repeated hammer blows. *"Wenn das Judenblut vom Messer spritz, dann geht's nochmal so gut…"* Let Jewish blood squirt from your knife and see how good it feels…

Friedman didn't need a translation. He put down the glass of champagne and sat staring at the new enemy, his radio.

"Attention! Attention! This is Proconsul Edmund Veesenmayer speaking. The Führer has appointed me plenipotentiary of the Reich in Budapest, in charge of forming a new Hungarian government. Regent Horthy has dismissed the traitor Kállay and has, with my approval, appointed General Döme Sztójay as prime minister. At the request of your new leaders, the German army has entered the country to purge the government of traitorous elements attempting to sell out the Hungarian people and their brave soldiers fighting side by side with their German allies on the Eastern Front.

"Martial law is declared. You will stay tuned for proclamations, announcements and orders. Violations will be met with the most severe consequences. *Heil* Hitler!"

Programs followed denouncing and vilifying the Jews and announcing the institution of a Jewish curfew and the promulgation of regulations requiring Jews to wear yellow stars and register at stations to be set up by the Gestapo.

Friedman looked out the window again. This time the first German army trucks and tanks and other tracked vehicles appeared. Planes roared overhead. He looked up. Messerschmitts filled the sky over Budapest. Turning from the window he faced his wife. "You were right. How stupid I was not to have left with my family before this happened! I must get us out of Hungary or we are doomed—neither the Hungarian government nor Regent Horthy will protect us."

Friedman stood over the radio, looking miserable. His wife wrapped her arms around him to comfort him.

Eichmann's Entrance into Budapest, Same Day

Occupying 140 vehicles, Eichmann and the Eichmann *Kommando*, the SS, and regular police recruited from all over Germany followed the First Armored Division of the Wehrmacht into Hungary. Eichmann rode in the rear of a large, black Mercedes-Benz. Nazi swastika flags on both front fenders flapping furiously in the backwash of dust from the convoy. The column slowed down as it approached Budapest. On this first day of the historic mission, Eichmann could hardly contain his excitement. This was also his thirty-eighth birthday and Himmler couldn't have given him a better gift than this assignment. He could, he thought, make his mark in history, outshining even *Obersturmbannführer* Hans Hoffle in the deportation of Jews. With a little effort, he'd reach 400,000 of them in Hungary alone.

He had another reason to be full of himself. Just before leaving Berlin, General Müller had advised him that Hitler had just awarded him a citation for his achievements in the field of exterminations and had also bestowed on him the title of Commander of Security Police for Hungary. Eichmann smiled. *I only wish I could rub my father's nose in it.*

They entered Budapest. Leaning forward, he tapped the driver on the shoulder. "Head for the Majestic Hotel on Schwab Hill, in the Buda section. You know how to get there?"

The driver nodded.

The Danube split Budapest. Buda, nestled in the hills sat on the west side of the river, was the home of the aristocracy, the well-to-do, the embassies and the Royal Palace, a complex that had been the seat of Hungary's kings and was now the regent's residence and office. Buda overlooked the other half of the city, Pest, in the flat area east of the river, which contained a mix of residential neighborhoods and commercial and industrial establishments. Several bridges connected the two sections.

Eichmann looked forward to his creature comforts. He'd already lined up several high-priced whores to help make his stay in Budapest memorable. Truthfully, he enjoyed life a whole lot more outside Berlin, where his wife and children weren't an inconvenience to the style of living he'd earned through his position in the Gestapo. He'd enjoyed the women, horses and drinking in every city in which he'd served—he expected Budapest would be no exception.

Death by hanging was the penalty for any SS man who appropriated Jewish property for himself instead of turning it over to the Third Reich. But those high enough in the Gestapo, if they were careful and shared the loot with the Reich treasury, could safely expect to accumulate wealth. Eichmann had been able to amass a modest estate, mostly from wealth confiscated from the Jews. All the leaders of the SS did it—Goering and Himmler were millionaires and would turn a blind eye to similar prerogatives exercised by their top officers as long as they weren't too greedy or ostentatious about it.

The Mercedes pulled up to the entrance of the elegant Majestic Hotel. The driver rushed around to open the door for Eichmann. The colonel, stiff from the long ride, stepped out of the car and stretched his limbs. Approaching the mirrored doors to the hotel lobby, he examined his reflection in great detail. He admired what he saw: an impeccably dressed Gestapo officer in a tailored silver-gray SS uniform, jacket, black Sam Browne belt, silver-braided peaked cap, black-striped jodhpurs and highly shined black jackboots. In a burst of compulsion, he straightened his jacket to smooth the fabric. Finally satisfied, he made a grand entrance into the lobby.

Proconsul Veesenmayer greeted him. Eichmann was polite but certainly not overjoyed at the prospect of working through the Foreign Ministry to rid Hungary of its Jews. The ridiculous fiction that Hungary was an equal ally was a tedious illusion that von Ribbentrop insisted be maintained so that his Foreign Ministry could retain jurisdiction to "negotiate" a consent from the Hungarian government to deport its Jews. Eichmann had been instructed to follow the Foreign Office's lead. In conquered countries, he thought ruefully, the SS and Gestapo ruled the roost with no interference from the weak sisters of civil government like the Foreign Ministry— interference he did not need. Despite the government's professed optimism on the war, he knew better; he didn't have much time to complete the job.

Buda, Majestic Hotel, Eichmann's Office, the Same Day

Majors Wisliceny and Krumey saluted Eichmann sitting behind his desk. Eichmann returned the salutes with a quick *Heil*. "Tell me, have you arrested that traitor Kállay yet?"

Wisliceny shook his head. "He's taken refuge in the Turkish Embassy."

Eichmann slapped his forehead. "Damn it, must I do everything myself?"

"Our Hungarian allies were supposed to arrest him at the radio station," Wisliceny explained, "but troops loyal to Horthy intervened and spirited Kállay away."

In the middle of this explanation, Eichmann searched the drawers, found a cloth, bent down and wiped the dust off his jackboots. Wisliceny wasn't surprised; this was classic Eichmann, a compulsive fussbudget.

Wallenberg is here!

Eichmann looked up at Wisliceny. "Well, just make sure if he leaves the embassy, that he's arrested. Is that understood?" Wisliceny nodded.

Eichmann turned to Krumey. "What's happening with the Jews?"

Krumey coughed. "I'm afraid word's gotten out on what 'deportation' means. We are working to convince the Jews that we recognize the sacred distinction between Magyarized, or Hungarian Jews, and Eastern Jews. We've been telling the Hungarian Jews that it's the Eastern Jews, not them, that will be shipped out of Hungary."

Eichmann nodded. "Whom do we have to head the *Judenrat*?"

"Samu Stern. We have treated this Jew, who also happens to be a member of Horthy's Privy Council, with exquisite courtesy and he has agreed to head the Jewish Council."

"Excellent. Let's leave the impression with the Jews that we're corrupt. Before we deport them, we'll be able to milk them of all the wealth they'll be trying to hide."

Krumey smiled. "You will be happy to know I am already negotiating to receive perhaps as much as $250,000 from Philip von Freudiger to get his family out. He's one of the *Judenrat* members."

"And a group called the Jewish Rescue Committee," Wisliceny interrupted, "has offered us $20,000 merely for the privilege of meeting with me and some of our SS counterintelligence people. They even promised those at the meeting an additional tip of $1,000 each after I hinted at sparing all the Jews, except those in Poland, for a ransom of $2 or 3 million. The Jews are already talking about paying it off in installments."

Eichmann smiled grimly. "That was fast. Our coffers should be full before long. Good work."

Wisliceny smiled. And the good colonel, he thought, could enjoy the luxuries of fine accommodations, drunken binges, debauchery with beautiful women, chauffeured cars and horseback riding—and, of course, the hunting trips in the countryside promised by his new friends in the Hungarian Nazi Party. Yes, the colonel does have plans for a high lifestyle in Budapest.

Eichmann's commanding voice snapped Wisliceny out of his reverie. "Major, I want you, Krumey, and Hunsche, to meet tomorrow with the *Judenrat* to advise them of their responsibilities. You know what to do." Captain Otto Hunsche was Eichmann's legal adviser in his department.

Wisliceny nodded. "Yes, Sir. You plan to attend, Colonel?" Wisliceny never addressed Eichmann by his first name. They had been on a first-name basis when Wisliceny was Eichmann's superior and later, when they were of equal rank. But once Eichmann was promoted over him, Eichmann expected to be addressed by his rank.

Eichmann rubbed his chin. "I don't think so. They know I'm in town. Let them wonder and fear what *Der Bluthund* is up to." Eichmann relished his reputation among the Jews as "The Bloodhound," the one who ferrets out and deports the Jews with chilling efficiency.

Eichmann looked at Krumey. "Do you have the list?" The list contained the names of more than 3,400 Jewish leaders and anti-Nazis in politics, business, law, the press and entertainment. Krumey handed it to Eichmann, who scanned it briefly and smiled. "Good, our Hungarian friends should be especially cooperative when we hold out the prospect of sharing liberated Jewish wealth with them. Have them assist you in arresting as many on the list as you can find, as well as any Jews found at the railroad stations or boat terminals. But leave the Jews on the *Judenrat* alone for now."

The "Hungarian friends" were the newly appointed officials in the Hungarian Interior Ministry under Minister Andor Jaross, and Deputy Ministers László Baky, head of the Hungarian Gendarmes, and László Endre, in charge of Jewish Affairs. The ministry, given jurisdiction over the solution of the Jewish question, was fanatically anti-Semitic and anxious to assist the Eichmann *Kommando*.

There was a knock on the door. Krumey stuck his head outside the office, then turned to Eichmann. "Colonel, Minister Endre is waiting in the other room."

"Send him in."

***

Eichmann sighed; he had no patience for protocol but knew he had to spend time playing up to the ministers of Germany's "allies." Veesenmayer and the rest of the Foreign Ministry would throw fits if he refused. Besides, he needed the help of the Hungarians to round up Jews.

László Endre bounded into the room, his face flushed, sporting a large grin. "Colonel Eichmann, what a great pleasure. Welcome! We've been waiting a long time."

Eichmann rose, bowed and clicked his heels. "We look forward to your help in solving Hungary's Jewish problem."

Endre laughed. "I'm eager to begin. My men are poised to round up Budapest's Jews as soon as possible."

Eichmann eyed the Hungarian official. "Yes—well—we first plan to deport the Jews in the provinces and save Budapest for last"

Endre gestured excitedly with his hands. "But Colonel, I assure you, it will pose no problem for us to start deporting the Jews in Budapest at the same time the provincial Jews are rounded up.

"Patience, Minister Endre," Eichmann soothed. "We don't have enough rolling stock. Besides, we don't want to roil the diplomatic corps in the city and offer an excuse for propaganda campaigns by the hostile neutral press. We will, however, begin the process of registering the Jews here in Budapest. It will save time when we are ready to deal with them."

Endre frowned. "We had really hoped to get started now."

Eichmann flashed a brief look of annoyance, then simply shrugged. "We will advise you when to start."

Buda, Astoria Hotel, Wehrmacht Headquarters, March 20, 1944

The three German Gestapo officers, Majors Krumey and Wisliceny and Captain Hunsche, received the representatives of the Jews at the headquarters of the Wehrmacht. After being kept waiting for an hour, thirteen Jewish men, led by Samu Stern, filed into the meeting room. Stern, a seventy-year-old businessman, presided over the exports of most of Hungary's agricultural products—the Nazis called him the King of Milk and Eggs. Long an adviser to the regent, he had failed in his recent frantic attempts to get through to him. His pleas had fallen on deaf ears. The message he had received indirectly was clear: the regent had no intention of intervening on behalf of the Jews.

Two German guards in the back of the room stepped closer, aiming their submachine guns at the Jewish group standing in front of the table behind which the three Gestapo officers sat.

Krumey, a large man, loomed over the group. He smiled. "Gentlemen, please relax. Excuse my over-zealous guards; they are nervous because they have never before been in a room with so many Jews." At his nod, the guards stepped back a few paces, lowering their weapons.

Krumey examined his papers. "You are advised that all Hungarian Jewish affairs are now the responsibility of the SS." Looking at Stern, he added, "And it's no use appealing to the Hungarian government."

Stern's raised his eyebrows.

"Yes, Herr Stern," continued Krumey reassuringly, "I know all about your attempts to reach the regent." An edge crept into his voice. "You will not get off on the right foot with us doing things like that and, I might note, such conduct could be very injurious to your health. Now you have been warned, that should be enough. You get my meaning, Herr Stern?"

Stern didn't move or respond.

Krumey slapped the table with his riding crop, the visitors flinching at the sharp crack. The guards moved in a step and raised their weapons. "I'm waiting for a response, Herr Stern!"

Stern nodded his head.

"If that's a yes, say so or you're liable to lose your tongue with one swipe of my dagger." Krumey fingered the scabbard of the SS dagger chained to his Sam Browne belt.

"Yes, Major," Stern said in a firm voice.

"Good. You do not seem to grasp that the Gestapo has swept away all the old conventions. Together with our new friends and collaborators in the Hungarian government, we are operating on completely different assumptions—ones that you'd better learn rapidly. Now, since we are responsible for all Jewish affairs, we will impose some economic restrictions, and you, as the responsible individuals, should have no trouble seeing to it that they are observed by the Jewish population."

The Jews exchanged glances, shifting nervously in place.

Krumey spread his hands in an exaggerated placating manner. "Don't worry, the restrictions should be no more than the necessities of war require. Religious and cultural activities may continue."

Wisliceny picked up a sheet of paper from the table and waved it in front of the assembled Jews. "This is a letter from Rabbi Weissmandel of Bratislava advising the Jewish leaders of Budapest that they could save their fellow Jews a lot of grief by complying with our instructions and orders." He handed the letter to Stern. "Read it and pass it on."

Wisliceny waited until all the Jews had read it. "One of our first orders is, Jews are forbidden to leave Budapest without a permit. Anyone caught doing so will be shot without further question."

One Jew raised his hand. Wisliceny snapped, "Well, what do you want?"

"Excuse me, sir, but why have some Jewish leaders and Jews on trains been arrested?"

Wisliceny growled, "Because there's a war on and hostages are being taken. But nothing will happen to them if you Jews behave yourselves and don't move around."

Krumey handed Stern a blank sheet of lined paper. "Have everyone in this room put his name on this paper. The *Judenrat* is now established. It shall be comprised of this group. This council will be the only Jews authorized to negotiate with the German authorities."

A voice came from the back. "Excuse me, Sir, but my health is not good. I don't think I can serve on the council."

Krumey rose and walked over to the speaker, his hands on his hips. "I strongly suggest you reconsider. I doubt if Auschwitz would be more beneficial to your health."

The man nodded.

Krumey looked over the group. "This meeting is over. We will inform you of another meeting within a day or two. Do not fail to show up. You are dismissed."

The guards prodded the Jews out of the room.

***

The door to the office closed, Krumey turned to Wisliceny and Hunsche with satisfaction. "If the Jews think we're a problem, wait until they have to deal with the Hungarian Arrow Cross. They don't realize yet just how lucrative to the Hungarians we have made hatred of the Jews."

Wisliceny slapped Hunsche on the back. "They think the Hungarian government will protect Magyarized Jews. They're in for a big surprise when they discover the magnitude of Hungarian rapacity." He started laughing and it was infectious. Krumey and Hunsche joined in.

Buda, Eichmann's Office, Majestic Hotel, March 31, 1944

At nine in the morning, Eichmann sat behind his large, ornate desk, confiscated from some Jewish executive. He straightened out his papers, writing implements, pads and paperweights. Everything was in perfect alignment and if anything on his desk were moved, he would know. He couldn't abide sloppiness, chaos and disorder in his office.

Wisliceny entered, accompanied by Franz Novak, the transportation specialist, and sat down. Novak, a fidgety little man, whose constant twitches and jerky movements greatly annoyed Eichmann, remained standing. Eichmann had briefly considered shipping him off to a concentration camp as a defective but had thought better of it, realizing how much he relied on Novak's genius in transportation planning.

Novak nodded toward the door. "Who are all those people in your waiting room, Colonel? They look like Jews."

"They are," smiled Eichmann. "They're the cream of the Jewish leadership, here to meet with me for our 'frank' talk."

Novak smiled knowingly. "Ah, the *Judenrat*. You haven't wasted time putting together a Jewish Council, have you?"

"We don't have the luxury of time that we had in Vienna, Paris and Slovakia. That means you must leave for Vienna immediately—today—to finalize the last technical details with the railroad authorities and work out a rail routing schedule for the deportation of the Hungarian Jewish vermin to Auschwitz. The transportation authorities must understand we have priority, even over the military. This is pursuant to the orders of the Führer himself. I intend to exercise that priority at every opportunity. You may go."

Novak clicked his heels, gave a brief *Heil* salute and left. Wisliceny remained seated across from Eichmann, who picked up one of his glass paperweights etched with swastikas. He stared at the Nazi symbols, squeezing the glass ball in his fist as if to pulverize it. "Some call me obsessed by this mission. So be it. If I succeed in destroying the biological foundation of the Jews in the East, Jewry as a whole will never recover from the blow. The extermination is

Wallenberg is here!

necessary to preserve the German people from the destructive intentions of the Jews."

"But Colonel," protested Wisliceny, "the Reich minister of Armaments said he desperately needs workers. He has been screaming for slave labor. Shouldn't we segregate the healthy Jews—at least the young males?"

Eichmann's eyes flashed with anger. "I will permit their use only for temporary labor needs, until I'm ready to ship them out. However, I am unalterably opposed to exempting wholesale from deportation to Auschwitz, able-bodied Jews. That would jeopardize the whole concept of the Final Solution. If we preserve these young, healthy Jews, the strongest of their stock, they'll some day come after us with revenge in their hearts. Now, unless I get direct orders from the Führer or *Reichsführer* Himmler, I don't want to hear any more of that claptrap. Do I make myself clear?"

"Yes, Colonel," Wisliceny said softly.

Eichmann was determined to exterminate the Jews rapidly, while the Nazis were still in control. The Nazi propaganda didn't fool him. As early as 1943, he had begun to doubt the probability of any German victory, and certainly not the glorious one predicted by Goebbels. He had smiled at Goebbels's euphemism for the German retreat, "an elastic pulling back." Eichmann was a loyal Nazi, but he had eyes and ears and could draw his own conclusions.

These doubts, of course, he never verbalized. He'd seen men shot for lesser offenses than that, especially after the Führer had privately assured the SS of Germany's secret weapon, which, when unleashed, would turn the tide of war. Eichmann wouldn't bank on that assurance as far as the Jews were concerned. He intended to complete his mission as rapidly as possible while hoping the secret weapon was not wishful thinking on the Führer's part.

Eichmann pointed to the door. "We have kept the Jew-dogs waiting long enough, show them in." Familiar with every document in the neat pile of papers on his desk, he quickly found the one he wanted, the list and biographies of the Jewish leaders waiting to see him. He scanned it briefly—all were former leaders in industry or the professions: Samu Stern, Dr. Ernö Boda, Dr. János Gabor, and Dr. Karl Wilhelm. He paused when he saw the name, Pinchas Freudiger, the Jew who was trying to buy his people's way out of the death camps. Eichmann smiled. He would wring him dry and then send him and his family up in smoke in Auschwitz.

Eichmann carefully posed himself in front of his desk, straightening his silver gray Gestapo working uniform. The double lightening insignia reflected their silver threads off the overhead lights. Feet wide apart and well anchored in his highly polished jackboots, Eichmann rested one hand on the flap of his black leather holster. He was satisfied he looked the part—*Der Bluthund*.

Wisliceny led the Jewish leaders into the room. They stood quietly in front of Eichmann. Krumey joined Wisliceny behind the Jews, who nodded in greeting but waited to be addressed.

Eichmann grinned. "You know who I am, don't you? I'm the one known as the Bloodhound." He laughed. Krumey and Wisliceny snickered. None of the Jews smiled.

His hands on his hips, Eichmann addressed them. "Gentlemen, my mission is to raise the output of the war industries. If the Jews work hard at achieving my objectives, no harm whatsoever will befall them. But I must have your cooperation in providing volunteers. If I do not get it, I will take your people by force. Do you understand?"

Samu Stern spoke, "Yes, Colonel, you make yourself quite clear."

Eichmann looked into the faces of the other Jews. Each nodded his assent.

"Good. I am not an adherent of violence because I value manpower, but any opposition will be broken immediately and without fail."

Eichmann rubbed his chin, eyeing the group. He unsnapped the flap on his holster and removed the Luger, examining it and admiring its lustrous blued steel finish. Waving it at the Jews, he growled, "If any of you are thinking of joining the partisans or applying their methods, I shall have you mercilessly slaughtered." He reholstered the Luger and smiled broadly, spreading his arms. "But let us not dwell on such unpleasantness. After the war, the Jews will be free; all the Jewish measures will be abandoned and the Germans will again be good-natured as before.

Behind the Jews, Eichmann could see Krumey shaking his head, smiling.

"You gentlemen are the *Judenrat* for Budapest." Eichmann ran a hand through his hair, talking in a soothing voice. "You can trust me and talk freely. As you see, I am quite frank with you. If the Jews

Wallenberg is here!

behave quietly and work, you will be able to keep all your community institutions."

The Jews exchange glances. Eichmann caught it.

"I want you to develop your own school system and give me a list of the necessary requirements for buildings and other technical matters." Eichmann smiled encouragingly. "You see, we're not the monsters portrayed by Allied propaganda, are we?"

The smile faded and Eichmann's gaze focused on Samu Stern. He took the SS dagger out of its scabbard and, without taking his eyes off Stern, ran his finger lightly over its sharp edge. "But understand this and have no illusions; in the past, where you Jews opposed us, there were executions. That's been my experience and I will not hesitate ordering the most severe measures. Do you understand what I'm saying?"

"Very clearly, Colonel," Stern said in a low voice. The rest of the Jews nodded silently.

"I have certain expectations. This is wartime. As a war measure, Jews will have to wear yellow badges, beginning at five o'clock this afternoon. See to it. This will be your first task as the *Judenrat*."

Freudiger cleared his throat. "Excuse me, Colonel. We will have to confer with the other Jewish leaders…"

Eichmann slammed down his dagger, scattering the carefully aligned stack of papers on his desk. "Now see what you have done. Enough of this, Jews. I have appointed you the leaders—there are no other leaders as of now. My requirements are not optional. You must order your people, not ask."

The Jews stood there as Eichmann carefully straightened the papers into neat piles. "I'm giving you the power to impose taxes. Take money from the converts; they are the richest." He snorted. "I'll treat them as Jews, anyway.

"You will print a Jewish newspaper to communicate our orders to your people. I'll make every Jew subscribe to it, which will be another source of income for you. For your first issue, you will advise your readers that no Jews may leave the precincts of the capital nor may they change their address. They must wear visible canary yellow stars at all times and ride only in the back of the last car of the trolleys. They are forbidden to sit on park benches, attend theaters or movies or use the public pools.

"That is all for now. You will report to me in two days on the progress that you are making to implement my orders. You will be advised of the location of the next meeting. You are dismissed."

The Jews filed silently out of Eichmann's office. He sat back in his chair, satisfied that his camouflage maneuvers had worked again. Before the Jewish leaders knew it they would be hopelessly enmeshed in his dragnet. There would be no Warsaw Ghetto revolt, no mass escapes and no mercy. The Jewish pigs would be the instruments of their own destruction.

Budapest, Outside the Central Synagogue, March 31, 1944

Stern lowered the brim of his hat to protect his eyes from the unusually bright morning sunshine at winter's end as members of the newly created *Judenrat* walked up Dohány Street toward the Central Synagogue.

Boda turned to Stern, shaking his head. "He's not what I expected. This Eichmann does not sound like a mass murderer. All he seems to want is for us to work hard."

Stern snorted, "You are daydreaming Ernö. Look what happened to the Jews in Poland."

Boda poked Stern in the chest with his right index finger. "Did you ever think, Samu, that maybe the Jews of Poland had not responded to the appeal for quiet behavior? I say let us try it out and see what happens." The others grunted their agreement.

Stern shrugged. "Remember when Dr Kastner sent a clandestine delegation to Kraków, Poland, to see that German industrialist. What was his name?"

"Oskar Schindler."

"Yes, Schindler, that was it," Stern agreed. "Kastner's purpose, if you recall, was to convince us through Schindler and the Jews working in his plants that the rumors about Auschwitz were all too true? We listened to the report they brought back of atrocities and murder of Jews. We laughed in their faces–even called the story a fantasy and fabrication. Even if true, we said," Stern shaking his head exaggeratedly, "it couldn't happen to us. Our Hungarian government would never permit anything like that. But now, having read the report of the two Jews who recently escaped from Auschwitz, do you really think we won't suffer the same fate?"

Wallenberg is here!

"I don't think so, Samu. There's a big difference. After all, Hungary is an ally of Germany; Poland was an enemy of Germany, as was France and Holland. We are Magyarized Jews—Hungarians—our government would not let them sent us to the concentration camps. Especially if we are productive and help the German war effort."

Stern shook his head. "Just look at the men Horthy put into power, Jaross, Endre and Baky, all virulent anti-Semites. They will gladly help the Nazis ship us out to the death camps." He sighed. "I just hope your optimism is warranted. Me? I don't think so."

Freudiger put his hand on Stern's shoulder. "Samu, I think the key to our survival lies in the greed and venality of SS officers like Wisliceny. We have talked privately with him and he is amenable to trading Jewish lives for money. For a few thousand American dollars, he's already agreed to set up meetings with high Nazi officials. I think we can strike a deal to save the Jews of Budapest for a few million dollars. Wisliceny told us to have the first installment of $100,000 ready."

Stern was not impressed. "I'll tell you a true story. A few years ago, I met a man in Czechoslovakia. It was at a time when Eichmann was permitting some emigration to Palestine. His brother had paid Eichmann to approve visas for his entire family. At the last minute, Eichmann withdrew the approval for the man's parents and sister. 'They are hostages,' Eichmann told him, 'so I can be assured you will not speak ill of Germans or allege that they treat the Jews cruelly.' The brother left for Palestine with his wife and without his parents and sister. A short time later, Eichmann shipped them to one of the death camps."

Freudiger's eyes narrowed. "What's your point, Samu?"

"My point," Stern hissed, "is that they will take all your money and then they will gas you." He put his arm around Freudiger's shoulder. "I am afraid, my dear Pinchas, money will not save you, and there is no help, no savior, in sight. We are alone in our unequal struggle."

Budapest, Central Synagogue, April 2, 1944

At eleven in the morning a black Mercedes limousine, red Nazi flags on the front fenders snapping furiously in the wind, and its motorcycle escort, screeched around the corner onto Dohány Street and pulled up to the front entrance to the Central Synagogue, braking suddenly. Making a grand entrance, the motorcyclists gunned their engines, roaring in unison before falling into dead silence.

Eichmann and Wisliceny emerged from the limousine, resplendent, this time in their black Gestapo dress uniforms and black peaked caps. As they climbed the steps to the synagogue's main entrance, the heels of their boots clicked on the stone in almost perfect unison.

Eichmann stopped midway up the steps, looking up at the tall, slender turrets, soaring above the center of the synagogue, and the huge, imposing Star of David cut out of tan brick trimmed with dark brown, high above the front entrance. Looming over the star was the great metal dome of the main sanctuary. The two officers entered the building and then the sanctuary to confront the reception line of the *Judenrat*.

Stern stepped forward. "Welcome, Colonel. If you wish, we can give you a tour of the synagogue."

Eichmann looked around the massive sanctuary, at its inlaid mosaic tile aisle flowing into the huge gold and red Ark, with its eternal flame flickering above the bema, flanked by massive candelabra, lit for the occasion. Intricately wood-carved balconies were suspended along each side, intersected midway by smaller, gilded pulpits under golden crowns etched with the Stars of David. Eichmann already knew this was considered one of the great synagogues of Europe. He shook his head. "No tour is necessary, I can see it all from here. Very impressive. Now, let's get down to work."

Stern led the procession into a meeting room off the central courtyard in back of the synagogue. They took seats around a U-shaped table, Eichmann and Wisliceny sitting with Stern at the head of the table. Both Germans declined glasses of sweet red wine.

Eichmann took off his cap and placed it on the table so that its smiling death's head faced most of the *Judenrat*. He began speaking softly. Some of the older council members had to lean forward, straining to hear. Eichmann saw them but did not bother raise his voice. "I am a reasonable man—if I am not crossed. You must trust me and keep your people calm. After the war and the Third Reich's glorious victory, you will be able to go back to your normal lives." He paused and then raised his voice, "But only if you help me now. Are you willing?"

Most of the council nodded their heads vigorously. Stern did not. Instead, he addressed Eichmann. "Colonel, what type of help are you contemplating?"

Eichmann smiled. "It's fairly simple. As a start, I require three hundred mattresses and six hundred blankets for the Germany Army and I want them in ninety minutes!"

Freudiger shook his head. "It's impossible to obtain that many items in ninety minutes, Colonel, be reasonable."

Eichmann stood, first banging his fist on the table, then strutting around, his jackboots resounding on the wooden floor. "Listen you pigs," he shouted, "if I could figure out how to load thousands of Jews onto the trains for deportation in ten minutes, ninety minutes should certainly suffice to comply with my demands. And after you have made that delivery, you will evacuate all Jewish buildings such as schools, factories and places of worship. Henceforth those buildings are the property of the Gestapo."

At a look from Eichmann, Wisliceny rose. Without another word, both men marched out of the courtyard gate directly into the street to the waiting staff car. The long, black vehicle roared to life and sped away with its unmuffled motorcycle escort.

Stern shook his head. "And it was good seeing you, too, Colonel Eichmann," he muttered. Leaning over to Boda, he asked, "You still think we can deal with this madman? We, my friend, are in deep, deep, trouble. And we have nowhere to turn."

Boda looked down. "And just how do we avoid becoming instruments in the murder of our own people?"

Stern frowned, staring at Eichmann's receding limousine. "I don't know, my friend. To tell you the truth, I feel like the captain of a large sinking ship with one small, leaky lifeboat."

***

A few minutes later, the air raid sirens wailed. Stern and the others hurried to the synagogue basement. Very soon, wave after wave of Liberators from the Fifteenth United States Army Air Force arrived and dropped their bombs on Budapest. The British planes came at night. This Allied response to the German takeover would continue until the city fell to the Soviets.

Pest, Streets, and Buda, Majestic Hotel, Eichmann's Office, Early April 1944

Driver, pull over to the curb." The German staff car screeched to a halt, as did the car following it. Eichmann pointed to a well-kept white brick building. "A very important rabbi lives here."

A perplexed Krumey knitted his brow. "Excuse me, Colonel?'

Eichmann smiled thinly. "I met this rabbi from Budapest a few years ago in Berlin. He was introduced as 'an important Jew in the Budapest community.' I looked up his address. Let's see if he remembers me. Have the Gestapo bring him out."

Krumey climbed out of the car and conferred with the Gestapo agents in the other car. Three agents got out. One rapped hard on the front door of the rabbi's house. When the door opened a crack, they forced their way in. A minute later, they led out a very frightened man.

Eichmann opened the staff car window, stuck his head out and looked over the bearded man with a skullcap. "You recognize me, Rabbi?"

The man shook his head.

"So—you don't remember me, heh, important Jew?"

Eichmann rolled up the window. Krumey looked at the rabbi. "You would have done well to have remembered—that was Colonel Adolph Eichmann." He ordered one of the agents, "Take the Jew to Eichmann's office."

***

Eichmann took a deep drag on a cigarette as he watched the rabbi being shoved into his office. Eichmann's glare matched that of Hitler in the portrait hanging behind him. He leaned forward on his large mahogany desk. "After today you will never forget me again, important Jew." He nodded to Krumey.

The doors to the office opened. Three German soldiers dragged in two boys, one about thirteen and the other, eight. A Gestapo officer carried in a year-old infant.

Wallenberg is here!

Eichmann looked at the rabbi. "These two boys struck a German soldier who had business with their mother. This officer will teach them a lesson." He nodded toward the officer, who handed the baby to a soldier and lit a cigarette. He grabbed the eight-year-old boy's hand and held it securely against the flat surface of the glass-topped desk. He pressed the glowing end of the cigarette against the back of the boy's hand but not hard enough to extinguish it. The boy screamed, but the officer continued to hold the cigarette firmly against the skin. A burning flesh stench filled the room. The rabbi turned from the sight. The boy tossed his head in every direction, struggling to free his hand. When he fainted, a soldier dragged him out of the room.

The Gestapo officer then picked up a large cigar lighter sitting on the desk and flicked it on. He unsheathed his SS dagger and held the tip of it over the flame until it glowed. He approached the older boy, whose arms were pinned back by the soldier. The officer grabbed the boy's right upper eyelid and raised it revealing the full pupil, dilated in terror. The officer inserted the hot tip into the boy's eye. The victim continued to scream as he was pushed out of the office.

Eichmann leaned back in his chair, taking deep drag and watching the smoke curling towards the ceiling. As the rabbi moved away from the German soldier, Eichmann laughed.

"Oh, don't be afraid. We won't harm you now. After all, you are an important Jew, are you not?"

"You've made your point, Colonel," the rabbi said softly.

"Not quite yet, Rabbi. The Jewish scourge must be destroyed. The way to do it is to destroy your young. The old people will destroy themselves. Pay attention."

Eichmann turned to the officer. "Shoot the infant, now."

The Gestapo officer hesitated. He unfastened the flap of his holster but did not remove the pistol. He looked at the infant, then back to Eichmann and shook his head. "I'm sorry, Colonel, but I cannot. It's only a helpless baby."

Eichmann leaped up, his face turning crimson with rage. "That was an order, Lieutenant! Report to your captain immediately." When the officer turned to leave, Eichmann put up his hand. "No, wait a second. You need a little toughening. After all, Lieutenant, that brat is only a Jew." He walked around his desk to the soldier holding the smiling infant. He drew his Luger pistol.

Turning to the rabbi, he said, "Now watch. You will never forget me again, important Jew."

Eichmann pressed the pistol against the child's skull. The soldier winced and held the infant away from his body. Without hesitation, Eichmann squeezed the trigger. The baby went into a spasm. Eichmann looked at the baby's blood on his Luger and tossed it to one of the soldiers. "Clean this up, and send someone in to mop up this Jewish mess," pointing to the blood and brains on the floor.

He turned back to the rabbi. "The infant's meat will feed my dogs and his bones ground up into fertilizer."

"You monster, I'll kill you," screamed the rabbi lunging at Eichmann's throat. Eichmann sidestepped as the soldier's pistol butt crashed into the rabbi's skull. Two soldiers grabbed the rabbi under the arms and looked to Eichmann for instructions. The colonel lit another cigarette. "Put him on a truck and ship him to the concentration camp—and make sure his entire family joins him." He blew the smoke at the barely conscious rabbi. "Goodbye, important Jew."

CHAPTER 5

Mukachevo, April 13, 1944

Eichmann arrived in Mukachevo, a large town in the middle of the sub-Carpathian agricultural area of Hungary. Climbing out of the car and looking around, he didn't like what he saw—an ugly place with thatched huts and houses lining the main street. Peddlers, most of them farmers, hawked vegetables and fruit from broken-down horse-drawn wagons and pushcarts. The town consisted mostly of dirt roads and peasants scratching out marginal livings. It had none of the culture or beauty of Budapest, not that he expected it to have. But it had one thing of great interest to Eichmann; it was home to thirteen thousand Jews. So he had selected Mukachevo to initiate and test the roundup procedures for the provinces.

Eichmann looked at the filthy street and then at his boots, which were already sullied. About to bend over with a cloth, he thought better of it—no sense cleaning them until after he left this godforsaken place.

Major Krumey, who had arrived from Budapest the day before, welcomed him. Krumey handed Eichmann a list of Mukachevo Jews. He scanned it, briefly. "Are they all wearing the yellow stars?"

Krumey nodded. "For over a week. The gendarmes have been going from house to house, driving the Jews out into the street and herding them to the local synagogue. Later they're marched to the railroad siding. One trainload has already left."

"Are the Hungarians finding the Jews' money, jewelry and other valuables?"

"They are doing a thorough job," Krumey assured.

"Himmler will want a full report. Give me the details."

"It's the same as we did elsewhere. Hungarian gendarmes are storming the Jewish houses, torturing the occupants until they reveal the location of all their valuables. You know the routine—wives are beaten in front of their husbands, children tortured in the presence of their parents, and so on. And God help those Jews who have no valuables to reveal; they are likely to be beaten to death. The gendarmes are quite skilled at inflicting pain. It's an efficient collection system."

Eichmann nodded. "Are they checking for items the Jews may have hidden on their persons?"

"Of course. Such valuables are being collected at the synagogue and all good clothing is taken from them. Then they are marched to the ghetto area. After the homes are vacated, we have trained local civil servants to search the houses for other hidden valuables. You'll be interested in a rather novel method of locating valuables buried in basements. They soak the dirt floor with water. Where the water first sinks in reveals freshly dug earth and a likely hiding place."

Eichmann frowned. "That's all well and good, but I don't trust those Hungarian scum; they'll try to keep most of it for themselves."

"What else can we do?" Krumey asked. "We don't have the manpower to do it ourselves."

"Unfortunately," Eichmann growled, "I can't squeeze any more men out of Himmler."

"We have another problem," Krumey offered. "We'll have to expand the size of the ghetto. We haven't been able to get enough trains to ship out the rounded-up Jews. There's not enough room for two thousand Jews, much less the thirteen thousand we are cramming in there."

Eichmann slapped his riding crop on the side of his jackboot. "No, no, we shall not enlarge the ghetto. It's a waste of resources—the Jews will be shipped to the death camps in short order, anyway. Let them stay outside."

"In this weather?" It was a typical damp and cold April day.

Eichmann snickered. "The ghetto will be like a sanatorium, providing the Jews with a healthier open-air life in exchange for their former mode of living."

"Are those further indignities necessary?" asked Krumey.

Eichmann's face clouded over. "Obviously, you have to work at stiffening your backbone if you are to continue doing this kind of work. Remember Himmler's admonition to the SS, 'You must be hard for this struggle to the death.'"

A disturbance caught Eichmann's attention. Two German soldiers were struggling with a powerfully built young Jew resisting their efforts to shove him into the back of a Gestapo car. A young officer came to their assistance. Eichmann recognized him as someone he'd

Wallenberg is here!

recruited for the Eichmann *Kommando*. Lieutenant Hans Kröner was the type of hard man the SS needed.

Kröner stepped calmly behind the Jew, smashing him in the back of the head with the butt of his revolver. The Jew's struggle ceased immediately. One of the soldiers handcuffed the stunned young man.

"Perhaps since the Jew does not want to get in the car, we can accommodate him with an open air-ride." Kröner said it loudly enough for Eichmann to hear. "Attach his handcuffs to the rear bumper and take him to headquarters."

Eichmann smiled. "That should teach the Jew a lesson, eh, Major? That Kröner is innovative. Keep an eye on him."

Krumey heard the car start up. He turned away from the sight of the screaming man. Eichmann slapped Krumey on the shoulder. "I'd say my men have the situation well in hand, don't you agree?" Krumey nodded without speaking.

Eichmann tapped the paper in his hand with his finger. "According to this schedule, the next trains are due here early this evening. Have you been having any trouble getting the Jews on the trains?"

"Some of the Jews, mostly young males, have taken to sitting on, and clinging to, the rails. It takes a squad of soldiers to carry them to the freight cars and throw them in."

"We don't have the time or manpower to spare for such foolishness. Simply shoot the resisters as an object lesson and leave their bodies beside the tracks."

"I will pass that on, Colonel."

"And Krumey—our rolling stock is limited, so pack them in like herrings, with no more than two waste buckets and one bucket of water to a car. As the Jews are loaded onto the train, make them stand and raise their arms—that way, you can squeeze in a few more people. Then seal the cars."

"But, under those conditions," protested Krumey, "many of them won't even survive to the border, much less to Auschwitz."

"Well, isn't that the whole point, Major? It'll give Commandant Höss fewer people to deal with at the gas chambers. Don't you..."

Another commotion. Eichmann turned to look. A soldier approached, dragging a screaming old woman by the arm. She wore no yellow star.

"What do we have here, Sergeant, a Jew without a yellow star?"

"No sir, I caught this woman giving food to the Jews crammed on the trucks."

"Throw her on the trucks with the Jews. She can join their journey to hell."

"But sir, she's a Gentile!"

"That, Sergeant, is known as setting an example. It will discourage other peasants from trying to help the Jewish vermin."

"Immediately, Colonel."

Eichmann looked at Krumey. "Come back to Budapest with me. I don't know about you, but I've certainly had enough of this poor excuse of a town. Let's return to civilization."

In the back seat of the staff car, Eichmann watched the smoke from the long drag on his cigarette curl upward. "Thirteen days—that's what I calculate it will take to clear the thirteen thousand Jews out of Mukachevo. It will become a model for all the other towns. Next, we will start cleansing ten towns at a time. We must maintain our schedule." Reaching down to the bar behind the front seat, he poured himself a brandy and offered one to Krumey. "Life doesn't get much better than this, does it?"

Krumey grunted noncommittally.

Mukachevo, that Evening and the Next Day

That evening, the freight train rolled into the Mukachevo siding on schedule. Hungarian gendarmes lifted the locking bars, throwing open the sliding doors to the cattle cars. Lieutenant Hans Kröner, standing in the stationmaster's office, watched the activity. As he reviewed the list of Jews, his eyes widened when he recognized one of the names.

He picked up the telephone. "Sergeant, resume the roundup immediately. We must fill that train by morning. Pull them out of the houses at random, if you have to, but get me two thousand Jews to ship. Leave the Jewess Zöldi alone—no one is to disturb her or her house. Is that understood?"

Kröner walked down the main street. The scene bordered on the surreal. The peddlers were gone. In the fading light, people screamed and ran; mothers looked for children and children looked for parents. The gendarmes, in their tall, cock-feathered hats, grabbed anyone on the street with a yellow star—men, women and children—driving

Wallenberg is here!

them on the run with whips, rifle butts and truncheons towards the railroad siding. Jews who tried to flee were shot on the spot and left to soak in their own blood. Those who couldn't keep up, or who tripped or fainted, suffered the same fate. Kröner counted at least twenty bodies in the streets.

After dark the SS detachment set up electric arc lights around the Jewish quarter. Four-man squads of SS and gendarmes pounded on doors. Where there was no immediate answer, they broke windows and forced doors with crowbars or battering rams. Where families barricaded themselves in, they blew the doors off their hinges with grenades.

Kröner shouted above the noise: "Get those damn Jews out of the houses and down to the trains—now!"

He watched people being driven into the streets as they were, some in nightclothes, others in various stages of undress. Screams filled the air as people who resisted leaving their homes were kicked, beaten with whips and smashed with rifle butts.

A woman dragged out of her house screamed that her baby was still inside. The gendarme cracked her across the face with a club. He pushed her, staggering and bloody, to the middle of the street where other Jews were being gathered for the run to the train. Curious, Kröner entered the house. The empty front room looked comfortable enough; steam from a cup of still warm tea on the kitchen table curled lazily toward the ceiling. A plate full of sweet biscuits stood beside it. Kröner walked over to the table, picked up a biscuit and bit into it. It had a slight almond flavor. He finished it and stuffed the rest in his pocket. It would be a long night.

He moved into the bedroom, where he found the baby, wearing only a short shirt, curled up in a corner. The splattering pattern of blood and brains told the story. The baby had been flung or swung against the wall with considerable force, headfirst. Its little head had been crushed. Kröner, looking at the results without visible reaction, fished into his pocket and began chewing on another biscuit.

In the street, the SS and gendarmes continued to run the people to the railway siding. Kröner had to trot to keep up, skipping from side to side to avoid the pools of blood and the dead bodies strewn about. Mothers carried dead children in their arms; children pulled and dragged dead parents by their arms and legs down the road to the siding.

When out of the range of the arc lights, the SS set off flares to illuminate the street to keep the beaten, hounded and wounded Jews from slipping away. Rail car after rail car was crammed full, one hundred to a car. Women fainted, children cried for water. Those Jews with the foresight to bring containers of water had them unceremoniously spilled out on the ground by the SS, on orders of Lieutenant Kröner. The vents of the cattle cars were boarded up. The doors clanged shut and the locking bars were slammed into place.

***

A small band of the Jewish underground, led by a man known only as Solomon, grimly watched the horrifying scene from the edge of the forest that surrounded Mukachevo. Reuven, a short, powerfully built man in his mid-twenties, had tears in his eyes. "Solomon, we can't just stand here and watch our brothers and sisters being slaughtered like so much vermin."

"What would you have me do?" replied Solomon, not without a little anger. "We are only a few partisans with a limited amount of small arms. If we attack the Germans now, they will wipe us out with their tanks and heavy weapons and we will not be around later to avenge our people. We must grow strong in numbers and arms. Right now we are just forming our resistance groups."

"How could we have been so complacent?" Reuven spit out. "We knew what the Nazis were doing to the Jews in other countries."

Solomon shrugged his shoulders. "Misplaced faith, I suppose, that Hungary would protect its own Magyarized Jews. I was as guilty of this fantasy of protection as anyone. Now we are paying the price. We must quickly build up our numbers with young, dedicated fighters."

Reuven, white lipped, persisted. "We must do something now; let's kill a few Germans, for starters."

Putting his hand on Reuven's shoulder, Solomon cautioned, "The Germans must not know we exist—at least not yet. What you and several of your men can do under the cover of darkness is help some of the young men escape the roundup and join with us. In the meantime I'll figure out how, without revealing ourselves, we can eliminate the German officer in charge of carrying out these outrages."

***

The next morning, as the fireman stoked the locomotive to work up a head of steam, Kröner and his orderly, inside the stationmaster's office, could still hear screams from the cars. Those near the boarded up vents, begged, through the cracks, for water.

The orderly smiled. "Good Morning, Lieutenant. How are you this fine day?"

"Tired but fulfilled."

The orderly unfolded a clean white cloth and placed it on the heavy wooden table. He served the lieutenant a hot breakfast, starting with a cup of steaming coffee. Kröner wolfed down the meal. Sipping the coffee contentedly, he watched the long train, groaning as the couplings absorbed the strain and initial shock of acceleration, start to roll out of the siding. It slowly picked up speed. He continued to watch the diminishing outline of the last car until it disappeared, merging into the horizon.

Fatigued from the long but successful night's work, he yawned. "The Colonel would be pleased," he said under his breath. "Perhaps he'd even promote me to the rank of captain." But first, there were nine thousand more Jews in Mukachevo to process. He looked forward to meeting the Jewess, Frau Zöldi—but that would have to wait for now.

Mukachevo, Two Weeks Later

Teca Zöldi sat in her in-law's house on the edge of town, fingering the postcard she'd just received from her husband. She read it for the hundredth time: "All is well with us. I am working here. Sebo." She stared at the card, trying to find some subliminal message. She divined none. She turned the card over and stared at the colored picture of a place called Waldsee, described on the card as "A resort town in Austria."

Her husband and daughter had left the house on Monday morning, two weeks ago, looking for food. She hadn't seen them since. Shortly after they disappeared, she had heard that the Gestapo and the Hungarian gendarmes had rounded them up, without warning, in the first random sweep of the streets—any Jews they came across would do. During the two weeks, she could hear the SS outside screaming in German at the gendarmes to fill the waiting freight train. Since her family had disappeared, she guessed that most of the other Jews in town must also have been shipped out. But the Germans hadn't come to her house. She had sat there, waiting. Then the post card had come, slipped through the slot in the door.

At least her daughter, Evike, hadn't been separated from her father. For that, Teca was thankful. After all, Teca reasoned, hadn't her husband used the word "us" in the postcard?

Teca had grown up in a Hungarian provincial town like this. She'd lived with anti-Semitism all her life. True, there'd been no pogroms like those in Russia or Poland, but nevertheless, she could feel the hatred of the Gentiles toward her as a Jew, even as a child and she didn't understand it. The Gentile boys were the worst and she was told by her parents to keep away from them. Her mother, whenever she bought Teca new shoes, would bury them in mud overnight so when Teca wore them, no one would notice they were new and take them away from her.

Teca loved dancing. Her wise father had sent her out of the stultifying town to live with an aunt in Budapest, where she had had the opportunity to take ballet classes. She had made the most of it. Her talents were quickly recognized and on her seventeenth birthday the Budapest Ballet had hired her. After a few years, Teca became one of the prima ballerinas. She met Sebo Zöldi, a Jewish actor in the Hungarian theater, and married him six months later. Both had productive and exciting lives in Budapest. They hoped their daughter, Evike, would follow in Teca's footsteps and become a ballerina. Then the Hungarian Parliament had enacted a rash of anti-Jewish legislation in the early forties to appease their German allies. Nevertheless, both Teca and Sebo prospered until the latter part of 1943, when the ballet and theater companies had to fire them under the new restrictive regulations that banned Jews from the professions and the theater.

In March 1944, out of work and bored, Teca and Sebo had taken Evike to visit his parents in Mukachevo. In the worst of timing, they had arrived the day before the Germans occupied Hungary. The Gestapo rolled into town two days later and immediately prohibited all Jews from traveling. The Zöldis were trapped in Mukachevo.

Wallenberg is here!

Now, of the five of them, Sebo's parents and her family, she was the only one left in the house. The others had been taken early in the occupation. She didn't understand why, but so far, she'd been spared.

A sharp rap on the door interrupted her thoughts. A voice speaking Hungarian with a heavy German accent shouted, "Open up, Teca Zöldi, I know you're in there!"

She had hoped against hope, but she knew it was just a matter of time before they came for her. The rapping on the door became more insistent, more urgent. Trembling with fear, she forced her unwilling legs to lift her out of the chair, stumbled to the door and unbolted it. A German officer in a smartly tailored, silver gray everyday Gestapo uniform pushed it open and stepped inside, his peaked cap politely cradled in his arm. He deposited a large bag on the floor. She stood there, silent and thoroughly confused, waiting.

He looked at her. "Do you speak German?"

She nodded.

"Excellent. Frau Teca Zöldi, I presume?"

She nodded again.

He bowed and clicked his heels. "Lieutenant Hans Kröner at your service."

She saw the death's head emblem on his cap and the twin Sig Runes on his lapel—he was SS.

He caught her look. "Please, relax, I have not come to harm you. Tell me, you were a ballerina with the Budapest Ballet, is that correct?"

"Yes," she whispered.

His face lit up. "Ah, good, I thought that was you. I saw you perform once. You were superb." He took her hand and lightly kissed it. "It is my pleasure. This cow-flop town has no culture of any kind."

As Kröner began moving all the furniture toward the walls of the large room, Teca mustered up the courage to speak again. "What are you doing?"

The lieutenant smiled. "You shall dance for me."

She knitted her brow, puzzled. Then she understood. Her eyes blazed in anger. "Why should I?"

He tossed his cap onto a small table he'd moved near the door. "Because, Teca—may I call you Teca?"

She shrugged.

"Because, Teca, it will keep you," he smiled, "and your lovely family alive. Is that reason enough?"

She stood there, stunned.

The officer lifted an old phonograph out of the bag and set it on the table alongside his cap. "It's not exactly a modern device," he said, winding it up, "but at least it doesn't require electricity."

He fished several phonograph records out of the bag and examined them. "Shall we start with a selection from *Swan Lake*? It's one of my favorite ballets even though a Slavic barbarian wrote it. The quality of the record is marginal but sufficient."

He gently laid the record on the turntable, softly lowering the arm onto the outer edge of the fragile record, careful the needle did not bounce and mar the grooved surface. The scratchy strains of *Danse des Petits Cygnes* filled the room. For Teca, it might as well have been *Danse Macabre*.

"I have no dancing shoes," she said hoarsely.

Kröner smiled. With a jerk, he pulled a pair of ballet shoes out of the bag and tossed them to her. "*Voilà*, try these."

Despite herself, she felt a shiver of pleasure from forgotten feelings as she turned the precious satin slippers over gently in her hands, running her fingers lightly over the fabric. "These may not fit."

"Teca, just tell me your foot size and I will try to find other shoes. Now, please, no more objections. Dance!"

"I must stretch first."

He sighed and sat down. "Very well, I'll wait."

Teca danced. It had been more than a few months, but her technique had not deserted her. To her surprise, dancing proved therapeutic. Totally immersed in the music and the command performance, she forgot the war, the roundups and Lieutenant Kröner; her world now consisted only of the magical, graceful white swan.

The record ended. Kröner applauded vigorously. "Bravo, Teca. You are beautiful and most talented—even in those old clothes. Next time, I shall bring a lovely costume for my star ballerina."

***

Every day for a week, Kröner arrived precisely at five in the afternoon. He brought her food. "Eat, Teca," he insisted. "You must keep up your strength to dance." She'd don the ballet costume and

Wallenberg is here!

slippers while he wound up the phonograph. Teca was not the only one carried away into the land of enchantment. Kröner, the audience of one, also lost himself in the music and the dance. That was sufficient for him. He never entertained thoughts of abusing or forcing himself on her. That, he knew, would destroy the magic.

***

At the end of the week, Kröner arrived at his usual time, wound the phonograph and sat back in the easy chair he had delivered to her house for his comfort. Barely had the dancing begun when a heavy pounding on the door broke the spell. Angry, Kröner flung open the door. "What the..." The obscenity died on his lips.

A tall, blond, blue-eyed SS major stood framed in the doorway, hands defiantly on his hips. Kröner snapped to attention.

"Send the woman out immediately, Lieutenant, I must question her. You wait in the house. Then, I will send her back in for your enjoyment." The major smiled, but his tone most definitely did not invite questions or discussion.

Kröner *heiled* smartly, then motioned to Teca to leave. She grabbed her coat and stepped outside. The SS major slammed the door shut behind her. If Teca had become used to having Kröner around, this strange, new SS officer put her once again into a state of terror. "What do you want with me?"

Taking her firmly by the arm, he whispered, "Walk around the house with me; we must be out of earshot."

Teca looked at him, her brow knitted in confusion.

He smiled. "I am with the Jewish underground. I'm known as Solomon."

Her eyes widened. "The Jewish underground in Hungary? There's no such thing!"

"There is now," he reassured her, "and we will build it up into an avenging force."

Still doubtful, Teca asked, "B-but your uniform? You look just like one of them!"

He shrugged. "Runs in the family, I guess. My mother was blond and blue-eyed—I'm her little Aryan who's fluent in German. It helps acting the part of an SS officer. I assure you though, I'm thoroughly

Jewish—but we don't have time to chat about family histories. You are in great danger."

"He won't harm me, I'm providing his entertainment."

The ersatz major looked down at his feet. "The lieutenant is leaving in two days, all the SS and Gestapo are. They are about finished clearing the Jews out of here. They'll be moving to another town. You are among the last. You will be shipped out tomorrow—or shot—no exceptions. The curtain is ringing down, Teca. This is your last performance. You can join us, if you have the fortitude."

"What do you mean, the 'fortitude'?"

"You must demonstrate you have the stomach for partisan warfare. We can't afford the luxury of weakness. You must show me. Go in there and kill him." He held out his Luger.

She shook her head violently. "I can't!"

"Why, do you care for him?"

Her eyes blazed with anger. "How can you think that? I hate him, but he is protecting my child and husband."

He shook his head slowly. "When did the Germans take them?"

"Three weeks ago."

"Then the lieutenant lied. They are dead," he said flatly, meeting her glare without looking away.

Teca bit her lip as tears welled. "You are wrong." She fished into her coat pocket and pulled out a creased, worn postcard. "Look, from Waldsee."

He didn't look at the card. "I already know what it says. 'All is well with us. I am working here.'"

Her knees buckled. She grabbed his arm. "How...?"

He shook his head slowly and grimaced. "Ah, Teca, my naïve girl, the cards, they are all the same. The Jews were forced to write these cards in Auschwitz. They were dictated by the SS, shortly before the card writers were gassed."

Now, the tears flowed freely down her cheeks. "I don't believe you—I can't believe you." She shook her head violently. "They're at Waldsee, my little girl..."

He sighed. "The SS intended the cards to dispel panic among those not yet rounded up—just so you'd grasp at straws and hope your man survived. But some of the victims managed to send cards that carried a different, secret, message. They signed the cards with Hebrew words such as *R'evim*, meaning 'hungry,' or *Blimalbish*, 'without clothes.' The Germans were none the wiser since they couldn't read Hebrew."

Teca, sobbing, covered her face with both hands. "Oh, God."

He put a gentle hand on her arm. "And Teca—there's no such place in Austria as Waldsee. It's pure fiction."

Seizing his sleeve, she cried out, "But I'm not like the Nazis, I can't just kill someone."

He grabbed her shoulders firmly, his blue eyes boring into her. "Shh, you mustn't let the lieutenant hear you. He may seem cultured to you, but Teca, this Kröner is a sadistic animal who revels in torturing, degrading and killing our people"

Teca nodded, biting her lip, casting her eyes down.

"Teca, look at me."

She raised her head.

He spoke quietly but with emotion. "We aren't like them either—you've got to believe that—but we must do what we must to survive. Do you doubt that?"

"No," she whispered, dropping her eyes.

"Good. Now, you can go in there, kill him and join us, or"—he shrugged—"dance for him until you go up in smoke in Auschwitz." He lifted her chin with a light touch and looked in her brown eyes. "Teca, it's your choice." He placed the pistol in her coat pocket and patted it.

Teca did not respond. She turned and disappeared into the house. The impostor major waited. The familiar strains of *The Waltz of the Flowers* wafted out from the open window. He sighed, shrugged and started to walk away.

The sound startled him. It shouldn't have. The underground fighter was as familiar with the retort of a Luger pistol as he was with the strains of the Tschaikovsky ballet. He recovered quickly, smiled and walked back to the house to fetch Teca, the underground's newest member.

BUDAPEST

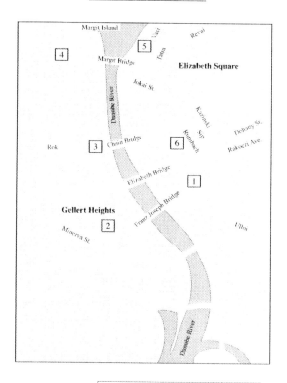

1) Wallenberg Headquarters, Section C
2) Swedish Legation
3) Royal Castle
4) Rose Hill
5) Swedish Safe Houses
6) Central Synagogue

Streets of Budapest, a Day in Early May 1944

Samu Stern, on behalf of the *Judenrat*, requested a meeting with Eichmann to discuss treatment of the Jews in the provinces. Eight members of the council walked to Gestapo headquarters. Boda quickened his pace to pull alongside Stern. "Samu, the Germans have cut our food rations, confiscated our money and valuables and forbidden us to leave our apartments. And the Hungarian Nazis are no better. They have frozen our bank accounts and confiscated our radios, telephones and typewriters. Now Eichmann is demanding 1,500 vacant apartments and a Jewish labor force to repair SS facilities damaged by Allied bombings. Last week, the SS took over the synagogue on Kazincky Street and made it into a stable; the Rabbinical Seminary on Rök Street is now a prison for Jews. Can you believe it, the Rabbinical Seminary? How can we live like this?"

"We can't. But that's their whole point, isn't it? Those situations, however, are not the purpose of our visit to the colonel today."

"But Samu, Endre just assured us that the Jews in the provinces are safe." Boda pulled out the written communication from the minister to the *Judenrat*. "Let me read it to you."

Stern spread his arms. "I've already read it, but read it if you wish."

Boda cleared his throat, skipping the salutation. "'The Jews have not been taken out of Hungary, they have only been removed from the zone of operations at the request of the Germans. Three hundred and twenty-five thousand Jews have thus been concentrated in the interior of the country. If they behave well, no more Jews are to be taken to concentration camps, only to ghettos.' You see? The minister has assured us."

Stern looked straight ahead. "You know better. He's a liar, the Hungarian equivalent of Adolph Eichmann. Haven't you heard what's happening from Jews escaping the provinces, and from the Jewish underground?"

Boda hunched his shoulders. "Maybe they exaggerate, no?"

Stern shook his head, laying a hand on Boda's shoulder. He sighed. "Ernö, Ernö, don't we have enough on our consciences?"

Boda scrunched his shoulders and dug his hands into his pockets.

Stern gritted his teeth. "You have a short memory—or very large rose-colored glasses. Don't you remember Endre? In the late thirties, this virulent anti-Semite incited the Gentiles in the town of Õjpest into starting a pogrom where several Jews were slaughtered. Now he's a big official anti-Semite. This is the same man who, with Eichmann, urged us to send our brothers in the provinces letters advising them to cooperate with the Nazis, obey regulations, follow orders and remain calm. We did, they followed our advice and all it earned them was a one-way ticket to Auschwitz. No, my friend, there is no reason to believe we will escape their fate. But we will see shortly, when we meet with the colonel, won't we?"

Buda, Majestic Hotel, Eichmann's Office, the Same Day

Captain Franz Novak fingered the buttons on his uniform, making an effort to keep his fidgeting hands still. He could not, however, control his twitching left eye. Seated in front of Eichmann's desk, he leaned away from the colonel who stood over him, in a fury.

Eichmann's face turned crimson as he screamed, "Where are my trains, Novak? How the hell am I supposed to clear the Jews out of Hungary without rails? You're supposed to be my transportation man—a damn lot of help you've been!"

Novak waited. When things weren't going his way, Eichmann resorted to abusing and blaming his subordinates. It didn't surprise Novak.

Eichmann stopped for a breath and, bothered by Novak's constant twitching, looked away.

Novak cleared his throat. He wiped his twitching left eye. "Colonel, the Transportation Ministry refuses to release any more rolling stock. It's desperately needed for the war effort on the Eastern Front. Allied bombings have reduced the supply of railroad cars drastically."

"That is no excuse," Eichmann thundered. "The main thing is statistics—every Jew must be mercilessly seized and shipped out! That simpleton minister from the Transportation Department attended the Wannsee Conference—he knows the program. Getting rid of the Jews must take priority over the war effort—or else everything we are trying to accomplish will have been in vain."

Novak shrugged. "Believe me, Colonel, I have tried everything. Now, I need your help."

Eichmann slapped his thighs with both hands. "Why must I always step in to do things myself? The Führer's orders couldn't be clearer. Let me quote them to you: 'In respect to transportation vehicles, when state interests of exceptional importance are involved, the army may claim priority *only when it is advancing.*' The last I heard, General Weichs's army was retreating. I, therefore, have, and claim, priority."

Wallenberg is here!

He had started screaming again. Novak sat very still, not uttering a word. He would let the string play out. He knew that Eichmann could just as easily have him jailed and tortured.

Eichmann strode around the room, the carpeting absorbing the sound of his jackboots. "Violating the Führer's direct orders is traitorous. Heads will roll!"

Novak cleared his throat. "It's just a respectful suggestion, Colonel, but you may want to consider requesting the intervention of the *Reichsführer* to obtain the rolling stock you need. We can't arrest everyone in the Transportation Ministry or, for that matter, all the generals on the Eastern Front."

Eichmann flopped into his desk chair. "Flippancy will not improve my mood. If you had done your job properly, I would not have to bother Himmler." His voice was lower. He sounded resigned now. "Himmler will support me, he always has when it comes to the Final Solution. I will see to it. Dismissed."

Novak rose from his chair and saluted. Eichmann was right. If there was someone nearly as fanatical as the colonel regarding the Jews, it was the *Reichsführer*. Germany might lose the war as a result, but Himmler and Eichmann would kill their Jews. He closed the door to Eichmann's office, sighed and rubbed his twitching eye. He did not like undercutting his comrades on the Eastern Front, but to argue with the colonel would be foolhardy. Preoccupied with his own problems, Novak gave no more than a passing glance at the Jews, with their yellow stars, sitting in the anteroom. Their concerns didn't interest him in the least.

Wisliceny rapped lightly on the door and entered. Eichmann looked up and snapped, "What is it?"

"You need to sign the order for the routing of the trains, Sir. They're packed with provincial Jews and ready to leave."

"Prepare orders to route them all to Auschwitz."

Wisliceny shook his head. "But Colonel, I don't understand? Veesenmayer assured the prime minister, who had fifty thousand able-bodied Jews rounded up, that they were being shipped to the war armaments factories as slave laborers for the Reich and not to the extermination camps. And the Reich armaments minister is begging for the Jews; they desperately need manpower for the war effort."

Eichmann's dark eyes bored into Wisliceny. "The Gestapo does not have to answer to these weaklings. Ship them to Auschwitz. That's an order."

"Very well, Sir. I will prepare the appropriate papers for your signature."

Eichmann examined his fingernails. They were clean and properly filed. Nevertheless, he took the nail file out of the desk drawer and cleaned them again. He returned the nail file to its proper place in the drawer, stood up and strode to the door. Time to deal with the *Judenrat*.

***

The council had been sitting in Eichmann's anteroom for two hours. Through the heavy wooden doors, they could hear the colonel shouting. They had watched an SS captain leave Eichmann's office. He had ignored them. Then Major Wisliceny had entered the office, closed the door and come out a few minutes later.

Suddenly, the door burst open. Eichmann stood there, slapping a leather riding crop into the palm of his hand. "Now what are you Jews complaining about?"

Stern stood. "Colonel, we have been trying to see you for two weeks."

"I'm a busy man and I have no time for sniveling Jews. You have two minutes to tell me what's on your mind, after which time you will be thrown out."

The council followed the colonel into his office. Major Krumey joined them.

Stern stood there. He hadn't been invited to sit. "Colonel, we have received disturbing reports on the terrible treatment of the Jews in the provinces. We have heard that you have been shipping them out to concentration camps in cattle cars, under inhumane conditions. We must protest."

Eichmann moved directly in front of his visitors. He singled out Stern, his face just inches from Stern's. "You *protest*, you worm? Hear me. Not a single word of those reports is true, for I have just inspected the provincial ghettos, so I ought to know. The accommodation of the Jews is no worse than that of German soldiers during maneuvers and the fresh air will do their health a world of good!"

Stern held his ground. "But Colonel…"

Eichmann put up his hand, cutting off Stern in mid-sentence. "Enough, they are better off. Haven't you people been receiving postcards from them? They are happy, working and healthy." Eichmann examined his fingernails again. "So—just what, Herr Stern, is your complaint?" He didn't look up.

"It's still about the Jews in the provinces, Colonel—thousands are being shipped out every day in freight cars, over one hundred people are being packed into each car with little water, no food and no sanitary facilities. Many are dying in the cars. This is inhumane. You said to come to you if we were being harmed, so here we are."

Eichmann looked at Krumey. "Major, you hear the fairy tales of these Jews?" He slapped a sheaf of papers on his desk. "I have the full report right here." He strode to the desk, returned with the report and shook it in Stern's face. Stern backed up a step.

Eichmann raised his voice, "For your information, Jew, only fifty or sixty died on each trip. Many on the trains were children who don't need as much air or as much space." He laughed. "In that way, we were able to fit that number in a railway car quite comfortably."

János Gabor, a council member, spoke up. "With due respect, Colonel, that's not what we've been hearing. Jews have been thrown out of their homes, herded into open fields, stripped of their valuables, left without food and water, their homes looted by German soldiers, and finally, they've been packed into cattle cars."

Eichmann shrugged. "If there has been bad treatment of the Jews, it was not the fault of the Nazis, but of Minister Endre." He laughed harshly. "Apparently, Endre wants to devour the Jews with sweet pepper." Stepping back, he eyed the entire group with contempt. "I demand you stop bothering me with horror stories of deaths on the transports. If you insist on these Jew-fabricated lies and allegations, each of you will be dealt with as a rumormonger. Do you know what that means?"

None of the council members answered.

Eichmann pointed to the door. "Now get out. You Jews make me sick."

Outside Eichmann's headquarters, Gabor turned to Stern. "Samu, we're in trouble. Those postcards—we've seen the messages hidden in the Hebrew signatures."

Stern looked at Gabor, "So, János, what's your point?"

"So, my point is, we are doomed. We need a miracle—or a savior, maybe more than one."

Stern shook his head. "Just whom did you have in mind."

"The Nazi machine is too powerful," sighed Gabor. "No one can help us."

CHAPTER 6

Stockholm, Office of Ivar Olsen, June 1944

John Pehle, head of the War Refugee Board, appointed Ivar Olsen, a Norwegian-born American, as WRB representative in Sweden. Olsen was a Treasury Department functionary with shadowy connections to the Office of Strategic Services, the OSS, America's wartime spy agency. Without a diplomatic mission in Budapest, there was little the American government could do there directly. Therefore, at Pehle's urging and with FDR's backing, the State Department had asked the Swedish government to increase the number of Swedish diplomats in Budapest and to use all diplomatic means to halt the Nazi campaign of terror against the Jews. The Swedes had agreed to work with Olsen.

Olsen had been instructed to find a non-Jewish Swede with diplomatic standing to send to Budapest. This diplomat, whom the WRB would supply with ample funds, was to be empowered by Sweden to issue Swedish passports with the objective of bringing as many Jews as possible to Sweden. Initially, the Swedes had selected Count Folke Bernadotte as that diplomat, but Hungary had refused to accept his credentials.

***

Olsen looked at his watch. Kálmán Lauer, a Hungarian Jew who owned a large food export company in Stockholm, was due at any moment. Lauer had been pushing hard for the selection of one of his employees, a Raoul Wallenberg, who, he claimed, was perfect for the job in Budapest. Olsen wondered why anyone from the famous Wallenberg family would take on a mission so fraught with danger. The Wallenbergs had their finger in every major Swedish industry: steel, iron ore, timber, electronics, communications, banking, transportation and autos, to name a few. Why wasn't this particular Wallenberg being groomed for a position in the Wallenberg empire instead of toiling in a sales job for Lauer's food export business, Olsen wondered. It didn't make sense.

Olsen was not optimistic. Wallenberg had no diplomatic experience and Rabbi Marcus Ehrenpreis of Stockholm had a negative impression of him. The rabbi, who had interviewed Wallenberg, had reported that the young man had talked mainly about the necessity of having sufficient funds to bribe and pay off Hungarian and Nazi officials and doing whatever else was necessary, legal or illegal, to save the Jews. The rabbi complained that Wallenberg, a rich Protestant boy, was too young, inexperienced and brash and not the right person for the job. Olsen, however, thought as Wallenberg did—do whatever had to be done to save the Jews.

Ushered into Olsen's office, Lauer, a short balding man, held out his hand. He had a heavy Hungarian or Jewish accent. Olsen wasn't sure which.

"Mr. Olsen, thank you for seeing me."

Olsen smiled. "Thank you for coming. Tell me about your proposed savior of the Hungarian Jews."

"Wallenberg's a junior partner in my food export business and a hard worker. As a Jew, I can no longer safely travel in Europe, especially to my native Hungary. Wallenberg has taken over those duties. He's obtained valuable experience dealing with the Nazis. He's done business with them in Berlin, Paris, Budapest and virtually all over Europe."

Olsen looked up at the mention of Budapest.

Lauer picked up on it. "He knows Budapest—been there several times."

Olsen nodded. "I'm curious. Why isn't he in one of his family's businesses?"

"That you'll have to ask him," Lauer responded and then continued. "He's fluent in German, English, French and Russian. He speaks German so well that he could pass for one of them. He can imitate a Gestapo officer so convincingly you would swear he was one—a wonderful actor. Most important, he's fearless and has a burning desire to save Jews in Hungary. Wallenberg spend a year in Palestine, working for a bank in Haifa. He learned firsthand about the persecution of the Jews and took up their cause long before it became fashionable in Sweden. When you meet him you will be convinced. Trust me."

Wallenberg is here!

Olsen frowned. "I don't have to tell you, we're getting desperate. It's three months since the Wehrmacht overran Hungary and the Eichmann *Kommando* is sweeping the countryside clear of Jews. Budapest will be next."

Lauer pressed his lips together, obviously trying to keep his emotions under control. "You don't have to tell me. My family is trapped in Budapest," he said softly.

"Then we must find our man now and dispatch him immediately," Olsen replied. "I will meet with your Mr. Wallenberg. I pray he is our man."

Saltsjobaden, Sweden, Several Days Later

Olsen had planned the dinner at the great rambling hotel resort of Saltsjobaden, where the rich went in the summer to sun, swim and sail their boats. Coincidentally, the resort had been developed by Wallenberg's family fifty years earlier. Olsen had reserved a private dining room in a corner of the hotel's ornate restaurant. Lauer was shown in while Olsen nursed a drink. Right behind him came a thin young man in his thirties, of medium height, with curly brown receding hair, prominent nose and dark, penetrating eyes. Impeccably dressed in a well fitting suit, a conservative tie, and shoes shined to a patent leather finish, Wallenberg flashed a wide grin and shook Olsen's hand with a firm, dry grip as Lauer introduced them. If Wallenberg was nervous, he didn't show it. Olsen liked that.

During dinner, Olsen probed Wallenberg's background. He was a bachelor, currently unattached. That was good. Cold, hard logic told Olsen that the last thing he needed on the mission was a married man with children, not that many Swedes would have been willing to walk into the jaws of the Nazi death machine. His field of candidates was almost nonexistent.

Olsen glanced at some papers. "I see that you spent some time in the United States, at the University of Michigan. Tell me about it."

Wallenberg smiled. "Nothing much to tell. I spent four years there, graduating with a degree in architecture."

Lauer shook his head. "He's being overly modest. His grandfather told me he had graduated at the top of his class and had been captain of the school debating team."

Wallenberg shrugged.

Olsen eyed Wallenberg. "Did you get to see anything of America?"

Wallenberg nodded. "I hitchhiked across America several times."

"Why hitchhike?" asked a puzzled Olsen. He knew the Wallenbergs were wealthy.

"I didn't have an overly large allowance and it was the cheapest way to see the country. Besides, it brought me into close contact with so many different kinds of people." Wallenberg smiled. "It added quite a bit of excitement to my life."

"Excitement?" asked Olsen.

Wallenberg paused, examined his wine, gently twirling the glass and admiring the color. Then he met his host's eyes. "I worked in the Swedish Pavilion at the Chicago World's Fair one summer. To get back to school at Ann Arbor, I hitchhiked with two large suitcases and a bundle of cash, my World's Fair earnings. My first ride resulted in a car crash. We weren't hurt but the car was a wreck. But that, as it turned out, wasn't the exciting part of the journey."

Wallenberg took a sip of wine and put down the glass. "I was left on the road, at night, in the middle of nowhere. A car with Iowa plates and four men stopped and offered me a ride. They had no luggage. That should have made me suspicious, but I was desperate for transportation, so I threw caution to the winds and got in. I told them I couldn't pay anything. Very cleverly, I thought, I worked my poverty into the conversation." Wallenberg shook his head. "I was too clever by half, they robbed me anyway."

Olsen's eyes widened.

"They turned onto a country road," Wallenberg continued, "stopped the car and ordered me out. One of them waved a revolver in my face. They were very nervous, probably the first time they tried this. He demanded my money. I gave them what I had. They also wanted my papers and safe deposit key. I managed to keep the papers and key by some quick talking, claiming sentimental value. When they got back into the car, intending to leave me on that deserted road, I played on their sense of fairness. I said now it was their turn to show some goodwill by giving me a ride back to the main highway since it was late and my suitcases were heavy. They looked at each other and then motioned me to the front passenger seat and piled my luggage on top of me to keep me from trying any funny business."

Wallenberg laughed. "I think they were more scared than I, which I found interesting." Taking another sip of his wine, he continued. "Suddenly, they braked to a halt and pushed me out of the car and into a ditch and then tossed my luggage on top of me. I immediately flattened myself under a bush, fearing they might fire a farewell shot in my direction."

Olsen shook his head in amazement.

Wallenberg grinned and spread his arms. "I know, it's unbelievable and I would understand if you were skeptical of my powers of judgment. The best I can say about that experience is it was great practice in the art of diplomacy and negotiation."

That made Olsen smile. "On the contrary, I believe the story and frankly, I'm impressed. You'll need all the coolness and negotiating skill you can muster if you go to Budapest. I doubt I'll be doing you any favor if I choose you to go." Olsen examined his fingers, then looked up. "Perhaps it's none of my business, but why aren't you in one of your family's enterprises? It would seem to be a natural opportunity for you."

Wallenberg smiled. "I don't mind being asked. You have to understand that the Wallenberg family has a split personality. On one side, my uncles and cousins operate the Wallenberg businesses, while on my side of the family, they became diplomats and do-gooders. Besides, the fact is that I do not see eye-to-eye with my cousins Jacob and Marcus who guard their prerogatives within the Wallenberg empire with zeal. They are not inclined to share their fortune with the other, less affluent, Wallenbergs."

"What do you mean, you do not see eye-to-eye?"

"It's no secret. There's a great deal of pro-Nazi sentiment among the Swedish upper class and my relatives are no exception. I expressed my anti-Nazi views to them at every opportunity. I was particularly incensed at Cousin Jacob selling eight million tons of iron ore a year to feed the German war machine, plus a few million more tons funneled through countries friendly to the Nazis. Their answer: business is business. Besides, they pointed out, Cousin Marcus sold iron ore to the British. When I accused them of being immoral, they began to see me as kind of a black sheep in the family. So, Mr. Olsen, I doubt whether I would ever be welcomed into the business. My grandfather, when he was alive, told me as much."

Olsen looked deep into the young man's eyes. "I can understand that, but why in heaven's name do you want to insert yourself into Budapest's boiling cauldron? We can't really protect you, and your assignment will certainly put your life in danger."

Meeting Olsen's gaze, Wallenberg responded without hesitation. "If there's any way I can help these people, even to save just one of them, I will go. I'm not a religious man, Mr. Olsen, but I do remember the Bible stories about the children of God, and of justice and righteousness. The Scriptures describe the Jewish nation as the 'chosen ones.' These people who gave us so much, they're defenseless now against one of the mightiest military machines on earth. And what is their crime? Existing—simply being in the wrong place at the wrong time."

Olsen could feel the young man's energy radiating throughout the room. Wallenberg stood up and paced around the room. "I usually prefer light movies, the Marx Brothers and Charlie Chaplin, but a few months ago, my sister dragged me to see a Leslie Howard movie called *Pimpernel Smith*. It was about a mild-mannered professor who secretly saved Jews by acts of unbelievable courage behind Nazi lines. It moved me and I told my sister, 'That is just the kind of thing I want to do.'"

Olsen glanced over to Lauer.

Lauer smiled. "Who else but an idealist would take the job?"

Wallenberg wandered over to the window and looked out, then turned back to Olsen. "It's more than idealism. You have to understand that I am part Jewish on my mother's side."

Olsen's eyes widened in surprise.

Wallenberg continued. "I lived in Palestine among the Jews, and in traveling for Lauer, I saw firsthand what was happening to the Jews all over Europe. Berlin Jewry has been virtually annihilated, the Jews of France are being rounded up at an alarming rate, young French children—children, Mr. Olsen—are being shipped in freight cars to death camps as we speak, and that madman Eichmann is now in the throes of eliminating the Jews of Hungary. I have been to all these places and seen these things."

Olsen saw Lauer's clouded expression. He knew the Hungarian was thinking of his wife and child trapped in Hungary.

Wallenberg asked his host, "Have you read the *Auschwitz Protocols*, written by some Jews who escaped that concentration

Wallenberg is here!

camp?" Olsen nodded. Wallenberg's voice took on a sad tone. "It is simply horrible what some humans are capable of doing to millions of others. It is not enough for the Nazis to kill with cold efficiency, they must also torture, starve and beat their victims first."

Lauer's eyes filled with tears. Wallenberg spoke with a passion and earnestness Olsen rarely saw in young men these days.

"You—we—have no choice, Mr. Olsen. Send me. I have dealt with the Nazis and know better than most what makes them tick; I believe I have the ability to cut through Nazi red tape and anyone sent on this mission who cannot do that is doomed to fail. I have a feel for what moves the Nazis and what does not; I can be more German and more officious than any *Obergruppenführer*; I can speak louder and with more authority than a Gestapo officer. Authority, Mr. Olsen, awes Germans, and when necessary, I can project considerable authority. My acting abilities and, I hope, a diplomatic passport, will be my protection."

Olsen thought Wallenberg was already projecting considerable authority.

Lauer, who had been largely silent throughout the meal, cleared his throat. Olsen, mesmerized by Wallenberg's earnest plea, finally turned away from the young man when Lauer started speaking.

"Mr. Olsen, you should see him do imitations. Chinese generals, American politicians, German diplomats—anything you can think of, he can do. He delights children with his animal imitations. You won't find a more fearless and dedicated representative for the WRB. Time's running out for the Jews of Budapest—and my family. You must dispatch someone immediately—please."

The tears still welled in Lauer's eyes. Olsen turned back to the young Swede.

"Mr. Wallenberg, if we sent you, what would you need?"

"Funds—plenty of money for bribing well-connected individuals, for payoffs to the Nazis and Hungarian authorities, and for food, medicine and forged papers. I must have a free hand to do whatever is necessary to save lives—no rules, no reports, no answering to bosses and no diplomatic niceties. In other words, Mr. Olsen, I have to use daring, opportunity and imaginative approaches to deal with problems that defy conventional solutions. I must have diplomatic status without being a diplomat. Anything else will surely doom the mission to failure and the Jews of Budapest to death."

On their way out of the restaurant, well into the morning hours, Olsen pulled Lauer aside when Wallenberg disappeared into the men's room. "I'm impressed, Lauer. This young man is perfect for the job. I'm going to recommend him. I thank you for bringing him to me."

Lauer smiled, then frowned. "But what about Rabbi Ehrenpreis? He's against sending Raoul."

"Don't worry, I'll bring him around. He has no one else. Besides, he's not funding this mission, the WRB is, and if I have to step on a few toes to get this mission off the ground quickly, so be it. Eichmann has been in Budapest since March. We have no time left; the three months wasted already have cost the lives of tens of thousands of Jews in the Hungarian provinces. There are half a million Jews in Budapest. Eichmann is there right now congratulating himself on the lack of outcry from the neutral nations of the world. We must destroy his complacency."

CHAPTER 7

The Budapest Express, July 9, 1944

Catching only snatches of sleep, Wallenberg spent a restless night in the corridor of the crowded train, his thoughts returning repeatedly to his send-off at Stockholm's Bromma Airport and his sister's news about her pregnancy and the bombings in Berlin. *When will I see any of them again?*

In the early morning darkness, the Budapest Express crawled across the Austro-Hungarian border and pulled into Hegyeshalom, jolting to a stop. Jackbooted black-uniformed officers pushed open the doors of the railway car and climbed aboard, shoving through the tightly packed passengers. They shouted angrily for papers.

Wallenberg shook his head at this rude welcome to German-occupied Hungary. He pulled his Swedish diplomatic passport out of his breast pocket. While he waited, he gazed absently out of the window. It was too dark to see much beyond the station platform, which was crawling with the SS and smartly uniformed Hungarian gendarmes.

Wallenberg stared into the darkness beyond the platform and sighed, wondering whether there might be another train out there, waiting to head in the opposite direction, with its passengers packed into cattle cars. Hegyeshalom was also one of the switching stations for the human cargo, where the Hungarians turned over to the SS responsibility for the Jews on the way to the death camps—both the dead and the living.

An hour later, his train resumed its journey. He closed his eyes but his mind wouldn't quiet down, disturbed by his Swedish countrymen's shameful toadying up to the Nazis. German officers swarmed all over Sweden, enjoying its nightclubs and hotels just as if they owned the country; suspected Allied spies were scandalously incarcerated while German agents had free rein in the country. Many Swedes, including his cousins, Marcus and Jacob, were sympathetic to the Nazis and hostile to his mission. He wasn't surprised about

Jacob's attitude. After all, Jacob conducted, for the Wallenberg empire, a highly profitable business selling iron ore to the Germans.

He shifted his legs and vainly commanded his brain to shut down. The thoughts continued. But for the turning of the tide of the war, he doubted the Foreign Ministry would ever have permitted this mission. What the devil was the matter with the Swedes? Were they so preoccupied groveling at the feet of the Nazis to protect their sacred neutrality that they'd lost all sense of morality? And what neutrality? A pro-German one? He finally dropped off to sleep again, but he dreamed about Auschwitz and the gas chambers and that wasn't any better.

Restless shuffling by the passengers woke him. The morning sun streamed through the windows. Wallenberg ached, having slept scrunched over his knapsacks, despite the noisy, nervous chatter of the German soldiers on their way to an uncertain and surely unpleasant fate on the Eastern Front.

He stood up, stretched and patted his pocket. The revolver was still there. The train had slowed to a crawl as it passed though the rail yards and rolled into the Nyugati Palyaudvar Station. Thankful the uncomfortable rail journey was over, Wallenberg stepped off the train, knapsacks hanging from his shoulder. He pushed his way through the crowds in the cavernous, art deco, glass-and-steel-domed Budapest terminal in western Pest and jumped into a dark green cab.

"Understand German?" Wallenberg could speak very little Hungarian.

The driver nodded.

"Good, the Swedish Legation on Gyopar Street in Buda, please." Wallenberg checked his supply of *pengös*. He had enough for the cab ride.

As the city flashed by the cab window, Wallenberg observed ruefully that it was not the same Budapest he'd visited a year ago. With the exception of Horthy, all the moderate politicians were gone, replaced by those with allegiance to the Nazis. The streets were infested with German soldiers and thugs from the Nyilas Party, the Hungarian version of the Nazi Party and known as the Arrow Cross. The green-shirted uniforms were emblazoned with crossed arrows patches, the Hungarian variant of the swastika. No longer were the outdoor cafes along Váci Street crowded with boisterous patrons; no longer did finely dressed woman parade on the elegant Korso. Allied bombers had reduced to rubble large sections of Pest, the commercial center of the city. The SS had blanketed the city with their swastika flags and banners. The "Horst Wessel Song" and German military music blared continually over loudspeakers.

The cab crossed the Danube. Wallenberg leaned forward, resting his arms on the back of the front seat, peering out the front windshield. The hills of Buda, with their fine homes and fashionable shops, came into view. The cab's engine screeched its high-pitched complaint struggling up the steep cobblestone streets of Gellért Hill.

The cab pulled up to a large wrought iron gate, framed by a stone arch, behind which rose the turreted, four-story Swedish Legation, a red brick mansion surrounded by tall trees, their branches, like slender, graceful fingers, reaching up beyond the roof.

Long lines of desperate Jews on the street outside the building marred the impressive setting. Looking pale and haunted, they clutched papers and files, their bright yellow stars stark against the dark coats and jackets. They shuffled and waited. The driver blew his horn to clear the people from the driveway.

He turned to his passenger. "It's the damn Jews trying to leave the country. They think the Swedes will give them passports." He snorted. "Fat chance. Who'd want Jews, anyway?"

"Never mind," Wallenberg snapped. "Just let me out here. I'll walk to the gate." He dropped his knapsacks and flashed his diplomatic passport at the armed Arrow Cross guards. The large iron gate swung open, he entered and the gate quickly closed with a sharp metallic clang. The faces of the waiting crowd, with beseeching eyes, resumed staring through the bars.

Buda, the Swedish Legation

Lars Berg, attaché in the legation, gazed out at the long line of Jews in the driveway waiting for passports. He sighed. The legation could process only a few a day—most of them would wait in vain. He spotted a man walking up the main driveway, a knapsack hanging from each shoulder. Turning to the consular officer Denes von Mezey, he pointed out the window. "That must be our Mr. Wallenberg."

Von Mezey looked and shook his head. "I'm not sure I understand what his function will be. He's not a career diplomat, doesn't know any of the ruling Germans or Hungarians in Budapest and can't speak Hungarian. And he is supposed to stop the deportations?"

Berg smiled. "Well, we shall see shortly, shan't we?"

***

A young brunette, plump, pleasant looking, with sparkling eyes and hair down to her shoulders, curled at the bottom, sat behind the reception desk. She watched the stranger put down his knapsacks and remove his hat, revealing curly brown hair on a prematurely balding head.

Margareta Bauer looked him over. Thin, of medium height, with dark, piercing eyes and a prominent nose, he looked in his early thirties. She smiled slightly, thinking he looked more like a schoolteacher than a diplomat. Rising to her considerable height, she extended her hand. A much brighter smile now lit up her face. "Mr. Wallenberg?"

He nodded.

"Margareta Bauer, administrative assistant. Please call me Greta. We've been expecting you—welcome. I'll let Mr. Anger know you're here." She showed him into Per Anger's ground-floor office.

***

Wallenberg had looked forward to seeing his friend, who was legation secretary, again. He knew Anger and his wife from Stockholm and had visited with them when he'd come to Budapest on business. The office was empty. Wallenberg dropped his bags on the carpeted floor and plunked down heavily into a chair. For the first time since leaving the train, he relaxed. As fatigue set in, he closed his eyes.

A creak of the door brought him back to full alertness. Anger walked in, a thin man, much taller than Wallenberg, and perhaps a little older, dressed in a tailored white suit with a maroon silk handkerchief tucked in the breast pocket. Unlike Wallenberg, he had a full head of dark brown hair, offset by his deep blue eyes and heavy eyebrows.

Wallenberg is here!

Anger smiled, placing a cup of steaming coffee and a bowl of nuts on the table in front of Wallenberg. "I think you could use the coffee. And be sure to try Greta's homemade gingernuts. They're delicious."

Wallenberg rose to greet him.

"Sit, sit, Raoul, you look exhausted. I'm so glad to see you again." He extended his hand.

Wallenberg remained standing to shake Anger's hand. "And good to see you, too."

Anger scrutinized him. "So you're the man they sent."

He gave Anger a questioning look. "What?"

Anger picked up one of the knapsacks and stared at Wallenberg's hiking boots. He laughed. "The legation has been waiting a long time for you, but I'm sure you'll not be exactly what they expect."

Wallenberg shrugged. He sat down, taking a sip of the coffee. "My mission…"

Anger put up his hand. "Yes, they know about your mission and have been instructed to cooperate with you."

Wallenberg nodded. Anger patted him on the back. "You have an unusual task here in Budapest. You're very courageous to take this assignment."

Wallenberg pursed his lips, then suddenly his face lit up. "Before I forget, Nina sends her regards."

Anger nodded. "Ah, how is your sister? I knew her husband from the diplomatic corps.

"Nina is about to give birth. I'm waiting to hear if I'm an uncle."

"Your sister used to wax eloquent about your acting abilities, particularly your imitations of diplomats and politicians—she said you could be more German than a Prussian general or more pompous than a German ambassador. You've never treated me to a performance."

Wallenberg jumped up and swept his hair down over the left side of his forehead while he pulled out a small, black comb and inserted it between his nose and upper lip. He clicked his heels and gave a straight-arm Nazi salute, shouting in thickly German-accented English, "*Sieg Heil*! My dear citizens, it is a pack of lies that I, Hitler, don't want peace. Everyone knows I want a piece of Czechoslovakia, a piece of Greece and a piece of Russia." Wallenberg goose-stepped around the office. "I am no different from Chamberlain of Britain!

The only difference between us is that he takes every weekend in the country, and I take a country every weekend. *Heil* Hitler!"

Anger slapped his thigh, laughing.

Wallenberg smiled. "Those jokes only work in English. Actually, I do better imitations of animals. I will be glad to amuse your daughter when I have a chance to meet her."

Anger chuckled. "She can wait, she's only four months-old. But enough talk, Raoul. I'll introduce you to Minister Danielsson and then take you to the furnished apartment we obtained for you, courtesy of a Jewish businessman."

Cocking his head, Wallenberg looked questioningly at Anger. Anger smiled. "Actually, we're doing Jews a favor. It helps protect their homes and possessions from confiscation by the German and Hungarian Nazis. When our diplomats occupy their places, their assets are immune from seizure. You should see Lars Berg's residence, a mansion with a cook, butler and maid, all paid for by its Jewish owner, grateful that we can use his home. Me, I'm renting a house on Gellért Hill belonging to Baron Alfonse Weiss, one of the owners of the Manfred-Weiss Industries. The Jews have also lent us much of their personal and business property such as typewriters and furniture. Now let's meet Danielsson and then I'll take you home so you can get some rest today. We can start early tomorrow morning."

Wallenberg shook his head. "I don't have the luxury of time; thousands could die while I rest. I'm anxious to get to work—today. I've read your reports. But now, if you don't mind, I would like an update on the situation here in Budapest, before we see Danielsson."

"Very well. After the Nazi takeover in March, we downgraded our mission from an embassy to a legation in protest. Sometime in early June, the Pope and our own King Gustav cabled Regent Horthy, appealing to him to intervene to stop the deportations. Meanwhile, Roosevelt gave Horthy an explicit warning, demanding the cessation of the deportations and threatening military reprisals—he made his point by bombing Budapest a week later. The legation sent King Gustav a report that Eichmann intended to clear all the Jews out of Budapest by July fifteenth. The king, in turn, sent Horthy another telegram. Also, we delivered to Horthy, a copy of the *Auschwitz Protocols*, detailing the torture and murders in the concentration camps."

Wallenberg listened intently, sometimes jotting down a few notes.

"It had its effect" Anger continued. "On June sixteenth, Horthy fired Endre and Baky, undersecretaries at the Interior Ministry. Fearing a *putsch* against him, he ordered the Hungarian gendarmes, originally brought to Budapest to assist in the deportations, back to the provinces. Loyal troops enforced his orders and the gendarmes left without a fight. Two days ago, Horthy ordered a halt to all deportations. Veesenmayer publicly demanded the resumption of deportations. In defiance of the regent, Eichmann's troops grabbed a group of Jews already interned by the Hungarians and deported them."

Wallenberg nodded. "Where does it stand now?"

"At an impasse. Interior Minister Jaross has sided with Veesenmayer and Eichmann, insisting that deportations be resumed. But Eichmann doesn't have the manpower to start any significant roundups. He needs the assistance of the Hungarian gendarmes—and Horthy has blocked their return to Budapest."

"What is the legation doing to help the Jews?"

"I developed a Swedish protective passport, the *Schutzpass*. I had to convince Danielsson to issue them to the Jews. Of course, you realize the passports have no legality whatsoever to support them. At first, Danielsson, ever the consummate diplomat, wouldn't hear of it. He finally relented and let us issue passports, but he limited their distribution to those with family or business connections in Sweden. The documents seemed to work to protect those who had them. We have represented that these people will be 'repatriated' to Sweden at the end of the war. They were exempted from wearing the yellow star."

"Why not repatriate them now?"

"Be realistic," begged Anger, looking pained. "The passes are a fiction. The Jews would never survive the hundreds of miles of transportation through German territory. They'd be taken off the trains…"

"You are right, of course."

Now Wallenberg busied himself sketching on a page from his notebook while Anger looked on, a little perplexed at his visitor's distraction and explosion of nervous energy.

Wallenberg looked up. "Tell me, Per, how many of these *Schutzpasses* were issued?"

"By July of this year, about seven hundred."

"Seven hundred? Good Lord, man, they've already shipped 400,000 Jews to the extermination camps and we have a half a million here in Budapest—and we're fooling around with a few hundred passes?"

"Persuading the Swedish government, and Danielsson, to issue even seven hundred very undiplomatic passports was a struggle."

Wallenberg frowned. "I have in my bag the written authority from King Gustav himself to do everything necessary to save those people—and I intend to honor my marching orders—no red tape, no reports and no diplomatic niceties. If it were up to the Foreign Ministry and the diplomatic corps, no one would lift a finger."

Anger looked into Wallenberg's eyes. "Understand this, Raoul. Though I'm a career diplomat in the Foreign Ministry, it doesn't mean I'm against you." He grinned slightly, shaking his head. "I've even been known to issue a few hundred passes myself, without authorization. Once, I saved a group of businessmen who would otherwise have been deported on the next train."

Wallenberg smiled. "We'll be able to work together just fine." He held up the page on which he'd been sketching. "The first thing we need is an impressive passport, one that the officious Germans will respect. I have dealt with the Nazis for many years. They are impressed by official looking documents with stamps, seals and signatures. Here is one I've just sketched out to take the place of the one you're using."

Anger studied the drawing.

"It's strange," mused Wallenberg, "but people ready to send their fellow human beings off to untold suffering and death without a qualm, can be stopped dead by the sight of an official-looking document, especially the Germans, whose respect for authoritarian symbols knows no bounds."

"You are right, of course. The same holds true for the Hungarians. On one occasion, the Hungarian authorities were about to deport some Jews they'd interned. When shown the provisional Swedish passports, they hesitated, arguing among themselves. They delayed long enough for us to rescue them through diplomatic means."

Wallenberg smiled at Anger. "Excellent."

Anger met Wallenberg's gaze. "Like you, I'm also acquainted with the German psyche. For a few years, I was posted to the Swedish Embassy in Berlin. It was I who warned the Swedish government of the imminent German invasion of Norway and Denmark. But in its usual meek manner, the Foreign Office sat on it until the takeover became a fait accompli. I've experienced, firsthand, the passion of the Nazis during a Hitler speech from a balcony. I was in the crowd below and got hit in the head for not taking my hat off in the presence of the Führer."

Anger looked at the sketch again. "I hope you can convince Danielsson to approve and sign such a passport. They're of dubious legality, as it is."

"You leave that to me. I'll convince him. I'm more concerned that the passport convinces the Nazis—that it looks official enough to impress German soldiers and their poorly educated Hungarian lackeys, who are more likely to be taken in by an elaborate document."

Buda, Swedish Legation, One Hour Later

Anger and Wallenberg climbed the stairs to the first floor, heading for Minister Carl Ivar Danielsson's study. Wallenberg paused to admire the elegant, highly polished grand piano he saw through an open door. Anger nodded his head toward the room. "That's Danielsson's music room. He retires there to play the piano for recreation and entertainment. Now come, Danielsson and Lars Berg are waiting to meet you."

***

Wallenberg looked curiously at the heavy man with a large, round, deeply jowled face, who moved away from his paper-strewn desk to greet his visitor. The broad flat nose, baggy eyes and ears plastered flat against his almost bald skull, gave Danielsson the appearance of a pugilist who'd had one bout too many. His looks belied his reputation as a brilliant, tough and hard-working diplomat.

Danielsson motioned them to comfortable armchairs grouped around a fireplace. Berg, already seated and smoking a pipe, stood and offered his hand. Wallenberg felt the firm handshake of the tall, well-built, balding second secretary, next in command at the legation, after Minister Danielsson and Legation Secretary Anger.

Impatient with the polite small talk, Wallenberg wandered around on the plush carpeting in the tastefully decorated office admiring the Swedish wood wall paneling. He looked out the large window with its panoramic view of the Danube, the Ferenc József Bridge and across the river to the sprawling commercial area of Pest. A freight train crawled slowly across the railroad bridge. He wondered how many Jews were being shipped across that span. Below the legation, he could see a small portion of the St. Gellért Hotel between the thickly foliaged trees. Immediately below him, he also saw the long lines of Jews waiting for admission to the Swedish Legation.

"Please excuse my impatience and impertinence, Minister. I have been sent here to save as many lives as possible—but not at the languid pace of diplomacy. There is no red tape binding the hands of Eichmann and no quotas limiting the numbers he can deport to the extermination camps. I don't see why I should be more hamstrung than my adversary."

Danielsson stood and faced Wallenberg. "I've been instructed to extend you all reasonable cooperation. However, I still must run a diplomatic mission and see that Swedish citizens and diplomats are not unduly endangered. Five other countries, including the Soviet Union, have no representatives here and depend on me to represent them. I still have to deal with the Hungarian and German authorities in order to carry out *my* mission. As long as you understand that, we'll get along fine."

Wallenberg nodded. Without hesitation, he opened his notebook to the page he'd been sketching and handed it to Danielsson. "I can create a more effective *Schutzpass*. Foremost, my pass would expressly state that the bearer was emigrating to Sweden and was, therefore, a Swedish citizen, entitled to our protection. The document must look important."

Danielsson took the sketch.

Leaning forward, Wallenberg pointed to the symbols he'd drawn in his architectural free hand. "All those Swedish three-crown coats of arms will be in bright blue and gold. We will put on numerous official stamps and signatures—yours particularly, Minister."

Danielsson grunted.

Wallenberg continued, undeterred, focusing his gaze on the minister's large, floppy, bow tie. "We must create a document so visually impressive and official looking that even Colonel Eichmann

Wallenberg is here!

might have second thoughts about violating it. It will have the bearer's photograph with the Swedish seal pressed onto it, just like our regular passports. One thing I have learned doing business with German and Hungarian bureaucrats is their weakness for symbolism. Even the simple protective passes we've issued so far have confirmed this. Those documents have kept many from being deported. The psychology of the bureaucracy, especially the German variety, tells me that that the more official the *Schutzpass* looks, the more effective its protection."

Danielsson studied the sketched *Schutzpass*. "You did this free hand, just now?"

Anger laughed. "He's an architect, you know. This is child's play for him."

Danielsson laid the open notebook on his desk and glanced questioningly at Anger, who tapped the sketch with his index finger. "You know, Raoul, that Horthy will allow us to issue only 1,500 *Schutzpasses*."

Wallenberg slapped the arm of his chair. "Then we shall issue 4,500."

Danielsson stared at the new arrival. "Just you wait a minute, young man. We still have a legation to operate and we can't just ride roughshod over the wishes of the Hungarian government."

Wallenberg matched Danielsson's gaze without flinching. "Minister, if our king and others hadn't applied pressure to Horthy, the Hungarian government would unhesitatingly have delivered all the Hungarian Jews to Eichmann. We do have a card to play with the Hungarians. The new puppet government desperately desires respectability and international recognition. We must dangle that bait. We must plan, anticipate and act beyond 'diplomacy as usual.' These are not normal times and I am authorized—and prepared—to use unconventional means. I will try not to interfere with your mission, but my mission, Minister, is to save a nation."

Berg smiled. "Which nation, the Jewish people or the Swedish soul?"

Wallenberg looked down at his boots, speaking softly. "Perhaps both, my friend, perhaps both."

***

Closing the door to Danielsson's office behind them, Anger slapped Wallenberg lightly on the shoulder. "You're shocking the staid diplomats with your unconventional proposals."

"Including you?"

When Anger laughed, his eyes seemed to sparkle. "Oh my, no—well—perhaps just a little. As far as I am concerned, you're just what the doctor ordered. I've been sneaking passes to the Jews for months now. Frankly, I'm glad you brought it into the open with the minister. So—how many *Schutzpasses* should we print, a full run of 4,500?"

Wallenberg shook his head. "Print 45,000. I intend to issue at least that many."

Anger chuckled. "You really are something." His laugh had an infectious quality. Wallenberg found himself laughing along with Anger. He'd always liked this young diplomat.

"You will get a lot of support from Lars," Anger advised. "His sympathies are with you, no doubt about it—and he is fearless."

"Glad to hear it. What are his primary responsibilities at the legation?"

"He runs Section B, the department entrusted with protecting foreign interests no longer present in Budapest—countries such as the Soviet Union and Finland. You, my friend, will be in the newly formed Section C, whose mission is to save the Jews."

"Per, I will need a large staff to process *Schutzpasses*. My idea is to recruit intelligent, ambitious Jews to assist me. The first order of business will be to issue a special combination passport, work permit and identification for each Jew employed by the legation in Section C. We must first protect those who will give me the help to accomplish our mission."

Anger rubbed his chin. "Yes, I agree, but don't forget also to protect yourself, Raoul. You hold a diplomatic passport and are registered with the Hungarian authorities as a first secretary of the legation. In theory, you have diplomatic immunity, but I'm afraid it may not count for much in the climate that pervades Budapest. Be careful."

Wallenberg smiled. "Don't worry, I'm more like a *Hassenfuss* than a hero."

Wallenberg is here!

"You?" laughed Anger. "A timid rabbit? Not likely, Raoul, not likely. You may look unassuming, but that simply masks all that creative energy waiting to burst forth on the unsuspecting Nazis."

Buda, Offices of Section C, and Pest, Police Headquarters, Several Days Later

Agnes, through the intervention of her boyfriend in Sweden, had obtained one of the first *Schutzpasses* from the Swedish Legation. Agnes impressed Wallenberg and he made the attractive young woman a receptionist and file clerk in his office. Through his efforts, Jews working for the legation no longer had to wear yellow stars. But the stars had to be officially removed by the Budapest Police.

Wallenberg passed the reception desk and stopped. "Agnes, why are you still wearing your star?"

"I just couldn't bring myself to go into a police station. It terrifies me."

Wallenberg laid a hand gently on her shoulder. "Go, Agnes. I promise you, it's safe. Go to the district police headquarters; it's only a block from here. The police chief is a friend of mine. You will be treated courteously." He called over another worker. "Watch the desk for a while, Agnes has to do something for me." He gently shoved her out the door.

***

Agnes, the prominent yellow star on her jacket, approached the desk sergeant at the police station, papers clutched securely in her hand. The policeman leered at her, like there were carnal images flashing through his mind. "What's your business here?"

She raised her papers for the sergeant to see but would not let go of her treasure. She said nothing. He scanned the top paper and nodded. "Follow me." She did, into an office marked "Police Chief."

The chief looked up. "Another one?"

The sergeant nodded. The chief put out his hand for the papers. This time she relinquished them. He stared at her in silence.

The sergeant smiled. He knew the chief was mentally undressing his comely visitor. She shifted her weight from one foot to another. The sergeant figured she was nervous—probably terrified by the ordeal of having to confront authority, though the Budapest police certainly weren't brutes like the Hungarian gendarmes.

She cleared her throat. "Excuse me, sir, but I was instructed by the Swedish Legation to come here to have my star removed officially. I have a *Schutzpass* and work at the legation."

The chief could see "WORK PERMIT" stamped prominently across the document. He smiled broadly and exuded friendliness, using her first name. "Agnes, it is my pleasure." He picked up the small scissors on his desk, came around to where she stood and carefully cut the threads holding the yellow star to the cloth of her jacket. He patted her on the shoulder. "Now go, young lady, and give Wallenberg my best."

The woman left the room, closing the door behind her.

The sergeant stood, shaking his head. "Another bloody Jew has just escaped."

The chief shrugged. "What of it? I could never understand all the fuss made about the Jews. She must be the fiftieth one this week. That Wallenberg is something. He's gotten the Hungarian government to exempt those Jews with *Schutzpasses* from wearing the star. And he's paid us well to cut through the red tape. What the hell, Germany is losing the war and we might as well look good when the occupying forces arrive. At the same time, there is no reason why we can't profit from being reasonable."

The sergeant nodded. "Still, it's a shame so many of them are being protected like that. I would have liked very much to take that one to bed. The gendarmes, when they were here, used the Jewesses any time it pleased them."

Offices of Section C in Buda

Section C, located in a small red brick house high in the hills of Buda, overlooking the city, was a beehive of activity. Berg marveled at the frenetic scene, more like controlled chaos, with hundreds of workers at typewriters and file cabinets. He turned to Wallenberg. "No one can accuse you of letting any grass grow under your feet. It's only been a week. How many workers do you have here now?"

"Over 350, all with passes and all cleared by the police."

Berg ran his hand through his hair. "My God, Raoul. How in heaven's name did you get the Hungarian bureaucracy to move so quickly? They are notorious for enmeshing everyone and everything in red tape."

Wallenberg smiled. "Currency, a pile of Hungarian *pengös*, paid to the right people, can cut through red tape in dramatic fashion."

Berg laughed. "Bribery, payoffs—you, dear Wallenberg, have brought the high art of diplomacy down several notches, in just one short week."

His colleague rubbed his smooth chin. "I'll take that as a compliment. When you are dealing with rats in the gutter, you have to stoop to their level." He looked out of the window at the peaceful Buda scene. "We have to move these offices into Pest, where most of the Jews live. We are too far removed from the field of battle and too close to the legation—I fear we are interfering with its diplomatic mission. Section C needs to be made more accessible to the people who need us.

"It may be too dangerous in Pest" demurred Berg. "It's so close to Eichmann's activities."

"I suppose that's the point, isn't it? I have no choice. Eichmann's hammer will fall on the Jews any day now. Horthy can't keep him at bay much longer. Three trains filled with Jews left for Auschwitz within the last two weeks. We must get as many Jews registered with *Schutzpasses* as possible. We must also find safe houses and put them under the protection of the Swedish flag. That way, at least the Jews with passports can live in relative safety."

Buda, Swedish Legation, Minister Danielsson's Office, the Next Day

Wallenberg paced back and forth in front of the minister's fireplace. Danielsson, seated, followed his movements with his eyes. Watching the energetic, restless young man was enough to fatigue the minister and make him edgy.

Wallenberg stopped in front of Danielsson. "Minister, if we are to have any impact here, we simply cannot continue to issue *Schutzpasses* only to those Jews who have direct family or business connections in Sweden."

Danielsson grunted. "But at least the requirement gives us an arguable, if somewhat tenuous, basis for protecting these people under the authority of King Gustav. Issuing these passports to any Jew who wants one would have no legal basis whatsoever. Both the Foreign Office and some of my staff agree that, through overissue, these passes would become devalued. I want to help but..." He spread his arms and hunched his shoulders. "What am I to do?"

Wallenberg rubbed the back of his neck. "First of all, Minister, I was sent here by authority of the king with instructions to save as many Jews as I could, not as many Jews as had connections to Sweden. To do any less would not be in keeping with the king's orders or morally acceptable to me. Furthermore, the Swiss envoy, Charles Lutz, has agreed to start issuing protective passes to the Jews, without restriction. And the papal nuncio, Rotta, has convinced the Vatican not to limit its passes only to converted Jews. How can we Swedes do any less where Nazi laws make Jews guilty of a capital crime merely for existing? We have no choice, we must be aggressive with our passes."

Danielsson closed his eyes and rubbed his temples. "Ah, I see that now, Raoul, you have assumed the diplomatic function of contacting other neutrals like the Swiss and the Vatican. Are you taking over my responsibilities for that, as well?"

"Minister," Wallenberg said softly, "if that's what you think, then I apologize. My only objective is to expand issuance of passports in order to save lives. I cannot accomplish this by observing diplomatic niceties and, quite frankly, I don't have the time for protocol—I'm sorry."

Danielsson sighed. "I see why you were on the University of Michigan debating team. You put forth your position persuasively. My diplomatic instincts tell me to rein you in because your energy and activity could put this entire legation in mortal danger. My emotional and humanitarian sense, however, sides with you. Against my better judgment, I'll meet you half way. You may issue your *Schutzpasses* to Jews with minimal connections to Sweden. And God help us."

Budapest, the Following Days

Lars Berg, in addition to running Section B, helped Wallenberg supervise the processing and issuing of *Schutzpasses* by the Section C workers. His aid enabled Wallenberg to turn to setting up safe houses for those who received these Swedish protective passes—his Jews. He

Wallenberg is here!

desperately needed more houses. Those already donated by the Jews were full. Wallenberg had mounted a Swedish flag on each of these houses, proclaiming them "mission houses" and Swedish territory. He packed them with sometimes seven to eight hundred to a house. At some houses, he posted SS-uniformed Jews as guards.

Berg sat across the desk from Wallenberg. Wallenberg leaned back in his chair eyeing Berg. "Lars, I really appreciate all your help. It's beyond anything I had a right to expect."

Berg smiled. "No problem, I really believe in what you are doing."

Wallenberg waved some *Schutzpasses* at Berg. "Issuing *Schutzpasses* and finding housing is only half the battle. More important is to instill hope in the Jews. Nazi propaganda and actions have so debased these Jews that many have lost the will to survive. We've seen hundreds of thousands killed, almost without resistance. I intend to change that attitude in Budapest. We must strengthen their will and give them a glimmer of light at the end of the tunnel.

"Think about it, Lars. Without Jewish cooperation, there would be chaos trying to identify and round them up. Jewish compliance facilitates Eichmann's task. At the right time, they must rid themselves of their yellow stars, stop giving the Nazis lists of Jewish inhabitants and end the *Judenrat*'s cooperation with the Nazis. We don't have much time either. The word in the street is that Eichmann is poised to resume deportations on a grand scale. I must see the *Judenrat* as soon as possible."

***

Every evening at about eight o'clock, Wallenberg and Berg would show up at the legation with hundreds of passes for Danielsson to sign. True to his word, the minister stayed until every last *Schutzpass* had his signature.

On this evening, Greta Bauer, the legation receptionist, burst into Danielsson's office during the signings, waving two *Schutzpasses*. "Minister, a Gestapo officer and several German soldiers are downstairs with two Jews. The officer claims their safe conduct passes are forgeries. He demands to see you."

Danielsson sighed, put down his pen and held out his hand. "Let me see the passes."

Bauer handed him the passes. Wallenberg peeked over Danielsson's shoulder. Danielsson looked up at Wallenberg. "The officer is correct. Those are not my signatures. They're both fakes. What will happen if I tell him that?"

Gripping the minister's shoulder tighter than he meant to, Wallenberg told him, "The holders of these passes will be deported to the extermination camps, or if they're lucky, they'll simply be shot on the spot."

Danielsson threw up his hands. "Wonderful choices: to lie or to murder." He nodded to Bauer. "Show the Gestapo gentleman up to my office."

The Gestapo officer, in his gray working SS uniform, entered, clicked his heels and bowed.

Danielsson stood, walked over to the officer and handed him the passes. "Captain," Danielsson said in flawless German, "the signatures are authentic."

The officer looked disappointed, then angry, his searching eyes never leaving Danielsson's face. "Are you sure, Minister? They look like forgeries to me."

Danielsson frowned. "Captain, I should be able to recognize my own signature, shouldn't I?"

"Very well, Minister, but you are warned. We will uncover forgeries and punish the perpetrators most severely, where and when they are found."

"No doubt you will. Now, if you don't mind, I have a lot of work to do."

The officer about-faced smartly and marched out of the room. Bauer followed, closing the door behind her.

Danielsson picked up his pen and resumed signing the passes. Without looking up, he growled, "You are teaching me to become an accomplished liar."

Wallenberg smiled. "And you received an 'A' on your first exam."

Danielsson continued to sign his name. "Very funny. Here, I'm saddled with a green diplomat just out of diapers—and he thinks he's a comedian."

Wallenberg is here!

Pest, Offices of the *Judenrat*, a Day Later

Wallenberg walked rapidly down narrow Sip Street. A block away from the Central Synagogue, he found the number he was looking for. It was a small four-story building housing the *Judenrat*. He tried the front door. It was unlocked. He entered.

***

An elderly man sat at a table, engrossed in a book with large Hebrew letters. Despite the July heat, a worn, heavy cardigan sweater, a large yellow star sewn over the left breast, hung from his small frame. He looked up and saw a young man carrying a brief case, well-dressed in a smartly tailored dark blue suit—with no star. The man walked up to the table. Speaking German with authority he said, "I would like to see the members of the *Judenrat*. Would you summon them? Raoul Wallenberg is here to see them."

The old man shuffled out of the room, closing the inner door behind him. Samu Stern, engaged in an intense discussion with another member of the council, grunted when the old man tapped him on the shoulder. "Later, Micah. Can't you see I'm busy?"

"But Herr Stern, an important German out there is very insistent on seeing a representative of the *Judenrat*. I think he's a Gestapo agent."

Stern frowned. "How do you know he's Gestapo? Did he show you his badge or warrant disk?"

Micah shook his head. "No, but he sounds and looks like Gestapo—quite aggressive and commanding."

"Tell him we're busy carrying out Colonel Eichmann's orders. If he's Gestapo, he'll barge right in."

Micah nodded and shuffled out.

***

Wallenberg looked at his watch. He'd been waiting three quarters of an hour. At his urging, the old man had gone back several times only to return shaking his head. Wallenberg glanced up when he heard the front door open. As a man entered from the street, he called, "László, László Pëto, is that you?"

"Raoul, what are you doing here?"

"Waiting to see the *Judenrat*."

"Why are you in Budapest?"

"I've been sent by the Swedish government and King Gustav to help the Hungarian Jews."

"One man against Eichmann, the Butcher of Hungary?"

"I've got help and a few ideas."

Pëto nodded. "I'll get the council to see you right away. Come with me." Taking Wallenberg by the arm, he led him through the inner door, ignoring the protestations of the old man.

Stern, annoyed, looked up at the interruption.

"Samu, this is Raoul Wallenberg, a friend of mine and of my father. We shared a room at a hostel at Thenon-les-Bain. He's come to Budapest to help us. You must speak to him right away."

Stern sighed. "May I be blunt, Herr Wallenberg?"

"By all means."

"I've heard of you. What I see in front of me is another young, rich Gentile, not likely to be of much help, regardless of his good intentions. No offense intended."

Wallenberg smiled. "None taken. But here, read this letter from Rabbi Marcus Ehrenpreis of Stockholm, explaining my mission."

Stern pursed his lips, taking the proffered letter. "I've heard of this Ehrenpreis." He read the letter and passed it to his colleagues. He sighed. "Your goals are very impressive and high-minded. But if you don't mind my asking, what hope can you offer against the power of the Reich and the wrath of Adolph Eichmann? My friend, you're just one man against a mighty war machine."

Wallenberg held Stern's gaze. "First of all, I'm a Swedish diplomat. More important, I have the authority to issue protective passports, *Schutzpasses*. I have already issued hundreds of them to Jews who are working for me. They, in turn, are busy preparing lists of other Jews and filling out passports for them. I have negotiated an agreement with the German and Hungarian authorities whereby Jews possessing Swedish *Schutzpasses* and working for me are exempt from wearing the yellow star. I promise you, I will do everything in my power to stop the deportations, including facing down Eichmann, if I have to."

Boda, who had just read Ehrenpreis's letter, demurred. "The Nazis are too powerful. It's like pissing into a hurricane."

Wallenberg is here!

Wallenberg shook his head. "That attitude, if you will forgive my saying so, is prevalent among the Jews in Budapest—and it will get you killed. The Nazis are not all powerful—you must believe that and pass the message on."

Boda smiled faintly. "You're joking, of course, Herr Wallenberg."

The visitor gave him a steely look. "Do I look as if I were joking? Without the assistance of the Hungarians, and the Jews themselves, the Germans are impotent to round up and ship out all the Jews. By themselves, the Germans can gather only a few thousand. And that, gentlemen, is their weak point. I have the money, the initiative and the support of the Swiss and the papal nuncio. I can put pressure on Regent Horthy. What I do need is your help. You must believe that you can survive. Only then can you do the things necessary to save yourselves. There will come a time—not now, but soon—when you will be asked to sow confusion among your enemies by taking away their ability to identify you by your yellow stars and your lists of Jews."

Wallenberg caught the council members exchanging glances. "You must pull your people out of the depths of despair and reinstill the will to resist and to live, not by force of arms, but by guile. We must attack the Germans' vulnerabilities—they are losing the war and fear retribution by the Allies. I will play on those fears. I have already started with some encouraging results; with your help we can identify those Germans and Hungarian susceptible to bribes and blackmail; we need spies, sympathizers and informants in the bosom of the enemy. I have obtained a few names from my sources in Stockholm."

Wallenberg looked at the members of the *Judenrat*. Their change in demeanor was palpable.

Peto nodded. "We can help—we have our spies, too. I've cultivated the friendship of the young Miklós Horthy, Miki, the regent's son. He is our eyes and ears in the palace and has his father's attention. There is also an active Jewish underground—young men and women from the city, the countryside and other overrun nations—and the Haganah from Palestine. Miki Horthy has been in contact with them."

Wallenberg thought a minute. "I need to make contact with the underground–I have some ideas to foul up Eichmann's plans. Certain underground people may possess physical characteristics that would be most helpful."

Stern touched Wallenberg's elbow. "And we know which of the Gestapo in Budapest will take bribes."

Wallenberg rubbed his hands together. "Excellent, we are off to a good start. It's crucial that you inform me of any actions by the Gestapo and the Hungarian gendarmes to resume the roundups. I will have to react immediately, before things get out of hand."

CHAPTER 8

Pest, Offices of Section C, Budapest, August 5, 1944

Wallenberg succeeded in moving Section C to Pest, where most of the Jews lived. Nearer to the Jewish population centers, the new offices could be reached more safely by his workers and those seeking *Schutzpasses*, though moving outside was still dangerous with all the Arrow Cross thugs roaming the streets. The new offices were on Üllöi Street, close to the Ferenc József Bridge, which offered easy access to Buda.

Per Anger visited the office for the first time. When he saw Agnes, the receptionist whom he had known at the legation, his face lit up. She greeted him warmly, and he gave her a hug. Entering the huge main room, he was amazed at what seemed to be hundreds of typewriters, clacking and hundreds more people scurrying around filing and carrying papers. That they worked with single-minded purpose was no surprise—their lives depended upon the success of Wallenberg's mission. Anger could not imagine how Wallenberg could have organized so many people in such a short time.

He crossed the room, rapped gently on the far door and then opened it. Wallenberg looked up and smiled as Anger slumped into the chair near the desk and began his report. "Eichmann is still making his presence felt. Since clearing the provinces of Jews, he's been champing at the bit to get at the Budapest Jews. I checked out a recent report that the Hungarians raided some Jewish houses and took Jews for forced-labor battalions. It seems that the SS intercepted and disarmed those Hungarians, took a few hundred of those Jews and immediately deported them to Auschwitz. I inquired at Gestapo headquarters, but they're not saying anything."

Wallenberg sighed. "We can't let these secret deportations continue. I have an appointment to see Regent Horthy tomorrow."

"How did you arrange that?" asked Anger, raising his eyebrows. "Few diplomats have seen him since the German takeover."

Wallenberg held up a single sheet of paper with the Swedish royal emblem. "I came with a letter to the regent from King Gustav, requesting an audience for me. The Hungarians are desperate to get some recognition from the neutrals, so Horthy's honoring the king's request."

Anger smiled. "How many more surprises do you have in your back pocket?"

"Oh, a few. But they wouldn't be surprises if I told you, would they?"

Buda, Royal Palace, August 6, 1944

Deciding that he needed the exercise, Wallenberg headed for Buda on foot. He walked several blocks north along the promenade paralleling the Danube, Belgrád Rakpart, and crossed the Chain Bridge. He proceeded briskly up cobblestoned Castle Hill to the sprawling palace, home of the Hungarian monarchs for six centuries. He was shown immediately into the regent's office. The ornate room with its huge chandeliers, Wallenberg guessed, had once been the throne room—he could fit all his 450 workers in this one room with ease.

The elderly regent came to the door to greet his guest.

"Herr Wallenberg, your king has been quite insistent that I see you. I like your king. Out of respect for his wishes I've taken the time from my busy schedule. Please be seated. Now, what can I do for you?" Horthy returned to his desk.

Wallenberg bowed and took a chair. "Thank you for seeing me, Regent. As the king said in his letter, he urgently requests that you intercede to stop the deportation and killing of the Jews."

"I have done all I can to stop the killings," protested Horthy, his eyes flashing with anger.

"But Regent, it appears that the Germans and the Arrow Cross are starting to resume their activities."

"That is out of my hands. Moreover, I resent the interference of the neutrals, particularly Sweden, in our internal affairs. These are Hungarian Jews, not Swedish or Swiss ones. Now, Herr Wallenberg, if that is all, I have work to do."

"Bear with me for another moment, please, Regent. I know your government is anxious to obtain recognition of Sweden and other neutrals. It would be easier to accomplish if you protected your Jews."

"That is presumptuous talk from a very junior Swedish diplomat. I wouldn't expect such a breach of diplomacy from Minister Danielsson, much less from you."

"You are right, Regent, but with all due respect, considering the lives at stake here, I must sometimes leave the diplomatic niceties at home. Let me offer you this thought: the Germans are losing the war. Surely you see that. Things might not go well for you with the victorious Allies if you do not stop the killings. Hungary's assistance to the German program to annihilate the Jews would be used against it. Regent, consider the example of Rumania, which resisted Nazi attempts to deport its Jews. That puts the lie to any Hungarian claim that it can do nothing in the face of German might. The Nazis need your manpower to help them round up and deport the Jews. Deny that to them, please."

Horthy slammed his fist on the desk. "Such arrogance. I will hear no more of this. Please take your leave at once."

***

Per Anger was still at the Üllöi Street office when Wallenberg returned. "I'm on pins and needles. How did the meeting with Horthy go?"

"I got my points across, all right, but I made the regent very angry. He'll probably give Danielsson hell."

Anger laughed. "Why should I be surprised that you were your usual blunt self? But tell me, what was your impression of the regent."

Wallenberg scratched his head. "Well, he's an imposing figure, very regal. But to tell you the truth, although he stood a head higher than me, I felt morally taller."

Buda, Hungarian Ministry of the Interior, a Day Later

The Deputy Minister of the Interior Endre and his aide sat waiting for Wallenberg. The minister spread his arms in frustration. "The Jew-lover is coming in again, no doubt to demand a new increase in the quota of *Schutzpasses* or some new exemptions for his Yids. This is the eighth time in two weeks. His persistence knows no bounds.

Every time I think I've seen the last of that fanatic Swede, he's back again with new requests."

"Just throw him out, Sir."

"I'd love to but it's easier said than done. Minister Jaros would have a fit. Our government still seeks recognition from Sweden and this Wallenberg is a registered diplomat." He shrugged. "I'm instructed not to offend the king of Sweden."

A light rap on the door announced the minister's secretary, who ushered Wallenberg into the office. The minister stood. "What now, Herr Wallenberg? You were just here yesterday."

Wallenberg held out a sheaf of papers. "I have a report here that the Hungarian government is planning to cancel the order exempting the Jews working for the Swedish Legation from wearing yellow stars and observing the curfew."

"True, that's one of the things we are considering, Herr Wallenberg."

"These Jews are part of the staff conducting the official business of the Swedish government. They cannot perform their duties if they are harassed because they are required to wear yellow stars and are not allowed in the streets except for only a few hours a day."

The minister hunched his shoulders. "My hands are tied, Herr Wallenberg. Civil law, enacted by our Parliament, now requires all Jews to obey those rules. Your quarrel is with Parliament, not with me."

Wallenberg, speaking in authoritative German, leaned on the front of the minister's desk, putting his face close to the minister's. "You are hindering the official duties of the Royal Swedish government. That, Minister, is unacceptable. You give me no choice; I will have to report this to my government."

"Calm down, please, Herr Wallenberg," said the minister, putting up his hands. "I will have to consult with my superiors and come back to you."

"I will not be put off like that," replied Wallenberg in a menacing tone. "If you can't give me an answer now," he moved to the door, "I'll see the regent about this. You leave me no option but to bother him about this trifling matter."

"Very well, Herr Wallenberg, I will exempt your legation Jews. I hope that satisfies you." The minister sighed.

Wallenberg is here!

"I appreciate that, Minister, but you haven't addressed the other requests of my government."

The minister cleared his throat and looked questioningly at his aide, who shrugged.

"Now what, Herr Wallenberg? I don't know what you are talking about." The minister spread his arms in frustration. "Does nothing satisfy you?"

"Aren't you kept fully informed by your office?"

"Yes—of course. Didn't we just deal with your problems—no yellow stars and no curfew for your Jews?"

"The Swedish government has also demanded that the Jews working on legation business be permitted to live in their own homes and not be moved to the ghetto or other houses set aside for Jews."

The minister scratched his ear and ran his hand through his hair. He busied himself straightening out things on his desk. "I know nothing of this."

Wallenberg persisted. "Minister, if I have to report back to my foreign minister that your ministry is ignoring reasonable requests of our government, Sweden will have to file an official complaint about your actions."

The minister sat there in silence, stunned by this audacious junior diplomat, who leaned forward in his chair. "Minister, may I speak to you in private?"

The minister nodded toward the door. The aide rose and left the office. Wallenberg spoke softly. "If you can resolve this minor matter quickly—simply a small concession on your part, you will find yourself amply rewarded both monetarily and with the support of the Swedish government on your behalf with the Allies after the war."

The minister nodded again. Wallenberg stuffed his papers into his battered leather briefcase and left.

The aide stuck his head in the door. "He's finally gone, Minister?"

The minister grumbled, "Thank God. What does it matter if we exempt a few Jews to get that vulture off our backs? No harm is done."

"But he'll be back, Minister, you can count on that."

His superior shrugged. "I'll lodge a protest with Minister Danielsson about his colleague's undiplomatic harassment of this ministry. We'll just see if we can't rein in the Jew-lover."

Buda, Swedish Legation, Danielsson's Office, August 8, 1944

Minster Danielsson nodded toward the window as he addressed Wallenberg and Lars Berg. "The Jews are besieging the legation again, seeking protection. It had gotten much quieter until the last few days."

Joining Berg at the window, Wallenberg looked out and then turned to face his boss. "The city is full of rumors that the deportations will be resumed. And more bad news—the word is out that the Hungarian government will honor provisional passports only for those Jews with family ties in Sweden, that it will rescind its order to not intern Jews holding foreign protection papers. I think they intend to start interning them by the end of the month."

Danielsson shook his head. "What will you do now?" he asked.

"We have to acquire a lot more safe houses under the protection of the Swedish flag. Minister Lutz says the Swiss will follow our lead and create their own protected housing."

Danielsson looked at Wallenberg, smiling. "I know your trying to do your job, but I have half the Hungarian government complaining to me about being flooded daily with requests and demands from that Wallenberg about *his* Jews. Just this morning, I received a protest from the Interior Ministry. You're a bulldog, I'll grant you that—you grab hold and never let go until you get what you want. You know what they call you? 'The pest.' They want you recalled. I must ask you to pull back a little. You're making it impossible for me to have normal diplomatic relations with the Hungarians."

Wallenberg's cheeks reddened and an angry edge crept into his voice. "You'll pardon me for asking, Minister, but are uneventful relations with the Hungarians more important than saving thousands of lives? Nothing works better than stubborn persistence—it wears the Hungarians down and has gotten me important concessions, particularly for the Jews who work for me—it has kept our team together and worked effectively to save other Jews."

Berg sucked on his pipe, trying to re-light it. He gave up and took it out of his mouth, waving it in his fist. "Raoul is right, Minister, we can't let up now. Things are getting worse. The curfew has been increased. Now the Jews can go out for only a few hours in the afternoon. Hungarian patrols have stepped up the looting of Jewish apartments to confiscate valuables. Maintaining our vigilance and keeping the pressure on the Hungarian authorities, as Raoul is doing, is the only thing holding back disaster. And you must continue to dangle the bait of possible recognition of the Hungarian government by Sweden."

Danielsson threw up his hands, turning to Wallenberg. "It looks as if everyone in the legation sides with you. I don't seem to be making the decisions any more."

Berg finally gave up trying to re-light his pipe. With a few good taps, he emptied it in the ashtray. He looked at Danielsson. "That's because Raoul has the moral high ground—it's no contest, saving lives versus diplomatic inconvenience."

"Go on, Lars. You may as well say the rest of what you're thinking: 'Who is Danielsson to hinder the saving of lives?'"

After a few seconds of embarrassed silence, Wallenberg stood. "If you'll excuse me, Minister, I'll see if I can set up a meeting with Colonel László Ferenczy, chief of the Hungarian gendarmes. I must see about housing before it's too late."

On his way out, he heard Danielsson mutter, "Can you imagine? A diplomat of mine being called a pest. What next?"

Wallenberg smiled slightly but did not turn around.

Kistarcsa, Internment Camp, and Buda, Swedish Legation, August 9, 1944

The sun's morning rays began filtering through the shadeless windows of the barracks of the Kistarcsa internment camp, but they didn't awaken the exhausted sleepers. They were roused the Hungarian guards stomping through the large room, shouting and banging truncheons on the wooden bunks and on slow-moving inmates. Another day in the slave-labor camp had started.

Alice Breuer tumbled out her bunk and put on her shoes. Tired beyond caring, she'd slept in her clothes to give herself a few moments more of sleep. Soon, she'd be going out for twelve hours to clear the rubble from the last Allied bombing. This she did on a daily diet of a few hundred calories, consisting of some watery gruel or a soup made of potato peelings, a piece of stale bread and some foul-tasting ersatz coffee. In her work group alone, every day at least a half a dozen Jews collapsed from overwork. They either died on the spot or were carted away by the guards and never seen again. Weakened by constant gnawing hunger and utter exhaustion, Alice could not last much longer. The temptation simply to give up and lie down in the field overwhelmed her at times. That, of course, would have hastened her fate.

Alice stumbled out of the barracks in her tattered clothes and took her assigned place among the rows of Jews, waiting for the roll call. Dozing on her feet, she almost missed her name. A loud voice repeated it. That snapped her back to full consciousness. She stepped forward.

The guard grabbed her roughly by the arm, ordering, "Come with me." She shuddered, dreading to be singled out. If any survived, it would be the unnoticed ones. As the guard pushed her toward the camp gate, three other inmates, also called out of line and prodded by guards, fell in behind her.

Led out of the gate, they were motioned to a waiting Hungarian police car. Alice screwed up her nerve. "Where are we being taken?"

"Shut up and get in, Jew." The guard shoved her roughly through the open rear door. The three other inmates squeezed in after her.

The two policemen in front remained silent for the entire trip. Soon, the terrain became familiar. Puzzled, Alice recognized the outskirts of Budapest racing by. Soon they crossed the Ferenc József Bridge, climbing the steep streets of Buda. The car pulled up to a large wrought iron gate in front of an imposing mansion. Alice read the plaque on the stone pillar, "Swedish Embassy."

The two policemen got out of the car and conferred with the gate guard, who telephoned ahead. A minute later, the heavy gate opened and the police car drove up to the entrance to the building.

"Out," one of the policemen said. Alice climbed out and stretched her cramped legs.

A well-dressed, balding young man standing at the front door, held out his hand. "Welcome, Frau Breuer. I'm Raoul Wallenberg." He led her and the others into the Legation, each to a separate room.

Wallenberg sat down next to Alice, offering her a piece of chocolate. She devoured it. Looking at Wallenberg, she whispered, "What's happening?"

Wallenberg smiled, handing her an official looking document. "This is a *Schutzpass*. Congratulations, you are now a citizen of Sweden. You will be protected from the German and Hungarian Nazis."

"But how?"

"Your husband came to me and told me of your situation. From now on, you must remember your connection to Sweden—AB Kanthal Halstahammer. It's important if you're ever stopped and questioned by the Gestapo."

Alice nodded, tears running down her cheeks.

Wallenberg put his arm around her shoulder. "Now, hurry home to your husband and child, they are waiting. A legation car will take you."

Kistarcsa, Internment Camp, August 11, 1944

Early one morning, two days later, a German staff car and a convoy of Wehrmacht heavy military trucks screeched to a halt in front of the closed gate of the Kistarcsa internment camp. A Hungarian guard, rifle slung over his shoulder, shuffled over to the car.

SS Captain Franz Novak leaped out and ordered, "Open this gate immediately and then stand back." Heavily armed SS troops swarmed out of the three trucks, surrounding the three Hungarian guards.

The gate guard's eyes widened with fear at the array of weapons confronting him. "Ex-excuse me, Captain, but we are under orders to permit no one access to the camp. The Jews housed here are slave labor, in support of the defense of Budapest."

Captain Novak, hand on his holstered revolver, growled, "I'll take responsibility for those Jews. I am acting under the orders of Colonel Eichmann. Now open up."

"B-but captain, I-I have orders to release the Jews only for labor battalion work."

"Enough talk!" Before the Hungarian guard could react, Novak unholstered his Luger and smashed the guard across the side of the head with the butt of his weapon. The guard collapsed in his tracks. The other two guards raised their rifles.

"You will be shot where you stand if you don't lower your weapons and stand aside," Novak barked.

Looking down the barrel of fifty or more MP-40 machine pistols, the guards lowered their old, nonautomatic rifles and stepped back.

Novak nodded to the driver of the lead truck. The engine roared, the vehicle lurched forward, moved around the staff car and smashed the camp gate. The rest of the convoy followed.

One SS squad surprised the gendarmes in their barracks, disarming them without firing a shot. Other squads stormed into each of the barracks housing the Jews. Novak entered the first building, screaming, "Out, out, Jew pigs, or you will be shot here and now. Clear this building immediately and do not stop to dress or take anything."

SS rifle butts smashed slower-moving Jews. Within five minutes, more than two thousand dazed, half-dressed Jews assembled in the dusty yard. Several minutes later, three more Jews were dragged out of the buildings, bleeding profusely around the head and upper body.

"Captain, Sir, these vermin were found hiding."

Novak nodded. "Kneel, you dogs." Troopers kicked the legs from under the three Jews. Novak placed his Luger behind the head of the first Jew and fired. The Jew lurched forward into the dirt face first. Novak nodded to the SS sergeant. The sergeant stepped behind the two other Jews, quivering on their knees, and fired two shots.

Novak strutted in front of the rows of Jews. "That's what will happen to you if you try to escape or do not follow orders instantaneously. Is that clear?"

The Jews shuffled nervously in place saying nothing. Novak approached a short, young Jew in the first row. He could see the fear even through the Jew's thick wire glasses. He shoved the revolver in the Jew's mouth. "I said," the captain growled, "is that clear?"

The young man nodded his head rapidly and could only utter something unintelligible.

Novak removed the weapon and looked at the rest of the group. Heads started to nod and murmur yes.

"Good, then we understand each other."

The SS sergeant whispered to Novak, "A quick count shows about twenty-two hundred Jews. We can take only two thousand, at most."

Novak nodded. "Shoot every tenth Jew in line. That should solve your problem. Then have the remaining ones loaded on the trucks and head immediately for the railroad siding. I'll meet you there. No one knows about this train, so stop for nothing or no one, understand? Begin loading the Jews in the cattle cars as soon as you get there. Leave a detail behind to bury the bodies."

Wallenberg is here!

Pest, Offices of the *Judenrat*, August 11, 1944

A few hours later at the *Judenrat* offices, Pincus Freudiger fidgeted as he spoke to Wallenberg and the Swiss envoy, Charles Lutz. "I know how important it is to obtain more safe houses, gentlemen, we…"

The door to the meeting room flew open, and a short, middle-aged man burst in, breathless. "Eichmann…" he gasped.

Stern walked over to him and sat him down. "Sándor, calm down, catch your breath, you'll have a heart attack."

Freudiger whispered to Wallenberg, "That's Sándor Brody. He monitors the internment camps for the council."

The labored breathing abated. Brody grabbed Stern's lapels. "Samu, we must do something right away. Eichmann's men have shot two hundred Jews at the Kistarcsa camp and the rest were taken by force to the railroad yards. Two thousand of them have been crammed into freight cars and are being shipped to Auschwitz as we speak—two thousand Jews, Samu." He started to sob uncontrollably.

Stern grabbed Brody's shoulders. "Pull yourself together, man. How did you find out?"

"The Hungarian director of the camp…" he took several quick breaths to reassert control, "got a message to me. I'm sure it's true."

Lutz turned to Wallenberg. "We have no time to waste. If that train reaches the border, those Jews are doomed. I must call Horthy."

Pëto put his hand on the telephone handset as Lutz tried to pick it up. "Wait a second. It takes too long to go through the government switchboard." He fished through his wallet, throwing little slips of paper on the table. "Ah, here, I have the regent's private telephone number. It'll ring right through to his personal secretary."

Lutz dialed the number. "Regent Horthy, please, Swiss Envoy Charles Lutz here. We have an emergency."

Lutz drummed his fingers on the table as he waited. His face reddened as he listened. "Calling back later is unacceptable to the Swiss government. I demand to speak to the regent this instant!" There was a pause.

"Regent Horthy? This is Envoy Lutz. I apologize for the interruption but I have just received word from an unimpeachable source that the SS has taken two thousand Jews from the Kistarcsa camp and is deporting them by train to Auschwitz. The train has already left Kistarcsa. You promised to protect those Jews and use them only for labor. You cannot permit them to be murdered by the Nazis. Switzerland will hold you personally responsible."

Lutz hung up. "Where's Wallenberg?"

Stern pointed. "He's in the next room, making phone calls."

Wallenberg returned. "I've reached the Spanish and Portuguese legations. Their ministers agreed to call Horthy. So will Danielsson. I will try to reach the papal nuncio later—he was out."

Buda, The Royal Palace, August 11, 1944

Hungarian Minister of the Interior Andor Jaros stood in front of the regent's desk, shifting nervously from one foot to the other.

"What the devil is going on, Jaros?" the regent shouted, pounding the desk. "My phone is ringing off the hook with outraged neutrals. How did this happen?"

Jaros had never seen Horthy lose his temper like this. The regent looked on the verge of a stroke. "Regent, it was Eichmann's doing, we have no control over him."

Horthy rose to his full six-feet-plus height, looking down on Jaros. He stopped shouting but Jaros could hear the fury and menace still in his voice. "Don't you dare tell me you have no control. You have a police force, the Hungarian gendarmes and the Army. You have overwhelming numerical superiority over Eichmann's men. You stop that damn train. You hear me?"

Jaros shook his head. "But Regent, do you want to please the neutrals and risk Hitler's wrath by confronting the SS? After all, it's just two thousand dirty Jews."

"You listen and listen carefully, Jaros. I don't give a damn about the neutrals, but those are *my* dirty Jews—not foreigners. They are Hungarian citizens, you understand? I promised to protect them from deportation, and by God, I will. I've got the Russians at my doorstep. I have no intention of ending up in the dock as a war criminal for that little monster, Eichmann." He crashed his fist on the desk.

Jaros looked uncomfortable. "What do you want me to do?" he whispered.

"Stop that train and return it to Kistarcsa, even if you have to use lethal force. It's your head if that train makes it across the border."

Jaros turned to leave.

Wallenberg is here!

"And Jaros—fire those two Nazi ministers of yours, Baky and Endre. They are working for the Germans and Eichmann, undermining my orders. I am sure they are planning a Nazi coup to oust me and install the Nyilas Party in power. I won't have it."

Near Hegyeshalom on the Austro-Hungarian Border, August 11, 1944

Several hours later Captain Leó Lullay, with several detachments of Hungarian gendarmes, watched as the freight train from Kistarcsa slowed before reaching the barrier erected ten minutes earlier.

Lullay had been ordered by Colonel Ferenczy to muster all the men he could find to stop, at all costs, the SS train. He didn't understand why, but he would carry out his orders with determination.

Three hundred gendarmes armed with rifles and automatic weapons surrounded the train. The locomotive, angrily belching steam, locked its wheels and slid to a screeching halt a few feet from the barrier.

SS Captain Novak jumped off the train. Seeing all the weaponry pointed in his direction, he halted. Captain Lullay stepped forward. His eyes met Novak's.

"What is the meaning of this criminal act?" Novak barked. "Remove this barrier *now* so we may proceed."

"I am sorry, Captain, but I have orders to turn this train around and return it to Kistarcsa."

"How dare you interfere with a train of the Third Reich? We will proceed whether you like it or not."

Lullay shook his head. "I don't think so. I intend to use force if I have to, but you will turn this train around."

Buda, Majestic Hotel, Eichmann's Office, August 11, 1944

Eichmann sat in his office thundering at his subordinate. "This is an outrage, an absolute outrage." Wisliceny observed the veins popping out on the colonel's neck. "This cannot be tolerated. In all my long years in the SS, such a thing has never happened to me." Eichmann stormed around the office, slapping a leather riding crop in his open palm.

The blocked deportation trains, Wisliceny knew, would gravely injure Eichmann's prestige. Last May, Eichmann had foolishly advised his superiors that by the end of June, the liquidation of the Jews in Hungary would be an accomplished fact. Now it was already August. The closeness of the Soviet Army made Eichmann even more desperate. Kistarcsa was to be the initiation of a new wave of deportations. Without the assistance of the Hungarian gendarmes, however, Eichmann could not accomplish his goal. Now, the gendarmes were actually opposing the SS. It couldn't happen to a more deserving person, Wisliceny thought.

Eichmann put his face up to Wisliceny's. "Snap out of that daze, idiot. We've got work to do."

Wisliceny winced at the colonel's vehemence.

"I will have my way," Eichmann said menacingly. "Order the *Judenrat* to be in my office by eight tomorrow morning. I have an idea. Here's what I want you to do…"

Buda, Majestic Hotel, Eichmann's Office, August 12, 1944

Members of the Jewish Council in the waiting room to Eichmann's office stirred restlessly. Stern looked up at the clock—almost seven thirty in the evening.

Boda touched Stern's sleeve. "My God, Samu, what is going on? We've been here since eight this morning—just sitting. They haven't let us make any calls and they won't tell us why we're here."

Stern nodded. "I'm just as much in the dark. Last night, Eichmann called János Gabor and screamed, 'How dare you. I'll show you what it means to interfere in my affairs' and then hung up. You don't have to be a genius to know that whatever Eichmann is up to, it won't be good for us."

Boda frowned. "Well, I think…"

Stern put his index finger to his lips. "Shh, someone's coming out." The movement of the door handle caught his attention. Captain Otto Hunsche, legal adviser, emerged from Eichmann's office, smiling.

"Gentlemen, I am so sorry you were taken away from going to the movies or the theater, or perhaps a stroll through the park on this lovely summer evening."

Boda shook his head. "You know very well, Captain, we are not permitted to do those things." Stern nudged Boda with his elbow to keep quiet.

Hunsche laughed. "Ah, of course, how stupid of me to forget you are Jews, not normal human beings. It's a shame, you miss so much in life." He swept his arm toward the office. "Now gentlemen, if you please, step into the colonel's office."

Eichmann was standing by the window, looking out. "They should be out of Hungary by now," he said to no one in particular. He turned, smiling. "Excuse the wait, but it took all this time to get everyone in Kistarcsa back on the train again. Now it has been done. The train has just crossed the border and two thousand Jews that you thought you'd saved yesterday have left Hungary for good. That's what you can expect from now on for getting that Jew-lover Horthy to fire Germany's friends at the Interior Ministry. I will show you what it means to cross me. You may go now, gentlemen."

Buda, Majestic Hotel Restaurant, August 12, 1944

Later that evening, Eichmann sat at dinner at the Majestic. He always wiped his mouth and hands carefully with a napkin several times after finishing a meal. Tonight was no exception. He sipped the remainder of the Hungarian red wine, glancing at Krumey across the table.

"The foot-dragging by the Hungarians must cease. I have been in touch with the *Reichsführer*. He agrees that the Germany Embassy here hasn't been vigorous enough in resisting recent Hungarian ideas of shipping the Jews to Palestine instead of to Auschwitz. That course of action is totally unacceptable because it would give the Jews valuable biological material to restock their race, especially since many of the émigrés would be Zionists."

Krumey nodded. "So what's going to happen?"

Eichmann smiled. "Himmler obtained Hitler's approval to cancel all exit permits from Hungary. I will have those Jews before I leave Budapest. They'll not escape my grasp. I plan to resume the deportations next week. Inform Police Chief Ferenczy."

Krumey took a sip of wine. "What about Ferenczy's request to visit Auschwitz to assure himself that the stories of atrocities and mass exterminations are not true?"

Eichmann shrugged. "I told him it would be no problem so Prime Minister Sztójay ordered Ferenczy to inspect Auschwitz." Eichmann smiled. "When he was ready to leave, I told him that a visit at the moment was out of the question—that he could go there only thirty days after the last transport of Jews left Budapest." He chuckled, "I thought he'd have apoplexy."

CHAPTER 9

Pest, Offices of Section C, August 17 1944

Wallenberg put down his office telephone, scratching his head. Per Anger, sitting on the other side of the desk, frowned. "Bad news?"

"Very bad. That was Finance Minister Lajos Reményi-Schneller. A German commando force raided the Sárvár Camp, subduing the Hungarian guards. They deported another fifteen hundred Jews. Horthy asked him to call me to assure me that the deportations had been carried out without the knowledge or consent of the Hungarian government."

"In addition to the Kistarcsa raid?"

Wallenberg nodded.

"Can we do anything?"

"I'm afraid not. They're already across the border. It was a lightening strike, a night raid. The Germans cut off all communications to and from the camp." Wallenberg rubbed his chin. Then he got to his feet and paced in front of Anger. "I've received assurances from the Hungarian government that these raids will not be repeated." He ran his hands through his hair. "But we have to recognize that the promises are hollow. We have to get these Jews into protected safe houses. It's time to see the Hungarian police chief. László Pëto, a good friend of Horthy's son, tells me that Chief Ferenczy knows the Germans are losing the war and has expressed a desire to save his own skin."

"The same Ferenczy who is the Hungarian liaison to the Eichmann *Kommando* and whose headquarters are called the Hungarian Jew-Liquidating Command?"

"The very same," Wallenberg snorted. "Apparently, he sees his chances of being hanged as a war criminal increasing every day. This Hungarian butcher may be suddenly turning into a great humanitarian, eager to cooperate in saving the Jews."

"And you believe him?"

Wallenberg sighed. "It's unfortunate, but we have to deal with anyone who can help us, regardless of their past baggage." He flashed a sardonic smile. "We may be hypocrites, Per, but it's for a good cause."

Anger suddenly put his hand on Wallenberg's. "Raoul, I have news about your friend's family."

By the look on Anger's face, Wallenberg knew it wouldn't be good news. "Kálmán Lauer's family?"

Anger nodded. "I just found out. They were shipped to Auschwitz over a month ago."

Wallenberg's eyes watered. He wiped them with his hand. "Even the child?"

"Yes, even the child."

"How can I tell Kálmán that? I simply can't do it," he said brokenly. "I swear, Per, I will stop this slaughter—with my own life, if necessary."

Buda, Office of Police Chief Colonel László Ferenczy, August 17, 1944

Later that day, Wallenberg, Switzerland's Charles Lutz and Elizabeth and Alexander Kasser of the Swedish Red Cross entered the foreboding headquarters of the Hungarian Police. The building bristled with armed policemen.

As their wait lengthened over a half an hour, Wallenberg felt his anger increase. Elizabeth Kasser patted his hand. "Patience, Raoul. Remember our objective is to obtain housing, not alienate Ferenczy." Wallenberg nodded.

Finally, an aide ushered them into a large room. Ferenczy motioned them to be seated at the oval conference table. On the long wall behind him hung the crossed-arrow banner of the Arrow Cross.

"Colonel, we'd like to set up separate housing for the international Jews," Wallenberg said.

Ferenczy snorted. "International Jews?"

"Yes," answered Wallenberg calmly, restraining himself. "Those Jews with protective papers from neutral countries. We propose to house them by buying and renting houses in the former Jewish Quarter in Pest—houses that were expropriated by your government. To create an international ghetto, if you will."

Ferenczy stood, leaning on the table. "I just don't understand why you want to help the dirty Jews. They're the devil's brigade, the

Wallenberg is here!

Christ killers. You should be ashamed of helping such despicable people. My job, as you well know, is to see that all the Jews are shipped out. So why come to me with this scheme?"

Wallenberg ignored the tirade. "Very simple, Colonel. With this 'scheme,' we can get these Jews out of your hair by putting them in these houses, which will fly the Swedish, Swiss or Portuguese flags. They will be the territory of those neutrals and thus no longer your concern." He paused to assess Ferenczy's visceral reaction. "To be perfectly blunt, you need to build up your postwar credits with the Jews and their friends if you don't want to be punished as a war criminal."

"I don't react well to threats," Ferenczy growled.

"You misunderstand, Colonel. Think of it not as a threat but as an opportunity. I'm simply pointing out, for your own benefit, the hard facts that should concern you."

"And just how will I be protected from the Allies?"

Lutz spoke up. "We, the neutral nations, will intercede on your behalf and testify as to your cooperation in saving lives."

Wallenberg leaned forward on the table. "Sell us back the houses you took from the Jews. We are prepared to pay a fair price."

Ferenczy shrugged. "Very well, you may buy back three houses."

Wallenberg rose abruptly, almost knocking over the chair. "Forget that pittance. That is not cooperation, that is an insult!"

"Ten houses, but no more."

Lutz looked at Ferenczy. "In fairness, we demand ten houses for the Swiss as well."

Ferenczy nodded.

Wallenberg sat down.

Alexander Kasser cleared his throat. "Excuse me, Colonel…"

Ferenczy started to smile. "Don't tell me—you want to buy houses also. You do not even represent a nation, Herr Kasser."

"That's true, but it can't hurt you to have the prestige of the Swedish Red Cross supporting you, can it?"

Ferenczy threw up his hands. "Are you sure you're not Jews? You certainly bargain like them!"

137

***

Outside Ferenczy's headquarters Wallenberg, grabbed Elizabeth Kasser by the hand and the dignified Swedish diplomat and the proper Swedish Red Cross representative danced down the street. Then he slapped Lutz on the back. "We did it, old friend, with nothing but bluff and words. We must waste no time cementing the understanding and setting up these protected houses."

Pest, Offices of Section C, August 17, 1944

A few minutes later, Elizabeth Kasser sat in a straight-backed chair in Wallenberg's office reviewing the list of available houses in the former Jewish Quarter. "Between the Swiss, the Swedish and the Red Cross, we'll have thirty more safe houses."

Wallenberg nodded. "And that's just for starters. I'll keep returning to Ferenczy to get more housing. For all his bluster, you can see he's both scared and looking, albeit surreptitiously, for a nest egg when the war is over."

Swiveling in his chair to face his large typewriter, supplied by a Budapest Jew seeking to protect his possession, he added, "I need more money. I'll have to write to Ivar Olsen. The WRB will have to replenish my special bank account to cover the cost of these new houses." He stood up and looked out of the window to Ullöi Street. An Orthodox Jew in traditional dress—a long black coat, wide-brimmed black hat, beard and long locks of hair, fringes hanging from his waist—emerged from the building. Wallenberg smiled. Elizabeth Kasser went to the window to see the source of the humor. Wallenberg pointed to the man below clutching tightly to what must have been his *Schutzpass*. "There goes another Swede." This time they both laughed.

Elizabeth Kasser poked him on the arm playfully. "Raoul, you're impossible. You can find humor in any situation."

"Not any, but most. It's the only way I keep my sanity in this Kafkaesque city."

"I've been thinking," she said, holding her chin in her fingers, "we should involve the International Red Cross in this housing project."

Wallenberg snorted. "The International Red Cross? What have they ever done to help the Jews? They gave concentration camps,

Wallenberg is here!

specially selected by the Nazis, a cursory inspection and wrote glowing reports. Look what happened in Theresienstadt. The Nazis first shipped two thirds of the Jews from there to Auschwitz to be murdered, cleaned up a part of the camp and invited the Red Cross to view this 'uncrowded, model' camp. The Red Cross fell for a ruse that a child could see through. When it would have counted, the Red Cross refused to protest the treatment and murder of the Jews in Germany, Poland and France because it said it would not interfere in the 'internal affairs' of those countries. Even in Hungary, when hundreds of thousands of Jews were being deported to the extermination camps in record time, Premier Sztójay convinced the International Red Cross representative visiting from Berlin, Robert Schrimer, that the Jews were being treated 'humanely.' Apparently, Schrimer was the only one in Budapest who believed it."

Kasser looked at Wallenberg. "Raoul, the past is the past. I know they're convinced now."

"Fine, then let them issue their own protective passes."

"They're concerned about the legality," Kasser warned.

Wallenberg slapped the side of his head. "See, that's what I mean. Of course there's nothing official behind the our passes but the seals and signatures—and they're probably illegal and a breach of diplomatic rules." He raised his voice. "But damn it, they've been effective in saving people. Can't they get that through their thick heads? Believe me, I'll have no qualms whatsoever explaining myself after the war. When the truth is known of what the Nazis were doing in the name of law, *my* actions will be justified, even by the politicians and bureaucrats. Furthermore…"

There was a rap on the door. Wallenberg looked up. A short, middle-aged man, a yellow star sewn on his jacket, opened the door slowly and timidly entered, clutching papers. "May I come in?"

Wallenberg waved him in.

"I just wanted to thank you personally for my *Schutzpass*." He waved the papers.

"I'm glad I could do it for you."

The man hesitated. "One question, Herr Wallenberg, if you don't mind." He looked down at his shoes.

Wallenberg waited.

"Can I use the pass to go to the theater?"

139

Wallenberg exploded. He flew out of his chair and reached the man in three giant strides. The startled man jumped back.

"I give you a chance to live, and the rooms to live in, and all you are concerned about is going to the theater?" Wallenberg shouted. "It's people like you that will make an anti-Semite out of me!"

The man stammered his apologies and backed out of the office, gently closing the door.

Elizabeth Kasser looked at Wallenberg, shaking her head. "I think you overreacted. You frightened that poor man to death."

Wallenberg slumped back into his chair, spreading his arms wide. "I know, I know. With all those lives at stake, I have no patience with frivolity."

Elizabeth Kasser walked around the desk and put her hand on his shoulder. "You need some rest. Your nerves are frazzled. You can't keep going on three or four hours of sleep a night."

"Perhaps, but I don't have the luxury of time for eight hours of sleep. It could cost a thousand lives, maybe more."

Washington, DC, State Department, Office of John Pehle, August 23, 1944

The same day, several hours later, in Washington, Pehle pushed Ivar Olsen's report across the desk to Morgenthau. "Here, read it for yourself. This Wallenberg is amazing."

Morgenthau did not pick it up. "I have another meeting in an hour. Why don't you just give me a summary? I'll read the full report later."

Pehle nodded. "His operation has simply exploded. In no time at all, he has bought and rented homes that he's turned into safe houses—and he's gotten the Swiss, the Swedish Red Cross and even the International Red Cross to buy houses. He's formed a social services unit in Section C that set up clinics, soup kitchens and a clothing center for Jews in the safe houses. He's got two hospitals functioning with forty doctors, and his people have drawn up programs to meet the needs of the children, the sick and the elderly. He's even organized a children's home."

Morgenthau looked at Pehle. "What about stopping the deportations?"

Wallenberg is here!

"He seems to have done that, as well. Very few Jews were deported in July and August. But I must tell you, his unorthodox methods are driving the Swedish diplomats to distraction. His splashy style of diplomacy has them edgy. Olsen says they would have preferred to deal with the Jewish problem along traditional diplomatic lines, which means, of course, not helping the Jews at all."

Morgenthau nodded. "That's excellent progress. How are the funds holding out?"

"No problem. We're feeding Wallenberg funds as fast as he needs them."

Morgenthau knitted his brow. "I just wonder how long the Nazis are going to tolerate being frustrated by Wallenberg and Horthy. It's a thin line of defense."

Pehle shrugged. "The Russians are close. If we can string it along for a few more months, we'll be home free."

"I'd like to believe that, John," said Morgenthau, shaking his head, "but I just don't think so. I'd hate to be in Wallenberg's shoes if Himmler makes a move in Budapest."

Budapest, Late August 1944

The Jews of Budapest in the late summer of 1944 were experiencing mixed messages. They rejoiced when Regent Horthy fired his pro-Nazi prime minister, Döme Sztójay, and appointed General Géza Lakatos, a Hungarian patriot not intimidated by the Germans. They despaired when Ferenczy secretly reported to the Jewish leaders that Horthy had given his consent to limited deportations of Jews from Budapest, to begin on August 28.

Horthy's son, Miki, assured *Judenrat* member László Pĕto that the regent was trying to keep the Germans off balance by making repeated promises but doing nothing to keep them. That assurance hardly assuaged the Jewish leaders. They called Wallenberg.

Wallenberg did two things. First, he stepped up the issuance of passports to Jews with any connection to Sweden, however tenuous. Immediately Jews rushed to the post office, scrambling to the Stockholm telephone directory to find and submit the name and address of a Swede, any Swede. Thousands of *Schutzpasses* were issued. Second, Wallenberg immediately prepared, with the concurrence of the neutral nations, a joint note addressed to Regent

Horthy and signed by Minister Danielsson, expressing anguish over the rumored resumption of deportations. It called on the Hungarian government to put an end forever to such actions.

A day later, news reached Budapest that the Russians had broken through German-Rumanian defenses in Moldavia. The Rumanian king demanded that the Germans leave so that he could conclude a separate armistice. The Germans responded by bombing the Royal Palace in Bucharest.

Horthy dispatched Ferenczy to meet Eichmann to tell him that the scheduled deportations were canceled for the time being.

Pest, Offices of Section C, Late August 1944

Charles Lutz sipped steaming coffee in Wallenberg's office while his host examined a Swiss protective pass. He turned over the document, shaking his head. "I don't understand. A 'Palestine Pass?'" He waved it at Lutz.

Lutz smiled. "Since we opened the Glass House on Vadász Street to process requests for passes, the Zionist underground came in and printed these up. We issued about seven thousand of them."

Wallenberg put up his hand. "But Charles, these are clearly bogus. Great Britain, not Switzerland, holds the mandate to Palestine."

"I know, but the Zionists followed your lead and made the passes very official looking with stamps and signatures. I'm also covering those seven thousand Jews with a Swiss collective passport."

"What the devil is a collective passport?"

Lutz's face lit up. "You think you are the only one who can be innovative? We are interpreting the passport as applying to family heads and encompassing all members of the family. The seven thousand passports should expand the protection to forty thousand Jews."

Wallenberg nodded. "The Zionist underground also has been issuing forged Swedish protective passes under their Operation Hazalah."

Lutz looked puzzled.

"*Hazalah* is Hebrew for 'rescue.'" He picked up a forged document and showed it to Lutz. "I more or less gave them my tacit approval—as far as I am concerned, anything that saves lives is legal."

"Does Danielsson know about this?"

Wallenberg laughed. "I try not to discuss such matters with diplomats trained to work within the letter of the law," he put up his hand, "present company, of course, excluded. I'm sure Danielsson suspects it but prefers not to be told."

Buda, The Royal Palace, August 28, 1944

Lakatos, the new prime minister, shoved the report in front of Horthy. "Read it for yourself, Sir. The Germans are refusing to resupply our troops with food and ammunition. They're also looting our army's produce and livestock. Who needs allies like that? This cannot continue."

Horthy nodded wearily. "I know, but the Germans are still too strong for us to take them on directly. I will chart two courses of action. First, I will announce publicly Hungary's firm intention to adhere to our alliance with the Third Reich and our continued participation in the war. That should buy us a little time. Second, I want you contact the Allies, covertly of course, to negotiate an armistice. It's a dangerous game, but I know of no other way to restore Hungarian sovereignty."

Lakatos rubbed his chin. "What about the Jews?"

"I will continue to fend off Veesenmayer's demands to resume the deportations." Horthy smiled. "After all, we lack internment camps, transportation facilities, guards and supplies."

"He won't believe you."

Horthy shrugged. "Then I will yell and scream about Hungarian sovereignty." Looking up at the ceiling, he added, "And I have a few cards up my sleeve yet to play.

"But it's not Veesenmayer I fear, it's Eichmann. He's a loose cannon and may strike out on his own. I'm going to try to get him out of here."

Lakatos rose to leave.

Horthy put up his hand. "Stay, Prime Minister. Veesenmayer's in the waiting room. I've summoned him." Horthy buzzed his secretary twice. A few seconds later, Proconsul Edmund Veesenmayer, German plenipotentiary of Budapest, entered. The secretary closed the door behind the proconsul.

Veesenmayer bowed courteously to both men. Horthy motioned him to a chair. Wasting no time, the regent declared, "I insist that the Reich restore responsibility for Jewish affairs to Hungary and that Jewish possessions in German warehouses be returned."

Veesenmayer's eyes widened. "That's impossible, Regent. Chancellor Hitler is already outraged at the suspension of deportations. I cannot guarantee what he will do if I forward such a message to him."

"Please be sure to tell the chancellor of my unalterable decision to remain loyal to the Reich. My message changes nothing in that regard. I hope the Führer will understand, however, that I cannot, in good conscience, reconcile the deportation of Hungarian Jews to Germany. We have heard reports of extermination camps on good authority—and Colonel Eichmann steadfastly refuses to permit my Hungarian representatives to inspect your facilities at Auschwitz for ourselves." Horthy spread his arms and shrugged. "What other conclusion can we draw, Proconsul? The Eichmann *Kommando* must be withdrawn from Budapest."

Both Veesenmayer and Lakatos looked surprised.

Veesenmayer leaned forward, his hands on the edge of the regent's desk. "This is totally unacceptable, Regent. On what basis do you think you can order the Third Reich around like a third-rate power? You, Regent, are courting total occupation of Hungary with such traitorous talk."

Horthy pursed his lips. "I would thank you to calm down and carefully consider your words. You are talking to an ally, not an enemy country. Think about this, Proconsul Veesenmayer. The Soviet forces have overrun the Rumanian oil fields. You desperately need the oil production from our fields in the Zala region, which we still control. You will need our help to maintain your supply lines through our country. It would not behoove you to make us the enemy. Please deliver *that* message to Berlin."

Buda, Hotel Majestic, Eichmann's Office, August 30, 1944

Wisliceny jerked backwards when Eichmann picked up a coffee cup and flung it down, sending shards of blue and white porcelain flying around the office. "This is outrageous. I sent you to Berlin to see Himmler to get that order countermanded," Eichmann screamed.

Wallenberg is here!

"Yes sir. I did the best I could but the *Reichsführer* was insistent. He has ordered the end to the deportations and has recalled us from Budapest. He suggests you return to Berlin for a vacation."

Eichmann grunted. "And after I reported to the Führer that Budapest was virtually *Judenrein!* I don't understand. Explain to me again why we are being recalled."

"According to Himmler, now that Hungary's Zala oil field production is indispensable to the Reich, it's not worth while to let matters come to a head because of the Hungarian Jews. Himmler told me to tell you it's only a temporary thing."

"But the Führer gave my mission priority over the war effort. I still don't understand why this is being done."

"To help our armies defend the Eastern Front," Wisliceny offered. He felt the colonel's withering gaze.

"Don't you understand, Major? Deporting the Jews takes priority." He crushed some of the shards of the cup under his jackboot. His voice dropped to a resigned whisper. "Unfortunately, I cannot disobey the *Reichsführer's* orders."

Wisliceny said, placatingly, "While Horthy is in power we won't get the help we need from the Hungarian gendarmes, anyway. And you know we don't have the manpower to round up all the Jews."

Eichmann grunted again. "We should have killed Horthy long ago."

"Will you go to Berlin, Sir?"

Eichmann shook his head. "László Endre, the fired Hungarian deputy minister, has invited me to his country estate. I may as well take advantage of the excellent hunting on the Austro-Hungarian border while I bide my time. But I'll be back for the more important prey, make no mistake about that."

Wisliceny nodded.

Eichmann's mood changed abruptly. He slapped Wisliceny on the back. "Come, Major. Let us get drunk at the Arizona Nightclub. Then you can order two high-class Hungarian women of the night to meet me at the Hotel Majestic. I will stay there tonight. If I can't dispatch Jews, I'll just have to show the women of Budapest a thing or two about SS prowess." He laughed.

Carl L. Steinhouse

Buda, Apartment of Baron and Baroness Kemény, September 2, 1944

Baron and Baroness Gábor Kemény gave a large reception for the international community of Budapest. A butler took Wallenberg's homburg and led him into the large drawing room filled with elegant antiques. The room expressed the cultivated grace and style that he encountered in many homes on the rich side of his family, although he himself had lived much more modestly as one of the diplomatic Wallenbergs.

A woman about his own age with deep blue eyes, in a low-cut, red gown, cleverly altered to offset her obviously pregnant state, approached him, her small manicured hand extended. The dazzling, dark-haired beauty of the Baroness Elisabeth Fuchs Kemény took his breath away, as he bowed and gently touched her cool, ungloved hand.

Wallenberg spoke very little Hungarian, but he needn't have worried. The baroness greeted him in perfect English. "I am so glad finally to meet you. I have heard about your exploits in Budapest." She laughed easily. "Somehow, from the way the Germans and the baron tell it, I expected you to be at least eight feet tall."

Wallenberg smiled, responding in equally flawless English. "I'm sorry to disappoint you, but I'm afraid it's my big mouth rather than my physique that's gotten me into all the trouble that apparently has made me the topic of conversation."

The baroness squeezed his arm. "You are too modest. I look forward to speaking with you—perhaps later this evening. Right now, duty calls." She left his side to greet other arrivals.

The tall, handsome baron, in military dress uniform bedecked with medals, braid, sword and sash, curtly introduced himself to Wallenberg and moved quickly on to the next arrival. There was no love lost between the two men. The baron's sympathies were with the Germans. As an important official in the Arrow Cross, he would, undoubtedly, be appointed to a high position in government if his party came into power—and the Germans represented the best chance for that to occur.

The evening would turn out to be important to both Wallenberg and the baroness. After dinner, she took Wallenberg's arm and led him out onto the balcony, shutting the double glass doors behind her.

out of the hearing of her other guests. As they chatted for the next hour, they discovered that they had a lot in common—love of hiking, cycling and movies, and an intense dislike of hunting and cruelty to animals. He told her how, as a teenager, he'd liberated the hounds from their kennel the night before a big foxhunt. The story delighted her. He waxed passionate on the subject of boats, particularly World War I battleships, and his inability to follow in his father's footsteps as a naval officer because he was color blind, which his art teacher pointed out to him when he painted green horses grazing on a field of red grass. The baroness threw back her head and laughed, trying to picture such a painting.

Then she frowned. "Mr. Wallenberg, I've spent too much time away from my guests. The baron will start wondering what happened to me. I enjoyed our conversation immensely and I hope we can do this again soon." Squeezing his hand, she left him to join the guests inside.

He remained on the balcony, feeling guilty about his attraction to this married woman whom he'd just met and perhaps just a little bit envious of the baron. Taking a deep breath to clear his head, he returned to the drawing room, found his homburg and left.

The Danube, Margit Sziget, September 11, 1944

In the next few days Wallenberg and Baroness Kemény met several times over coffee to talk. The baroness loved to speak in English and Wallenberg, not always comfortable in social relationships with women, found her a delightful conversationalist. On this September afternoon they walked, hand in hand, through the woods on Margit Sziget, a slender, two-mile-long islet in the middle of the Danube. This bit of forest surrounded by water and the concrete, cobblestone and brick of Budapest, offered, for many residents, a brief respite from the war and the German occupation.

"Raoul, I'm surprised some lovely woman has not netted you. To me, you seem to be a prize catch."

"I have been too busy organizing my professional life to think about marriage. To be honest, I did propose to someone in Stockholm, but she turned me down. She said she was too young to get married and I suppose she was right. She was only seventeen. It was just as well because then I got this assignment to Budapest. What kind of life would my wife have had? I certainly could not have brought her here."

"That was her loss." Then her face suddenly brightened and she brought her hands together in a clap. "I've heard all about your wonderful imitations of animal and people. You must give me a demonstration sometime."

"Certainly. But tell me how you, an Austrian, came to choose a Hungarian baron?"

"Oh, I led a pretty carefree life, cavorting across Europe with titled friends. I was skiing in Cortina when I met him. He was so handsome, dashing and romantic. He became my chief passion and eventually we got married." She looked up at the clouds. "Unfortunately, I didn't know about his interest in the Arrow Cross, or about his Nazism and anti-Semitism. Don't misunderstand me. I love him very much; it's just that…" She sighed.

Wallenberg looked in her eyes. "I know, you're part Jewish."

"You know?" she asked, wide eyed.

Wallenberg grinned sheepishly. "I admit it, I collected information on your background. Your Jewish grandfather was president of the Austrian Parliament in the Hapsburg days and your mother was a descendant of a pope."

She smiled ruefully. "Two popes, actually. Is my life that much of an open book?"

"Not really. I hope I haven't upset you. It just so happens you were on a list of people who might be of assistance to me in Budapest. The person who prepared the list apparently knew of your background."

The baroness looked down, pinching the corners of her eyes with her thumb and forefinger.

Wallenberg put his hand on her arm. "I have upset you, I'm so sorry."

Looking directly at him, she explained, "It's just that the baron doesn't know of my Jewish background and he's so narrow-minded about those things…"

"Don't worry, Elizabeth, your secret is safe with me."

She kicked a pebble as she walked. "Life as a baroness hasn't been easy. I'm bored with doing nothing. When I first came to Budapest, I was in publishing, working for this wonderful Jewish editor. At first, the baron tolerated it. When they took the editor's business away from him, as happened to most Jews, I was out of a job. The baron was just as happy and insisted that from then on, I should stay home to run his household and be by his side when he needed me. That, he said, was my place in life."

Wallenberg nodded. "Many wives face the same dilemma. In that regard, may I cheer you up with a funny story?"

The baroness nodded and smiled.

"Once upon a time, a beautiful, independent, self-assured princess happened upon a frog in a pond. She watched him hop from lily pad to lily pad." Wallenberg got down on his haunches. "Ribbit, ribbit," he croaked in his best frog imitation. "The princess paused. There was something different about this frog so she listened carefully. Sure she heard it say something, she bent down and put out her hand. The frog hopped up on it. It looked in her eyes. 'Ribbit, ribbit, I was once a handsome prince until an evil witch put a spell on me, ribbit, ribbit. One kiss from you, ribbit, and I will turn back into a prince and then we can marry and move into the castle with my mother. You can prepare my meals, clean my clothes, bear my children and forever feel happy doing so, ribbit.'

"That night, while the princess dined on frog's legs, she laughed and said, 'I don't damn well think so.'"

The baroness laughed so hard tears came to her eyes. "An excellent imitation of a frog, and a very funny story. I can certainly identify with it."

Her companion smiled, "I'm glad I brightened your day."

Finally, he had found someone in Budapest he could share his feelings with. For the first time since arriving two months ago, he could relax. As they continued their woodland walk, he told her about Swedish literature, Swedish food and the long Swedish winter nights. They discussed Goethe, Shelley, Keats and Schiller. She was surprised at his knowledge of, and love for, Shakespeare. He waxed eloquent on the Swedish opera. By this time, he was feeling something more than friendship stirring, something he would have to suppress, as he was sure she also was doing. How important their relationship was to be to his mission, Wallenberg would not realize until later.

CHAPTER 10

Budapest, September 1944

The Jewish community breathed a sigh of relief when Adolph Eichmann left Budapest and the deportations were suspended. SS Colonel Kurt Becher had convinced Himmler that although the Jews were no longer being rounded up, it wouldn't hurt to squeeze a few more dollars out of them in a new round of "goods for blood." Becher played on Himmler's desire to make the SS financially independent by getting into some profit-making industries. Becher, not tainted by direct involvement in the exterminations, was dispatched to Budapest to oversee the negotiations.

Jewish leaders looked on Becher's arrival with a mixture of suspicion and hope. He wasn't Eichmann, but Jews were still being harassed and murdered by the SS, which Becher represented. Becher came to negotiate and he did, greatly enriching the SS. In a masterstroke, he arranged the transfer of half the share capital in the Manfred-Weiss Works to the SS with himself as the head of the firm. In return, forty-eight members of the Weiss family were flown to Portugal in two German planes.

***

At the end of the month Wallenberg wrote to Ivar Olsen of the WRB reflecting a new optimism. He reported that most of the Jews had been released from work camps in the countryside. Jews now were ignoring the curfews, and many had removed their yellow stars. By the end of September, not a single Jew had been shipped out of Budapest. He concluded by requesting that arrangements be made for shipments of clothing and medicine to Budapest.

The report wasn't his only written communication to Stockholm. He began thinking of returning home. He wrote asking his mother to look for an apartment for him and confided in her his worries about supporting himself. Doubting whether he'd be welcomed into the Wallenberg business empire by his cousins, he wrote to his friend

Kálmán Lauer, asking him to make discrete inquires of his cousins' father-his own uncle and godfather-Jacob Wallenberg, Sr.

Velem, Estate of László Endre, September 1944

Ever since he arrived at Endre's estate, Eichmann had been drinking heavily. His host watched as Eichmann paced back and forth like a caged animal. "Relax, Colonel. You'll have a stroke."

Eichmann shook his head. "Who can relax while Himmler lets that traitor Becher barter away my Final Solution. I tell you László, it's a dirty business. But I'll get even, don't you doubt it."

"It's only a few Jews that got out of Hungary and it had the *Reichsführer's* blessing. Why worry about it?"

Eichmann's distorted features reflected his seething rage. He faced Endre, hands on his hips. "You just don't understand," he spit out. "Becher is allowing the most dangerous Jews, the prominent and wealthy ones to escape. He's undermining Nazi ideology and the Final Solution. He'll answer for this treachery, I'll see to it."

Endre put his hand on his guest's shoulder. "My sources in Berlin tell me that a German takeover and the ouster of Horthy is imminent. We will both be back in Budapest, before we know it."

"It can't be too soon for me."

The Hungarian smiled as Eichmann walked unsteadily to the bar. "Haven't you had enough?" It fell on deaf ears as Eichmann finished off the rest of the bottle of cognac. "I have brought in some nice young girls for the evening's entertainment to take your mind off things. I just hope you're in condition to enjoy it."

Eichmann stared at Endre through bleary, half-closed eyes. "Don't worry about me, I can outperform you with the ladies, drunk or sober," he snapped.

Endre shrugged and smiled.

Buda, SS Headquarters, Early October 1944

An SS clerk led László Hegedüs through the massive gray entrance to SS headquarters and down the hall to the office of Dr. Theodore Grell. Grell, now in charge of Jewish affairs in Budapest, was well known for his impatient desire to get the deportation trains rolling again. Hegedüs, a Jew and a Wallenberg aide who dealt in *Schutzpass*es and passports, hated going there. The place crawled with

SS and Gestapo officers. Swastikas and Hitler's image on the walls mocked him at every turn. The thick walls of the building's basement housed the interrogation rooms. Every time the Gestapo summoned him to this place, he had the uncomfortable feeling that he'd end up down there never to return.

The aide ushered him into Grell's office. Hegedüs thought this must be important because he didn't have to wait. He couldn't decide whether that was a bad sign.

Grell didn't ask him to sit. Instead, the SS officer leaned forward on his desk, shoving a paper at Hegedüs. It was a Swedish *Schutzpass* made out to a Dr. Arthur Kende. The name didn't ring a bell but he could see the document was a crude fake.

His eyes hooded, Grell asked, "Is this a forgery?"

Hegedüs stalled, pretending to study it. If he said yes, this Dr. Kende could lose his life, if he denied it, it could threaten the credibility of all the passports. "I do not recall this one, Dr. Grell. I will have to consult with Herr Wallenberg."

"Get out. I want an answer by tomorrow morning or I will send the Gestapo to fetch you."

Pest, Offices of Section C, An Hour Later

Wallenberg, sitting at his desk, turned the passport over in his hands and shook his head. "This fake would fool no one, not even an uneducated, provincial gendarme. Who is this Kende anyway?"

Hegedüs shrugged. "We have no record of a Dr. Arthur Kende. No one has ever heard of him."

"Very well, then. We can't put every Jew in Budapest in jeopardy for one man who we don't even know exists. Tell Grell the passport's a fake." Wallenberg grinned. "He'll probably fall off his chair."

Wallenberg still fought an uphill battle with other members of the Swedish Legation on the passes. Although originally they were issued only to those who had a strong connection to Sweden, he had found ways to give them to any Jew who requested one. Danielsson did not approve the practice, but he did nothing to hinder Wallenberg. A few in the legation, however, complained that the wholesale issuance of passes would negate their value. Determined to save lives, Wallenberg brushed aside those objections. In the end, he had gotten his way. Now, no one was turned away.

Wallenberg is here!

Pest, a House in the Jewish Quarter, the Next Day

A large black Mercedes roared up to the entrance of a house in the Jewish Quarter and squealed to a sudden stop. Four armed SS officers leaped out, three with revolvers drawn, one with a submachine gun. They banged furiously on the door. A man in his early twenties in an Arrow Cross uniform, armed with a rifle, opened the door a crack. The four SS, screaming orders in German, crashed through, knocking the man back.

They found three more Arrow Cross guards in the parlor. The officer with the submachine gun backed them against the wall. "*Schnell,*" he screamed. "Where is the bitch Jewess? We have come to take her for questioning. Are you hiding her?" He pushed the weapon into the belly of a guard.

"She is upstairs, sir. We were going to take her down to the Danube and shoot her."

"Idiot, she is withholding important information. She must be taken down to Gestapo headquarters." The SS officer motioned with his head to the stairs. The other SS rushed up the stairs and pounded on her door.

"This is the SS. Come out immediately."

They dragged a frightened woman out of the room and down the stairs. In the street, as the awe-struck Arrow Cross guards gawked, the officer with the submachine gun shoved the woman into the back of the Mercedes and climbed in beside her. The swastika flags on the fenders came to life as the staff car took off and disappeared around the corner.

The SS officer smiled at the woman. "Do not be frightened. I'm Pista; these men and I work for Wallenberg and the underground."

Totally confused, the woman stammered, "Wallenberg, the one from the Swedish Legation?"

Pista grinned. "The very same. Your niece Agnes sent word to Wallenberg less than an hour ago. She is waiting for you at his office. You're lucky he's efficient." He saw tears in her eyes. His also became moist.

Pest, Arrow Cross Headquarters, October 2, 1944

Ferenc Szálasi, head of the Hungarian Arrow Cross Party, rose from his chair, walked around his desk and greeted Emil Kovarcz, the organizer of the Arrow Cross militia. "What did you learn in Berlin?" He returned to his seat and motioned his visitor to a chair.

"Good news, Sir. Orders have been received for a coup. It should happen any day now."

"I've heard that before. I'll believe it when I see it."

Kovarcz leaned forward. "This time they're serious, I'm sure of it. We must have a meeting of the right-wing, pro-war, pro-German legislators to prepare the political and military justifications for seizing power. We don't want a vacuum when the Germans move in. We must have our people in place to assume control when the *putsch* occurs."

Szálasi nodded. "And what about the militia, is it ready to step in?"

"Certainly, Sir," replied Kovarcz as his face lit up. "I am uniting all the anti-Communist and right-wing youth organizations under the banner of the Arrow Cross. I have already established a network of party headquarters throughout the country. Each one of them is a repository for arms the Germans have provided to us."

"That's fine," said Szálasi, leaning back in his chair. "But what about the generals loyal to Horthy? They could present a serious problem."

"Leave it to me, Sir." Kovarcz assured him. "I have that contingency covered. General Dezső László will see that they're neutralized."

Szálasi rubbed his chin. "The Germans, no doubt, will expect us to assist them in resuming deportations."

"That will be no problem. They shouldn't have been suspended in the first place. My militia will be ready for the task. Everyone will rejoice when that dog of a regent is punished for his cowardly dealings with the Russians and the Jews."

"I expect your militia to be absolutely loyal to me, to carry out my orders swiftly and without fail."

Kovarcz gave a slight bow. "Certainly, Sir. My men are most anxious to get started. They have already been practicing by harassing and beating up Jews."

Buda, Royal Palace, October 15, 1944, Morning

Miki Horthy looked at his watch. "I have to leave soon, Father. A Tito partisan has arranged a meeting to coordinate our efforts against the Germans."

The regent frowned. "Is that meeting really necessary? You already know that we may be out of this war shortly."

"What's the latest developments on that?" asked Miki.

"After the Soviets overran Debrecen, I sent a three-man delegation to Moscow, led by General Gábor Faraghó, to begin preliminary negotiations for a cease fire. I have already directed my loyal generals to cease hostilities and pull back our forces to Budapest to protect us against the Germans. I will go on the radio shortly to announce the end of the war for Hungary."

"You're doing the right thing, Father. But you may not succeed. Therefore, we need to coordinate with the partisans to keep up the fight. Trust me, it will be an important meeting."

"Well, be careful Miki," warned the regent. "There are spies everywhere. If the Germans catch you..."

"The partisan representative and I are the only ones who know about the meeting."

"Nevertheless, I am providing you with a car and three bodyguards."

Miki shrugged. "Very well, Sir, but I really don't need them. They must be instructed to stay in the car. The partisans, as you might expect, are very skittish."

The regent nodded. Miki looked at his watch again and started toward the door. "I've got to go now. I don't want to be late for my meeting."

Buda, Outside the Royal Palace, October 15, 1944, Same Time

Lieutenant Colonel Otto Skorzeny squirmed uncomfortably in the passenger seat of the roughly idling truck. The cabs of German trucks were not built for six-foot-four bodies. The warm day only added to his discomfort because he had on a trench coat with a yellow star sewn on its breast. All his men wore the same uniform. Each had a hooded mask in his pocket. His men—the driver and the eight in the back of the truck—were paratroopers in Skorzeny's SS Special Forces Battalion.

Comrades called Skorzeny Scarface. The dueling scar ran from the bottom of his left ear, across the cheek down to the chin. He wore the scar as a badge of honor so he didn't mind the sobriquet.

Skorzeny had led several daring raids. The most spectacular, at the personal request of the Führer, was his rescue of Benito Mussolini. The Italian dictator had been imprisoned in a hotel atop the Gran Sasso, the loftiest peak in the Apennines, accessible only by funicular railway. Skorzeny and his paratroopers had used a glider for the dangerous landing. Without firing a shot, they had disarmed the Italian guards. Skorzeny spirited Mussolini off the mountain, piloting a tiny Fieseler-Storch plane that he had stowed in the glider. Such a feat made him the natural choice for this new mission.

The large sedan bearing the standard of the regent of Hungary emerged from the main gate of the Royal Palace. Skorzeny straightened up and pointed. "That's the one! Get moving."

The big truck lurched forward following the sedan down the hilly streets of Buda. Three blocks from the palace a roadblock forced the sedan to halt. Skorzeny rapped on the rear window of the truck's cab and eight men, now hooded, leaped out of the back of the truck, firing their weapons, killing the two Horthy bodyguards instantly and wounding the chauffeur. On the street, screaming people scattered in all directions. Skorzeny flung open the front passenger door, pushed the dead guard into the wounded driver, leaned over the front seat and smashed the regent's son across the temple with the butt of his revolver. He pulled the unconscious Miki Horthy out of the car.

On Skorzeny's signal, one of his paratroopers hauled a Persian rug from the truck, an idea Skorzeny had borrowed from George Bernard Shaw's play *Caesar and Cleopatra*. "Spread it out and roll him up in it, quickly. We have to get out of here."

The rolled rug was unceremoniously dumped in the back of the truck, which sped off and headed west. At the Austrian border, Miki Horthy, groggy but conscious, was unrolled out of the rug by Colonel Skorzeny and shoved into the back seat of a waiting Gestapo staff car. The colonel climbed in beside him.

Skorzeny smiled, the scar moving upwards on his cheek. "Well, Master Horthy, you've been a bad boy, trying to play grown-up games with the Yugoslav partisans."

Miki, his eyes drawn to the scar that was the largest and most pronounced he'd ever seen, stared at Skorzeny. "How did you find out? Only two of us knew."

"Because it wasn't a partisan you were dealing with. A German agent contacted you and you walked right into the trap. You should leave the business of war to grown men."

Miki Horthy slumped into his seat. "Where are you taking me?"

"Certainly not to the partisans," Skorzeny laughed. "I think the Mauthausen concentration camp will be more suitable accommodations, don't you agree?"

"You will kill me?"

"If that's what we wanted, you'd be dead already. For now, you are more useful alive."

Pest, Office of Section C, the Same Day, October 15, 1944

Wallenberg brought the radio into the main room of Section C, where his staff was busy processing requests and issuing *Schutzpasses*. Above the din of the workers, he shouted, "Quiet down everyone. Regent Horthy is about to go on the air. What he has to say may be significant." Wallenberg had heard through Miki Horthy that the Hungarian government was secretly planning to negotiate an armistice. He had kept the information to himself, not wanting to raise people's hopes.

One of the section workers ran in, breathless, announcing, "There's been fighting and gunfire reported near the palace. People on the scene say a bunch of Jews attacked a government car and killed some soldiers, then fled in a truck."

Wallenberg frowned. "That can't be. There's been no partisan activity in Budapest that I'm aware of."

Pista, a partisan, nodded. "You're right, we didn't want to embarrass the regent, so we pulled back. They weren't partisans or Jews that attacked. The attackers were just dressed like Jews."

"That's a bad sign," said Wallenberg and looked at his watch. "It's time to hear the announcement." He turned up the volume on the radio. They heard some static, then the Hungarian national anthem. The announcer, in the gravest tones, stated that the regent was about to make an important announcement. Then it was quiet, punctuated by more static.

"My fellow citizens, I am pleased to announce that for Hungary, the war is over. All the horrors perpetrated by the Gestapo and its puppets in the last few months will be ended, immediately." The room full of people stirred. "I have instructed our armed forces to disengage from the battle with the Soviets and pull back to their barracks in Budapest for the defense of the Motherland. With trust in God, peace shall prevail in our country for a thousand generations. Thank you."

The room erupted in wild cheering. Those who still wore yellow stars ripped them off. The radio blared out the music of Hungarian composers and, as if to emphasize the new order, *The New Hebrides* symphony by the Jew Mendelssohn, whose music had been banned by the Germans.

Several of the staff hugged Wallenberg, who put up his hands. "Quiet, please." He waited until everyone calmed down. "Before any of you starts to celebrate or do anything rash, please consider that we do not know how the Germans will react to Horthy's announcement. Remember this sobering thought. The Nazis are still a formidable presence in this city and all over Hungary. I don't want to throw cold water on your happiness but I suspect we haven't heard the last of the Germans. So please, continue working and let's see what the next few days bring."

Pest, Main Railway Station, October 15, 1944, the Same Time

The decision had been taken to send all wives and children of the Swedish delegation in Budapest back to Stockholm. While Wallenberg was quieting his staff, Per Anger was leading the Swedish dependents into the railway terminal already crowded with German soldiers. With the troops using the trains, reservations were exceedingly hard to come by, but he had managed it. Suddenly, the station loudspeaker called for attention. The regent was about to make an important announcement. With difficulty in the noisy terminal, Anger caught the drift of Horthy's statement—an armistice had been declared.

He conferred with the other diplomats seeing their families off. Some urged him to permit the families to return to their homes in Budapest. Anger was tempted, but seeing the terminal teeming with the Nazi military, he decided against it.

"We'll stick to our original plan. The families must go home. We do not know how the Germans will react. With such a strong Wehrmacht and SS presence in Budapest, I doubt they'll take this lying down. There could be serious violence. This may be the last opportunity to get our people out, so they must go."

As Anger and the other Swedish diplomats helped their families, including Anger's wife and daughter, to board, a German transportation officer appeared at the train door and barred their way.

"Halt. You must relinquish all your seats, as the German Army requires them. Disembark your people immediately."

Anger strode up to the German officer, their faces a few inches apart. "I will do no such thing. We are Swedish diplomats and these are our families. We have reservations and tickets. This outrage must cease immediately."

The German officer blinked, obviously taken aback by this unexpected resistance. Anger was sure the announcement of an armistice hadn't helped the officer's disposition. The German recovered quickly. "Remove yourselves without delay," he shouted, "or I shall have the Gestapo throw all of you off the train and I will not be responsible for the safety of your women and children. This train is commandeered."

Just as loud, and in fluent German, Anger shouted back, "I have no intention of taking orders from you. If you have any problems with that, you may take it up with Plenipotentiary Veesenmayer with whom I and the Swedish Legation maintain close diplomatic relations."

The name Veesenmayer stopped the German officer cold. He looked at his clipboard for a few moments. "Very well, you may proceed, but be warned that your families will be under enemy fire en route." He stomped off the train.

Anger stayed until he saw the train disappear out of the station. On its way back to the Swedish Legation in Buda, the Swedish staff car was halted in Pest, two blocks from the railway station. Roadblocks of German tanks and military trucks had sprung up all over the city. One diplomat turned to Anger. "You were right. Thanks for insisting on getting our families out of here."

Buda, Royal Palace, October 15, 1955, a Few Minutes Later

After his speech, Regent Horthy returned to his office and called in his military aide. "Have we heard from General Miklós or General Veress yet?"

"No, Regent, not a word."

Horthy frowned. "They should have started withdrawing by now." Horthy's secretary rapped lightly on the door and entered. "Sir, Proconsul Veesenmayer is here, demanding to see you."

Horthy sighed. "I suppose I can't refuse to see the German ambassador. Send him in." Veesenmayer entered and bowed. Horthy waved him to a chair. "My mind is made up, Proconsul. I will go through with the armistice."

Veesenmayer smiled. "I think not, Regent."

"Are you here to threaten me?" asked Horthy, knitting his brow. "I have ordered my armies back from the Eastern Front. They are arriving as we speak."

Veesenmayer shook his head. "You are mistaken, Regent. Your armies are still at the front, fully engaged in the battle with the Soviets. We knew what you were up to. Our friends in your military, Generals Vörös and László, successfully disrupted your communications to the Hungarian Army. Your generals in the field are none the wiser." Veesenmayer walked to the window overlooking Buda. "Come, look out the window."

Horthy sat unmoving.

"If you look, you'll see several German Tiger tanks with their guns trained on the palace. While you were making your announcement, the Twenty-fourth German Panzer Division moved into Budapest under the very capable command of General Erich von dem Bach-Zelewski." Veesenmayer paused, looking up at the ceiling. "He's famous for suppressing partisan activity throughout Europe and is more than able to handle any trouble in Budapest."

Horthy drew his revolver. "I will resist with every bone in my body. Your panzer division will have to kill me first."

"Such heroics are unnecessary, Regent. We have your only remaining son in our custody and will not hesitate, however distasteful as that may be, to kill him. Call off this ill-conceived armistice and you will see Miki again. It's your choice, his life is squarely in your hands."

Wallenberg is here!

Horthy slumped down in his chair, his hands supporting his head. "What do you want from me?" he asked hoarsely.

"You must resign and turn over power to the Arrow Cross Party. Its leader, Ferenc Szálasi, will handle the rest of our demands."

"That hoodlum?"

Veesenmayer looked out the window, then back at Horthy. "I prefer the term 'Hungarian patriot.'" He shoved papers in front of Horthy. "Sign these, now."

The defeated Horthy, his hand shaking, complied.

"Now you must leave with me. You will be transported to Berlin, where you will stay until the end of the war."

Horthy's eyes were moist. "What about my son?"

"You will see him in due time—if you cooperate."

Pest, Office of Section C, October 15, 1944, Hours Later

Wallenberg's warning to his staff to wait a few days to see German reaction turned out to be overly optimistic. An hour after the broadcast the Hungarian music ceased. Suddenly, German military marches blared from the radio, including the most hated of all, the *Horst Wessel Song.*

A deathly silence pervaded the office, even though there were more than 450 workers packed into the room. Those who looked out the window could see columns of German, not Hungarian, troops moving down the street. The Section C workers waited for the next announcement—it was just a matter of time—as German martial music continued to pour out of the radio. It came at six in the evening.

"This is the voice of Nyilas, the Arrow Cross, the Nazi Party of Hungary. In Operation Armored Fist, German troops have surrounded Budapest and have thrown out the criminal ruling clique. Arrow Cross has assumed power. Former Regent Horthy has resigned and left Budapest. Patriot Ferenc Szálasi, leader of the Arrow Cross, has been named prime minister and will lead the nation in continued warfare against the Soviets, side by side with our German brethren. There has been no armistice. I repeat, there has been no armistice. Now, we will pick up where we left off and, once again, fight against the Jewish-Bolshevik menace. Further announcements will be forthcoming. News bulletin: The Jews have been reported to have been signaling the Allied bombers, which then dropped explosive toys to be picked up by Hungarian children. The new government is investigating. We must defeat the enemy within! Hail to the Arrow Cross!" Martial music resumed.

Wallenberg put his head in his hands. It was starting all over again, he thought, and with the Soviets so close. This time it would be far worse without the buffer of a sympathetic Hungarian government. The Arrow Cross was worse than the SS. Looking sadly at his friend Pëto, he said, "László, I am afraid our celebrations were a bit premature. We're in deep trouble. We must redouble our efforts at issuing protective passports."

"We are already working hard," Peto replied. "The workers deserve some rest and recognition."

"We don't have time for rest," snapped Wallenberg. "If you and your people have performed well, continue in this manner and do not wait for thanks from me. We must save lives, not congratulate ourselves."

As everyone in the room stared at him, Wallenberg shook himself out of his funk. "Get to work everyone. We have a lot to do in the next few weeks. Avoid the streets unless absolutely necessary until we see what's going to happen. Arrow Cross bands will be out there looking for trouble. And take heart, we will weather this storm also." He felt nowhere near as confident as he sounded.

Buda, Office of Proconsul Veesenmayer, the Next Day, October 16, 1944

Ferenc Szálasi was shown into the swastika-festooned office of the German plenipotentiary. "I am very busy. You wanted to see me, Proconsul?"

"Yes. It appears you've been a little too busy."

Szálasi cocked his head in a questioning look.

"It seems your Arrow Cross men, whom the SS armed, did not waste any time starting to loot the palace. Call them off, immediately."

"But I thought we could..."

"Not you, us. The *Reichsführer* has claimed the right to the palace treasures as a prize of war. Your men are stealing from us and unless you want to argue with the Twenty-fourth Panzer Division, you will order a stop to the looting."

"But, Proconsul, the Wehrmacht is loading up Hungarian museum treasures and hauling them out of Hungary."

Veesenmayer glared at Szálasi. "It cost millions of marks to occupy Hungary for your benefit. Do you object to Germany trying to recoup a small part of the cost?"

Szálasi examined his boots. "No, Proconsul, I just assumed we could keep some of the bounty—as an encouragement to my men."

"You will have plenty of opportunity when we resume shipping out the Jews. There will be plenty of property to go around."

Szálasi nodded. "I've been looking forward to that. When do we start?"

"As soon as Eichmann arrives."

"Our men have already started shooting Jews found in the streets in revenge for their signaling the Allied bombers."

Veesenmayer smiled. "Well, save a few for Colonel Eichmann, or else he'll be very disappointed."

Szálasi laughed loudly. "As you wish, Proconsul."

CHAPTER 11

Pest, Offices of Section C, October 16, 1944

Wallenberg and his Section C huddled around the radio to hear the swearing-in of Ferenc Szálasi as prime minister of what the commentator characterized as the new fifteen-member government of "national solidarity."

Szálasi's words cut through the office like a scythe.

"Fellow citizens, we shall continue to fight side by side with our German brothers. We are resolved never to surrender our beloved nation to the Communists; we shall accomplish this by holding fast to our alliance with Germany. Make no mistake, this is a war of independence against international Jewry. Whoever impedes the nation's war effort and disrupts unity is a traitor and will be dealt with accordingly. I have been assured by the German chancellor that Reich military technologists are, at this moment, devising, and Reich armaments industries are producing, new weapons and war planes that will turn back the Soviets and their allies. To protect and defend the citizens on the home front, I have appointed Emil Kovarcz, former head of the Hungarian gendarmes, minister without portfolio, with responsibility to organize and arm a national military service of the Arrow Cross."

Wallenberg grimaced. He'd heard enough. He left the room, followed by Lars Berg. In Wallenberg's office, Berg nodded towards the window. "Kovarcz is a vicious thug. The SS is already arming his teenage toughs with automatic weapons. They parade down the streets in their green Arrow Cross uniforms, cockily showing off their new guns."

"Most of them have little education and certainly no training or discipline." Wallenberg rubbed his forehead. "And you're right, they are being led by an animal who won't hesitate to unleash them on Budapest. We have our work cut out for us. By comparison, the past few months will seem like a picnic."

Wallenberg is here!

Buda, Majestic Hotel, Eichmann's Office, October 17, 1944

Eichmann leaned back in his chair, taking in his old familiar office in the Majestic Hotel. He inhaled his cigarette deeply, permitting the calming effects of the nicotine to fill his lungs. He would enjoy this day—his triumphant return to the city. His sense of well–being stemmed in part from the half bottle of brandy he polished off on the drive to Budapest. The hunting, drinking and debauchery—he had never thought he would tire of them—but he had. The six weeks at the Endre estate waiting to resume his Jew-clearing program had been too long. He had a lot of time to make up to achieve *Judenfrei,* a Jew-free Hungary.

A smiling Wisliceny came bounding into his office. "Welcome back, Colonel."

Eichmann received the major's enthusiastic greeting in silence, thinking that the weak fool hated him for leapfrogging him in rank and for being so hard on the Jews. He was sure his return to Budapest had disappointed the major deeply. Without returning the greeting, he barked, "Did you set up the meeting I requested?"

"Of course, Colonel. I already have them sitting in one of the interrogation rooms. Shall I bring them in?"

Eichmann nodded and took another shot of brandy. Wisliceny led the members of the *Judenrat* into the office. Eichmann watched them file in, preparing to enjoy himself. He did not invite them to sit. Grinning broadly, he greeted them. "Well, gentlemen, as you see, I'm back. I suppose you thought that Hungary could do the same thing as Rumania and Bulgaria and capitulate to our enemies. You were wrong. You forgot the Magyars still lie in the shadow of the Reich. My arms are long enough to reach right into Budapest." He thrust his arms straight out toward the Jews and chuckled.

Eichmann chain-smoked, inhaling deeply and blowing smoke at the visitors. He got up and started pacing—or weaving—around the office. The effects of drinking gave him a glow. He blinked and refocused his eyes. "Now pay close attention. The government of the Arrow Cross under Prime Minister Szálasi takes its orders from us. I have selected Emil Kovarcz to be Hungarian minister in charge of the Jewish Question. You know him? A brute of a man." Eichmann laughed loudly.

Eichmann stood toe to toe with one of the Jewish leaders. "The deportation of the Jews will start immediately, only this time it will be on foot. The transport facilities are needed for other purposes now." He filled his glass again and raised it. "Of course, if you supply us with the necessary trucks, you can ride instead of march to the camps. Does that appeal to you?"

The Jews exchanged quick glances.

Eichmann took a sip of brandy. He smiled. "Ah, you're scared, aren't you?" Like a sudden thunderstorm blotting out the sun, his benign look became an angry glare, the smile on his lips curled into an ugly snarl. "We are finished with your fairy tales about American dollars buying you out of your fate." He rubbed his hands. "Now we are going to get down to serious work—efficiently and quickly. You are dismissed."

As the visitors started to leave, Eichmann raised his glass. "To your health, gentlemen," he roared raucously as the Jews disappeared from sight. Eichmann looked at Wisliceny. "I've waited a long time for that. It was most enjoyable, most enjoyable." He took another drink. "What do think of our new Hungarian puppet government?"

Wisliceny rubbed his chin. "Honestly? They're a bunch of uneducated, undisciplined hoodlums. The Arrow Cross doesn't know how to run a government. All they can do is coerce and intimidate. Arming these young hoodlums with machine pistols has created anarchy. Already, armed teenagers are roaming the streets shooting people. We estimate that at least two hundred Jews, and who knows who else, have been shot. Their bodies are still in the streets. Looting is widespread. It's not only dangerous in the streets for the Jews, but for other Hungarians, as well. Even we Germans had better be careful. These criminals are very undiscriminating in using their weapons. They ask very few questions."

Eichmann smiled. "Good. Then they will do a lot of our work and save us the trouble of transport. And if a few Hungarian Gentiles are killed in the process, so be it. Just inform our troops to kill the bastards if they threaten Germans in any way."

Pest, Offices of Section C, October 18, 1944

Lars Berg carelessly threw his damp raincoat and hat on the rack in Wallenberg's office. "It's a war zone in those streets. Arrow Cross toughs very nearly shot me. You can't believe it; they shoot at anything that moves. They stopped me and my driver. One hoodlum wanted to gun us down on the spot. I told them the prime minister would not be very happy if they shot a Swedish diplomat on his way to meet with him in an hour. That got their attention. They finally let us pass."

Wallenberg said gloomily, "It sounds as if the streets are not even safe for cars."

Berg smiled. "Well, they're a little safer for us now." He dropped some stickers on the desk. Wallenberg picked them up, looking puzzled.

"They're Arrow Cross identification decals for the car windshield. In theory, it's like a safe-conduct pass."

Wallenberg nodded. "I'll put one on my Studebaker."

"But there's no discipline or command structure out there," Berg sighed. "Arrow Cross commanders are contesting one another's areas of jurisdiction with random displays of force. They're even killing each other to establish territorial rights. It's a jungle."

"I'm not surprised. As soon as the *putsch* occurred, new Arrow Cross members had to be recruited fast. Kovarcz signed up the lowest scum in the city. The crooks and street trash came running to join. Why, then, should we expect any restraint now? The prime minister himself is a former convict. One thing you can say for the German Nazis: at least there's a spirit of discipline and order—and instruction in the proper use of firearms. The new Hungarian militia lacks all of that, but it matches the Germans in viciousness."

Lighting his pipe, Berg looked at Wallenberg. "I can't believe, after all our work, Interior Minister Gábor Vajna's announcement that safe conduct passes and foreign passports are no longer valid and that all Jews are subject to the control of the Hungarian state. He's told me he'll tolerate no interference, whether from within Hungary or from the neutral nations. What are you going to do now?"

Wallenberg's eyes narrowed. "I'm continuing to issue *Schutzpasses* to anyone who applies, with or without connections to Sweden. Then I plan to see Prime Minister Szálasi. I have an idea he may be amenable to some concessions because he, like Horthy before him, is seeking international recognition. Some gesture on Sweden's part, and those of the other neutrals, may be important to him. And then there's the new foreign minister, Baron Gábor Kemény. I know his wife."

Wallenberg laughed as Berg looked surprised. "Don't look at me that way, Lars. I met her at a few parties. She loves to talk in English, so we've met on several occasions over tea, a lunch, or a walk. It's purely platonic, I assure you. The way to the baron may be through her."

Berg grunted skeptically. He sucked on his pipe, trying to keep it lit. "The Jews have been prohibited from leaving their homes for any reason. They have a choice, starve or be shot. We have to do something or there won't be anyone left to save."

Wallenberg nodded. "I have stocked large quantities of food in secret warehouses around the city for just such an eventuality. We must try to get the food to the safe houses and other homes in the Jewish Quarter. It'll be dangerous. I'll have to ask for volunteers."

Pest, a Street, October 19, 1944

Wallenberg sat in the back seat of his tan Studebaker, portable typewriter on his lap, heading for one of the safe houses in Pest's Jewish Quarter. He inserted another blank *Schutzpass* and typed in the name of a Jew from a list of those living in that house, pulled it out of the carriage and inserted another blank pass. He'd already typed out thirty *Schutzpasses* when the Studebaker began slowing down.

"Herr Wallenberg?"

His passenger looked up. The driver, Vilmos Langfelder, pointed straight ahead. "Another roadblock." A Hungarian military truck blocked the residential street.

Wallenberg sighed. "Very well, let me do the talking."

Langfelder pulled up to the truck and came to a smooth stop. Several youths in green Arrow Cross uniforms approached, pointing their machine pistols at the car.

"Out of the car!" one youth ordered angrily. Wallenberg stepped out.

"You, too", the youth screamed at Langfelder, pointing the pistol into the front window.

Wallenberg, radiating rage, stood face to face with the youth giving the orders. Before his opponent could speak, Wallenberg shouted in fluent German that all could hear, "How dare you stop me?

This is an outrage!" He pushed aside the machine pistol. "And stop pointing those weapons at me. I'm a close friend of Colonel Ferenczy, whom I was on my way to see until you stopped us." He looked at his watch and frowned. "I will be late. Now see what you have done."

Wallenberg pushed the youth in the chest with his index finger. "What is your name?" Pointing at the other armed boys behind the leader, he asked, "And you—what is your name? And you?" He found a piece of paper in his pocket and took out his pen.

The Arrow Cross boys started to back up and look at one another, lowering their pistols. The leader of the group whistled sharply to the driver of the blockading truck and waved. The truck backed up onto the sidewalk, clearing one lane on the street. Wallenberg and Langfelder jumped into the Studebaker and drove off through the cleared opening.

Langfelder, still ashen, shook his head. "I don't know how many of these confrontations I can take. Thank God you sound like the Gestapo. That trash wouldn't have a second thought about shooting us. I'm surprised no one called your bluff about the meeting with the prime minister."

"Acting the authoritative, pompous German seems to be one of my natural talents. These Arrow Cross are not about to challenge such authority. But you are correct. It's getting too dangerous. Perhaps I should drive myself from now on."

Langfelder shook his head. "No, I won't desert you. Besides, having a chauffeur adds to the aura of authority and importance you want to project. It is safer if I stay with you." He pulled up to the curb and nodded toward the house on the immediate right. "That's the place."

Wallenberg jumped out of the car, carrying his typewriter. If there was anyone not on the list or one he'd simply missed from the list, he'd prepare a *Schutzpass* on the spot. He knocked. No response. That didn't surprise him. These days, the potential for death lurked behind every knock on the door. He shouted "Wallenberg here with your *Schutzpasses*!" After a few seconds he heard a bolt being slid back. The door opened a crack. Wallenberg held up a *Schutzpass*. The door swung open. A paunchy, middle-aged man held out his hand. Wallenberg shook it.

"You are here. Thank God. We've been waiting for you. All the residents are assembled in the parlor. Please—come in."

Pest, an Apartment in the Jewish Quarter, October 19, 1944

A mile away, in the Jewish Quarter, Keleman Kaplun looked out the window of his third-floor apartment. A large, tan American sedan sped by, disappearing down the street. Keleman was hungry. He was also terrified. So far, the terror kept him rooted in the apartment. Forbidden to go out, he and his family had exhausted their food supply. He'd never been a brave man, but he couldn't let his young son starve. Putting aside his fears, he decided it was time to find provisions. Turning to his wife, he said, "The streets seem quiet now; I must go out to find some food."

"Don't," she cried, grabbing his arm. "They'll kill you. Stay in, please Keleman, I beg you. Things will change soon."

"Gitta, be reasonable," he replied as he freed his arm. "It's been five days now since they have forbidden us to leave our homes, even for a few minutes. Is it better we should starve to death rather than risk going in the streets to look for food?"

Gitta shook her head violently. "Are you blind? You can see what's happening outside as well as I. The Arrow Cross are shooting Jews dead on the streets."

"We are out of food," he said firmly. "Our son must be fed."

"All I'm asking, Keleman, is that you wait another day or two. Is that too much to ask?" Tears welled in her eyes.

He flicked away the tear on her cheek with the knuckle of his index finger. "Gitta, I'm sorry but I must go. Things will only get worse."

"But you don't know that," she pleaded.

Keleman ripped off the yellow star on his jacket. "Now I'll be less of a target."

Gitta, hands on hips, blocked the apartment door. "Are you stupid? If the Arrow Cross doesn't get you, you'll be shot by the Gestapo for disobeying their orders."

Four-year-old Mozes hung back in the doorway to the bedroom, listening. He hesitated, then ran at his father, grabbing his belt. "Don't go, Papa," he cried.

Keleman patted his son's head. "Don't look so forlorn, my little Mozes. I will return safely with food, I promise. Now go back in the other room." Defiantly, Mozes hung on to his father's belt. Sighing,

Wallenberg is here!

Keleman gently disengaged Mozes's a little fingers and moved to the door.

"Please, Gitta, don't make this any harder. I must go, you know that."

"I don't know any such thing," she cried.

Keleman, a powerful, heavyset man, pushed the slightly built Gitta aside and forced open her fist that clutched the heavy fabric of his jacket. He closed the door firmly and started down the stairs. He could hear Gitta's pleadings, like nails hammered into his head. The heavy front door of the apartment house closed behind him, finally silencing the searing pleas. Standing with his back against the door he peeked out both ways before venturing onto the mean streets of Budapest—still empty. Steeling himself, he stepped out gingerly, every sense alert, like a deer traversing a forest clearing. He looked up to the third-floor window, where Gitta stood silhouetted, tightly hugging herself.

As soon as he looked down the street, he spotted it, a body lying in the gutter, shot and just left there. He bit his lip. Oh God, what was he doing. Gitta was right. He could still make it back to the house without being seen. No! He had to think of Mozes. There was a grocery store around the corner, a block away, if he could...

"HALT!" Keleman froze in his tracks. "Turn around, hands in the air, hurry!"

He raised his arms and slowly turned. Three youths, no more than sixteen or seventeen, in the green uniforms of the Arrow Cross, patches of crossed arrows on their sleeves, glared at him, each with a machine pistol aimed at his middle.

"Your papers," shouted the one who appeared to be the leader, his closely cropped blond hair barely showing under his dark green cap.

Keleman searched his pockets. He shook his head. "I'm sorry, gentlemen, I seem to have left them at home. I will go get them."

The blond boy snarled, "Don't bother you lying Jewish scum. You think we are stupid? I can see the spot where you tore off the yellow star."

"But gentlemen, I assure you..."

A dark-haired boy, his face scarred by acne, whined, "Let me shoot him, it's my turn." The leader shook his head. The dark-haired boy continued to complain, "It's not fair, you did the last three Jews."

The blond snickered and pressed the trigger. Ten rounds stitched through Keleman. The shots echoed through the street. Keleman was lifted up and thrown back against the brick building. They left his body there.

***

Gitta slumped to the floor under the window, in a daze. She curled up, still hugging herself tightly. Mozes peeked into the room, then trotted over to his mother. He touched her shoulder gently. "Mama, what is it? I heard loud noises." Gitta, her eyes unfocussed, stared straight ahead. Mozes stood on his tiptoes to look out the window. Quickly Gitta pulled him down, enveloping him in her arms. She sat there rocking him. Mozes folded himself into her lap, sucking his thumb. He didn't have to ask any more. He knew.

An hour passed and they were still on the floor, rocking. Insistent rapping on the door brought Gitta out of her trance. She gently placed Mozes, now fast asleep, on the rug and stiffly rose to her feet. She was beyond caring what dangers lay beyond the door.

"Who is it?" she asked, if only by habit.

A muffled reply. "Jewish representatives of Herr Wallenberg."

She opened the door a crack. Three men stood in the hall. One pushed a basket of food at her. "Here, courtesy of Herr Wallenberg and the Swedish Legation. We are bringing food to all the safe houses."

He pushed the door open and laid the basket on the floor. "Just in time, no?" Her hysterical laughter took them aback. They quickly retreated down the stairs shaking their heads.

Buda, Majestic Hotel, Eichmann's Office, The Same Day, October 19, 1944

Veesenmayer settled into the visitor's chair in Eichmann's office as the colonel poured a glass of cognac and offered one to his guest. Veesenmayer put up his hand, declining. Eichmann shrugged and downed his in one gulp. Veesenmayer stared at this boor who didn't even know how to savor a glass of cognac, but his expression revealed nothing.

Wallenberg is here!

Eichmann lit a cigarette. Veesenmayer pushed back his chair. He didn't need to breathe in the smoke from Eichmann's lungs. "Colonel, I must report to Berlin. What have you done to institute the steps for deportation?"

Eichmann blew some smoke away from where Veesenmayer was sitting. "I have reached an agreement of cooperation with the new Hungarian administration, specifically, Interior Minister Vajna. Fifty thousand Budapest Jews will soon be marched to the border and then we will send fifty thousand more."

Veesenmayer rubbed his hands together. "Excellent, excellent. The Führer will be most pleased by my report. You must proceed against the Jews without mercy."

Pest, Streets, October 20, 1944

Interior Minister Gábor Vajna sat in a Hungarian government car. A heavy rain was falling and he had no desire to be outside. His driver parked the car on a street that had several safe houses flying Swedish or Swiss flags, the ones scheduled to be raided. The day was just dawning—an uncivilized hour for a minister of his rank to be up and about—but the prime minister had insisted.

An armed Arrow Cross contingent, mostly teenagers, jumped out of the army trucks that had pulled up to the curb. The boys started banging on the front doors of all the houses. Lights started to wink on all over the street.

***

There were ten beds packed into one room, not atypical for a safe house. Living in such close proximity made for short tempers among the inhabitants. They bickered constantly about who should clean the bathroom or kitchen. Izsak Kamya had retired for the night in the midst of yet another argument. Darda Swartse, a perennial troublemaker, was accusing Izsak's wife, Viktoria, of not pulling her weight. Darda continually accused one or another of the women of shirking.

Hours later, Izsak had heard the banging but thought it was part of his dream. The persistent racket and yelling finally touched his consciousness. He sat up in bed, rubbing his eyes. Viktoria stirred.

Several other people were waking up. Izsak shuffled to the window. Green-uniformed soldiers were screaming to the occupants of the house to open the door, threatening to break it down. An involuntary shiver ran through him. Unbidden, he recalled his mother's *bobbe-myseh*, an old wives' tale: *The shiver means that someone has just walked over your grave.* God, he hoped not.

Izsak threw on a robe and moved to the front door. The banging increased. Several other men joined him at the door. A hand grabbed his shoulder. "Don't open it—they will deport or kill us."

Izsak shook his head. "You don't know that. Besides, it won't help not opening the door. They will break it down and shoot us out of pique." He slid the bolt back and turned the door handle.

The door flew open. Four Arrow Cross boys with rifles confronted Izsak. The leader stepped forward, pushing the barrel of his rifle into Izsak's abdomen. "All in this house will be ready, within an hour, equipped for a three-day march. Anyone in this building not in the street by then will be shot without hesitation!"

Viktoria had swung her legs off the bed. Wringing her hands, she asked, "What do they want, Izsak?"

"We've got to pack for a three-day march. Come, let us get ready. Dress for the weather, it's raining hard."

She cradled her head with her hands. "Oh, God, they're going to kill us."

Izsak shook her gently. "I don't think so. They wouldn't have asked us to pack for three days, they would have just dragged us out and shot us. Now come, get dressed. We don't have much time."

The ten houses emptied into Teleki Square. The Arrow Cross pushed men, women, children and the aged into the middle of the street with their rifle butts. Several Arrow Cross guards grabbed watches and rings from the Jews. They demanded money from many others.

An SS officer appeared with a megaphone. "Start running now, hurry!" He pointed out the direction.

Izsak slung Viktoria's bag over his shoulder along with his own and grabbed her arm. They ran several blocks, wiping the rain out of their eyes. They were joined by Jews sprinting in from other streets, until thousands were running and jostling one another attempting to stay in the middle of the pack to avoid the rifle butts and clubs of the Arrow Cross and the SS running along the perimeter. Many older people couldn't sustain the pace and stopped running or simply fell to the ground. The guards pulled them out. Izsak heard shots being fired. A middle-aged woman in front of him slipped on the wet cobblestones. He bent down to help her. The people behind him cursed, having been forced to veer off to avoid falling over them. Izsak felt a sharp pain in the back of his head. An Arrow Cross guard raised his rifle butt again and screamed at Izsak to keep moving. Viktoria grabbed him roughly, pulling him up with all her strength.

"You can't stop to help anyone," she cried. "They will kill us both if you slow down for anything."

Reluctantly, he left the fallen woman to her fate. Six blocks later, the Jews were halted and assembled into labor battalions. Izsak was separated from Viktoria. She went with the women's group and he and ninety-nine other men marched in the other direction for two hours.

They stopped at a large clearing on the outskirts of the city. A German soldier handed Izsak a shovel. "Start digging and don't stop until I tell you. One hundred men began digging a long trench for defense against the Soviet forces closing in on Budapest.

Izsak's muscles rebelled but he kept digging. Several Jews stopped to rest. They were kicked and beaten with clubs. Those unable to continue were dragged away. Out of sight, the diggers could hear the sharp cracks of a pistol.

On the third day, at midnight, Izsak returned to the safe house on Teleki Square, exhausted and almost beyond caring. He saw the women were already back. Viktoria was not among them. He walked through the house, searching. "Darda, have you seen Viktoria?" Darda shook her head and looked down at the floor. Izsak grabbed her shoulders. "What did they have you doing?"

"We cleared bombing rubble from the streets."

"Was Viktoria with you?"

Darda kept her eyes cast down. "For awhile." She volunteered no further information.

"Darda, tell me what you know, please."

Darda started crying. "A few Arrow Cross guards selected several of the younger women and took them away. We never saw them again."

"Those animals," he screamed. He ran into the kitchen and grabbed a large carving knife.

Darda cried. "What are you going to do? You'll get us all killed."

"It doesn't matter any more. We're already dead."

Izsak ran into the street. An Arrow Cross tough approached him, pointing a machine pistol at him. "Where do you think you're going, Jew scum? You're not allowed out."

Izsak pushed the weapon aside with one hand, surprising the inexperienced guard. The knife, in his other hand, flashed across the guard's throat. The guard went down, his only sound, a gurgle—then silence. Izsak had no awareness of the guard's blood spurting over him. He picked up the machine pistol and walked down the street, looking straight ahead. Turning the corner, he came face to face with a squad of German soldiers talking amongst themselves, their weapons slung over their shoulders. Izsak emptied the clip, dropping four soldiers. A hail of bullets threw him backwards, two rounds exploded his heart.

***

Within an hour, Teleki Square was filled with heavily armed SS troops, who surrounded the house out of which the avenging Izsak Kamya had emerged. The troops did not bother to knock. A grenade blew the door off its hinges.

The troops pushed, kicked and beat the men and boys out of the house. Those who tried to explain or protest lost their teeth from smashing rifle butts.

The troops shoved more than thirty victims against the wall of the house. Three soldiers leaped out of a military truck and set up, with expert precision, a light machine gun on a tripod. The gunner swung the weapon around to the Jews lined up by the wall. The SS officer nodded. The machine gunner opened fire. The Jews fell in a hail of bullets. Some rounds passed through the bodies and through the ground floor windows, killing a young girl and her mother.

The SS officer turned to his sergeant. "That should serve as a good example. Leave the bodies there for the rest of the Jews to see. Next time, we will kill a thousand for every German slain." The Wehrmacht trucks roared away. The troops left with the same suddenness that had marked their arrival.

CHAPTER 12

Pest, Streets, and Buda, Majestic Hotel, Eichmann's Office, November 4, 1944

Langfelder deftly maneuvered the Studebaker through rubble, courtesy of the American bombing of an hour ago. Tonight, the British bombers would be coming. Glancing in his rear-view mirror at Wallenberg, he smiled. "If we're stopped by the Arrow Cross rabble today, we can honestly say we're on our way to meet someone important."

Wallenberg nodded. Strange, he thought, that Eichmann should have invited him to his office. It should be interesting conversing with the man whose plans Wallenberg had been sent to frustrate. He had met Eichmann once, briefly, at the Arizona Nightclub. Eichmann had barely acknowledged his presence before turning away to continue his conversation with the woman sitting next to him.

Wallenberg pushed through the doors of the Majestic Hotel lobby. A Gestapo major motioned to him.

"Herr Wallenberg?"

Wallenberg nodded.

"Dieter Wisliceny at your service." The major clicked his heels and bowed. "Please follow me." He led Wallenberg into a large office, closed the door, and left the two adversaries alone.

Eichmann looked up from his papers, eyed his visitor, and motioned him to a chair. Then he arranged his papers in a perfectly aligned pile. "Why did you go to Palestine in 1937?"

Wallenberg pursed his lips. What a strange way to start a conversation. Well, he thought, two could play that game. "Because it interested me. And didn't you visit Palestine at about the same time, in 1937?"

Eichmann's eyes narrowed. "I see you've done your homework."

"I'm sure you must have found it quite an exciting place," Wallenberg remarked offhandedly. "Amazing what the Jews have done there developing the desert and expanding business and commerce. They've shown they should have a state of their own in Palestine, don't you agree?"

Eichmann exploded. "I know all about you, Jew-lover. You think we don't know that the Americans have put you in Budapest, and that you receive all your dirty dollars from that crippled pig, Roosevelt?"

Wallenberg sighed. Here comes the attempt at intimidation. "And we know all about you, Colonel."

"Never mind about me. You and the Wallenberg family are enemies of the Third Reich. Your cousin Marcus sells Swedish iron ore to the British."

Wallenberg smiled. "That's true. But, my dear Colonel, my cousin Jacob sells even more iron ore to the Germans, so there you have it."

Eichmann stood up, his face flushed. "Jacob? That swine and traitor? I can have you arrested simply because of your association with that assassin-lover."

In Berlin, where Jacob Wallenberg conducted business with the Third Reich, a close German friend of his had been arrested and later executed for participating in an abortive bombing attempt on Hitler's life. After that, Jacob Wallenberg had been warned to stay out of Germany.

Wallenberg shook his head. "The quality of your information disappoints me," came the calm reply. "My association with Jacob? If I had been close to my cousin, as you seem to suggest, I'd be rich and gainfully employed now in one of the Wallenberg businesses run by Jacob's side of the family." Wallenberg spread his arms. "Instead I'm here, in Budapest—with you."

Wallenberg's nonchalance only increased Eichmann's anger. "You can't fool me. Your so-called Swedish passports are all frauds! Those Jews you are protecting are enemies of the Reich. Sweden cannot be permitted to interfere in Hungary as it did in Denmark. You think we don't know that the Jews in Sweden are helping Jews escape from Denmark? I promise you, we will put an end to it all."

"I don't know why you fuss so much, Colonel. After all," he continued, shaking his head, "didn't King Christian of Denmark tell your Führer that there was no Jewish problem in his country, there were only his people? We Swedes are like the Danes—we've never considered ourselves inferior to the Jews, so we've never had such problems. I don't understand why you Germans feel you are inferior and therefore, have to do something about it. Do you?"

Wallenberg is here!

Wallenberg watched Eichmann walk around, lighting a cigarette and taking several deep puffs. While the German struggled for a response, the Swede changed the pace, reaching into his briefcase. He pulled out a liter of twenty-year-old Scotch and a carton of cigarettes. Eichmann wasn't corruptible, he knew, but perhaps this school dropout and small time salesman from Linz would be impressed sharing drinks with a Wallenberg whom the colonel considered to be aristocracy. Eichmann stopped pacing; his eyes followed his visitor as he placed the cigarettes on the desk, held up the bottle of Scotch to the light and then began to open it.

Wallenberg, his expression turning angelic, looked up at the perplexed colonel. "Glasses?" Eichmann smiled, despite himself. He reached into the cupboard behind his desk, pulled out two whiskey glasses and plunked them down in front of Wallenberg, who poured two shots without spilling a drop. The adversaries downed them silently. Wallenberg poured another round.

Eichmann sat down and leaned forward on his desk. "Wallenberg, you're strange, but you're not such a bad fellow. I have nothing against you personally. As a matter of fact, I rather like you. Perhaps if you could raise some ransom, I could allow a trainload of your Jews to travel to Sweden."

Wallenberg eyed his host. He frowned, shaking his head. "While you deport the rest to the death camps? I don't think so."

Eichmann shrugged. "Have it your way, but that trainload of Jews will be on your conscience, not mine."

Wallenberg's eyes hooded. "I hope that's just your attempt at a bad joke."

Eichmann put out his hand. "You're glib, Wallenberg, I'll grant you that, but this little meeting won't change anything for me, you know."

Wallenberg stood and shook his head. "Nor for me, Colonel, nor for me."

Buda, Swedish Legation, Danielsson's Office, November 7, 1944

Danielsson sighed. Without consulting him, Wallenberg had met with Eichmann on his own. An International Red Cross representative who had seen Eichmann the next day reported that the colonel had ranted that he was going to "kill the Jew-dog Wallenberg." After telephoning the Swedish foreign minister, Danielsson called German Proconsul Veesenmayer. The Swedish diplomat began without greeting. "Colonel Eichmann has threatened the life of one of my staff. That is unacceptable conduct and our ambassador in Berlin has lodged a protest with your foreign minister. For my part, I demand that this man be removed from Budapest for the safety of my staff."

With solicitous words but sarcastic in tone, Veesenmayer replied, "Minister, I'm sure Colonel Eichmann was merely joking. But you have to understand that the interference of the Swedish Legation in our Jewish matters is illegal. Perhaps Eichmann's irritation is somewhat justified, since Wallenberg's methods are highly unconventional, undiplomatic and not legally permitted. You should take the colonel's outburst simply as a warning that our patience with Wallenberg's activities is wearing thin."

Danielsson rolled his eyes. "Your condescension is insulting, Proconsul. I will hold you personally responsible for any harm to Raoul Wallenberg." He slammed the receiver down.

Buda, Veesenmayer's Office, November 7, 1944

Eichmann fidgeted under Veesenmayer's steely, unrelenting stare. "Have you lost your mind, Colonel? You have a loose tongue and it's going to get you in a lot of trouble with Berlin. I don't appreciate having to apologize to the damn Swedes for your intemperate ranting."

Eichmann cracked his knuckles. Veesenmayer winced. "The Foreign Office doesn't understand the situation. Wallenberg is very dangerous and must be dealt with."

Veesenmayer leaned forward. "No, Colonel, it is you who do not understand. You must never speak so carelessly again." He smiled ever so slightly. "Of course, if you should do away with Herr Wallenberg, it must not look as if we were involved. Do I make myself clear?"

Eichmann nodded.

Budapest, Streets, November 1944

Samuka walked as quickly as his short legs would permit. He had his *Schutzpass* and work permit identifying himself as a Section C employee. These days, however, no documents really assured safety

Wallenberg is here!

from the roving Arrow Cross gangs. He would have liked to make a dash for the office, but a running Jew would only attract more interest from the gangs.

A commotion a block down the street drew his attention. He stepped into a doorway until things clarified. Street confrontations spelled nothing but trouble. What seemed to be the focus of attention was something out of a horror story. A macabre figure in a priest's black cassock, bearing a huge crucifix in one hand and a revolver in the other, was marching toward him, exhorting his band of armed Arrow Cross youths. Samuka had heard stories about this strange defrocked Catholic priest, Father András Kun, who delighted in rounding up Jews on the street. He'd take them to houses where he could torture and then shoot them. Then he would dump their bodies into the Danube. Today, Father Kun and his crazed gang were pushing along several Jews, not noticing Samuka pressed hard against the door.

"Find more of them, this is not enough—try harder!" the priest screamed. In anger and frustration, he wheeled around yelling, "In the holy name of Jesus, fire!" shooting one of the Jews near the spot where Samuka stood. The bullet went through the Jew and ricocheted off the building, almost hitting one of the Arrow Cross men.

Samuka pressed his back hard against the locked door, as if, by osmosis, he could pass through to the other side.

The priest and his followers turned the corner and disappeared from sight. Samuka stuck his head out, looked around and continued his journey to Section C offices. He decided he had to do what most of the Section C people were doing—live at the office.

Pest, Offices of Section C and Streets, November 1944

Pista came bursting in to the Section C offices. Only Lars Berg was there.

"Herr Berg, the Arrow Cross has taken one of our workers, István Löwenberger. I need Herr Wallenberg."

"He's away on other business. Where's this Löwenberger being held?"

"In an Arrow Cross house, not far from here. I'll take you there." On the run, Berg followed Pista to a building three blocks away. Luck was on their side, they encountered no roving Arrow Cross gangs. Pista pointed out the house. "In there, Herr Berg."

Berg put his hand on Pista's shoulder. "You go back. If I don't return in a half hour, come with help from the legation." Berg tried the front door of the building. It was unlocked. He threw it open. The three Arrow Cross guards surrounding the seated Löwenberger jumped up. The prisoner looked up in surprise.

"Release that man immediately; he is a Swedish protected person." Berg flashed his diplomatic credentials.

The three guards looked at one another. One walked up to Berg. "We no longer recognize Swedish protective passes for Jews. We will not release him."

Berg straightened to his full height of over six feet, towering over the youth. "Your criminal conduct will not be forgiven. I will not leave without the prisoner. It's as simple as that."

The guard's face reflected his indecision. "We must talk this over. You will wait here." The Arrow Cross left the room, taking the prisoner with them. Berg waited.

Soon the leader of the group returned. "We will not surrender the prisoner and if you don't leave now, you will be shot also."

"Let me see the prisoner."

The leader smiled. "He's been taken out the back way. He's no longer here.

"I don't believe you." Berg pushed past the Arrow Cross guard and entered the back room. There were five more prisoners back there, including a German major, but no Löwenberger. The way the Arrow Cross was terrorizing everyone on the streets, Berg wasn't surprised to see a German hostage. Firefights between the Germans and the Arrow Cross were not unknown.

The angry guard raised his rifle, shoving it in Berg's ribs. "Now get the hell out of here or you will be taken out and shot like your Swedish-protected person."

Berg could see the guard wasn't bluffing. The presence of the German prisoner gave him an idea. Berg left the house and ran down the street looking for a German officer. When he spotted an SS armored personnel carrier with a squad of soldiers led by a Wehrmacht captain, he flagged it down.

Flashing his credentials, he asked, "Captain, you must come immediately. Arrow Cross men are holding a German Army major prisoner in the back room of a house. His life is in grave danger. I will show you where it is."

The captain reached out and helped pull Berg aboard the carrier, which drove quickly over to the house. The captain raced around to the back entrance with half the squad while the remainder attacked through the front. Berg heard firing in the rear of the house. The soldiers in front fired submachine guns into the door, splintering it to bits. Two Arrow Cross guards on the other side of the door died instantly. The guards in the back room were gunned down by automatic fire through the back windows.

The captain escorted the hostages out of the building. "Thank you, Herr Berg", he said, bowing in the diplomat's direction. "You probably saved the major's life. You are welcome to take home your five Jews."

While Berg had saved six lives, he was nonetheless disconsolate–the Arrow Cross had murdered poor Löwenberger.

Pest, Children's Orphanage, the Same Day

While Berg was trying to rescue Löwenberger, Wallenberg had his own hands full. A report of trouble with the Arrow Cross at an orphanage he'd set up for seventy-nine Jewish children put him into immediate action. In short order, the tan Studebaker pulled up to the orphanage door. One of the supervisors ran up to the car, crying. "They're all dead but one, Herr Wallenberg."

He grabbed her arm and shook her. "What did you say?"

"All but one of the children are dead, shot by the Arrow Cross."

"Oh God. When?"

"About two hours ago, they came. They shot some of the nurses and marched the children out into the woods in back of the building." The hysterical woman paused to catch her breath. "Then they just shot all those innocent babes in cold blood." She grabbed Wallenberg's lapel. "How could anyone shoot children out of hand like that? How, Herr Wallenberg?"

Wallenberg walked slowly into the orphanage. He couldn't bring himself to view the carnage back in the woods. He spotted the one little survivor, a boy sitting on the floor, jammed into the corner. A worker came up to Wallenberg. Nodding toward the cowering child, she told him, "Apparently, he hid under a big chair and somehow managed to escape out the back door and into the street without being discovered. He's the only child who survived."

Wallenberg sank to his knees, unable to stem the sobs that racked his body. The workers backed away, giving him the space to express his grief.

After a few minutes, Wallenberg composed himself, stood up and walked over to the woman. "I want to save a nation and the hardest thing for me is when they kill the children. But we will fight on with even more determination, more dedication and more fury." Squeezing her shoulder, he picked up the boy and carried him out to his car.

CHAPTER 13

Pest, a Swedish Safe House and the Streets, Late November 1944

George, a Section C worker, made it a habit to visit his parents and grandmother at least every other week. They lived in a Swedish safe house four miles from the Section C offices. More and more people were being crowded into a finite number of safe houses, and his family's living conditions became a source of constant concern to him. He would have preferred to check on his family more often, but the trip to their refuge was simply too hazardous to risk on a regular basis. When he did go, he brought along food for them from his own rations.

George had been preparing to study engineering when the anti-Jewish laws, the *Numerous Clausus,* established quotas for universities, effectively barring him from matriculating. He thought then that nothing worse could happen to him. He was wrong. The German takeover put his very life in danger.

In March, the SS had forcibly evicted George's parents and grandmother from their condominium in Buda. His father had taken it particularly hard. His home was a source of fierce pride—in 1933 he and his friends had built with their own hands the six-unit apartment complex. He enjoyed showing his visitors the spacious flat with the fine workmanship and the comfortable amenities he'd provided for his family.

Thrown out of their home on one hour's notice by a particularly nasty SS officer, George and his family found themselves and their four suitcases in the street with nowhere to live. A friend of the family invited them to stay with him in Pest. Eventually, the friend found a place for them in one of the newly designated Swedish safe houses. They were thankful for the space, but they had to share a bedroom with another family. There were too few safe houses and too many evicted Jews.

George had been sleeping in the Section C offices since the streets had become too dangerous to walk, even the short distance from his own safe house. On the night of this visit to his family, George spent a little more time with them than he intended, staying too late to risk the return trip. He slept on the floor in the bedroom his parents and grandmother shared with another couple.

Some hours later someone shook him hard. Unwilling to wake up, he rolled over, away from the source of the intrusion. A sharp pain in the ribs brought him to full consciousness. He opened his eyes to a boot a few inches away from his face. "Get up, lazy Jew, or my next kick will shove your face in."

George staggered to his feet. He looked at his watch—five in the morning. The soldier in the green Arrow Cross uniform had already turned his attention to the other sleepers in the room. An officer stuck his head in the door. "You have ten minutes to dress and assemble in the courtyard. Take nothing with you. And don't make me come look for you—that will upset me very much and you definitely don't want that to happen." He looked at the grandmother. "The old Jew bitch can stay here. We don't want her."

George, his parents and the rest of the occupants of the safe house were marched out of the courtyard, prodded by the rifle butts of the Arrow Cross guards. They joined others who had been routed out of other safe houses.

Fortunately, the pace of the march was not so fast—George's parents could keep up. Still, there were those who could not, and when they slowed down or stopped, they were beaten across the shoulders with truncheons or rifle butts. Those who couldn't continue were simply dragged away. George kept himself between his parents and the guards. He maneuvered himself so he walked beside a young Arrow Cross guard. He decided to risk conversation.

"Can you tell me where we are being taken?" George whispered, his eyes forward, never meeting those of the guard.

"Quiet, no talking allowed," the guard barked.

George persisted. "If you were rousted out of your home early in the morning and forced to march, wouldn't you want to know where you were being taken? It's not such a terrible question. I'm more concerned for my parents than myself. You can understand that, can't you?"

The guard kept walking, also looking straight ahead. "Shut up," he hissed. "You'll get shot if you keep talking to me."

"It's not asking for so much to answer my question."

Wallenberg is here!

The youth said flatly, still looking straight ahead, "The brick factory."

Just three words, but they spoke volumes to George. He bit his lip. This was going to be no labor battalion. The infamous brick factory was an assembly point from which the Jews were marched to one of the border towns to be shipped in cattle cars to Auschwitz or other death camps. His parents would not survive a seventy-mile march, much less the Auschwitz ovens. He'd have to escape to get help. Though his chances of a long life by staying where he was were nil, his strong survival instinct rebelled at the more immediate likelihood of being shot. He wrestled with a paralyzing terror of putting his life on the line now.

The ragged band approached the Margit Bridge—or what was left of it. The bridge crossed from Pest to Margit Sziget, the island in the middle of the Danube, and then to Buda. At the Pest end, the Jews marched onto a German-engineered pontoon bridge that replaced the section of the Margit Bridge accidentally destroyed by the Wehrmacht. The pontoon bridge emptied onto the island, where the Jews had to tramp through thick woods to reach the still standing section of the bridge to Buda. George saw his chance.

Heavy brush lined both sides of the path. Steeling himself with several deep breaths, he stepped in front of the guard, heading for the bushes. "I have to take a leak. It can't wait." Without waiting for an answer, he started walking to the bushes, unbuttoning his fly. He could be shot for this, he knew. He tensed for the impact of the bullet.

The guard swung his rifle towards George, then lowered it. "Well, make it quick and then get back in line."

George entered the thickest part of the bushes, where he watched as the guard walked on, keeping pace with the marchers, never looking back. Other guards either didn't notice George or didn't bother themselves about it. He went through the motions of urinating while backing deeper into the bushes. He emerged when all the marchers had cleared the island and retraced his steps to Pest. Then he ran as fast as his breath would permit, ignoring the danger on the street, especially for a running Jew. Wallenberg! He had to reach him.

Pest, Offices of Section C, an Hour Later

Wallenberg wryly acknowledged to himself his own naiveté in thinking just a few months ago that he'd be in Sweden by now, leading a normal life. Nothing he ever undertook, it seemed, stayed quite in the mainstream. Now, in November, all his earlier optimism had evaporated. His mission was more dangerous than ever since Eichmann had resumed shipping Jews out by train and, when rail transport wasn't available, by forced marches.

If Wallenberg faced a daunting task, the Germans and the Hungarians must have thought that they were dealing with an army of Wallenbergs—he seemed to show up everywhere large numbers of Jews were being held, and he plagued the Hungarian ministries with demands and protests.

Today, Wallenberg called Per Anger. "We have two life-threatening emergencies on our hands at once. I need your help. Can you cover the railway station at Hegyeshalom? The SS are going to load a few thousand Jews on a train bound for the death camps. I can't get there. I have to stop another death march in progress."

"I'm right on it," Anger responded without hesitation.

Outside of Budapest, the Brick Factory, Several Hours Later

Wallenberg took a deep breath as his Studebaker pulled up to the red building dominating the area, the huge brick factory swarming with Arrow Cross guards. A convoy of Red Cross trucks pulled up behind him. He had to steel himself for these dangerous confrontations. He felt like an actor before the curtain goes up, getting himself into character for the role and overcoming stage fright.

Climbing out of the car, he approached the nearest guard, a boy of nineteen or twenty. "Where is your superior, young man? I must see him immediately."

The flawless German and authoritative tone convinced the guard the man before him was not a person to be trifled with. Though the youth understood only a smattering of German, he quickly grasped the import of the request and pointed to the small office in the corner of the building.

Wallenberg barged right in and barked, "Give me a megaphone, right now. You have incarcerated illegally, and under inhumane conditions, people holding Swedish passports."

The baffled guards looked to the sergeant. Wallenberg strode over, putting his face into the sergeant's. "Well, are you going to cooperate or do I have to report you?" He copied down the name on the sergeant's identification tag.

The sergeant motioned to one of the guards, who disappeared and returned in less than a minute with a megaphone. Wallenberg grabbed it, looked at the sergeant and nodded toward the main floor of the factory. "Come, you will help me find the Swedish protected people."

The sergeant followed Wallenberg into the factory. The stench of feces and blood assaulted the Swede, who suppressed a gag. When his eyes adjusted to the darkness of the large, dank room, he flinched, unprepared for the scene. Hundreds of people, packed into this airless room and sitting in their own waste, seemed beyond caring. Shocked, even with his experience, by this new demonstration of Nazi depravity and brutality, he stood there silent and appalled. Then, some stirring caught his attention—it buzzed through the room. He caught the whisper, "Wallenberg is here!"

Shaking off his horror, he lifted the megaphone to his mouth. "Attention, those with Swedish passports step outside and form a line to the left of the courtyard, those with Swiss passports go to the right, and those with Portuguese papers line up in the center."

People began to rise, slowly, stiffly. They searched their pockets and held out their lifesaving documents for Wallenberg to see. Arrow Cross guards pushed them outside into the yard, directing them on how to maintain orderly lines as the Swedish diplomat instructed.

A short man with wire-rimmed glasses, pins still stuck in of his vest, approached Wallenberg. "The Arrow Cross ripped up my *Schutzpass*. I'm Berkowitz, the tailor."

"Of course, I remember you," said Wallenberg, who did not. "I initialed your document myself." Wallenberg turned to the guard. "Show this man to the Swedish line." Berkowitz followed the guard out of the factory.

Wallenberg felt a tug on his sleeve. He turned to face a middle-aged couple, Swedish *Schutzpasses* in hand. "You may join the others outside," he said, pointing to the door.

The woman tugged at his sleeve again. "Excuse me, Herr Wallenberg, we're George's parents, did he…?"

Wallenberg patted her shoulder. "He's safe. He's the one who alerted us about the march." Broad smiles lit up their faces.

Wallenberg gently pushed the woman toward the door. "Now, get yourself out of this hellhole."

In the midst of the exodus from the brick factory, the local police chief pushed his way in. Grabbing Wallenberg's arm, he announced, "I am Police Chief Andros. Just what do you think you're doing?"

"I am saving you from a very embarrassing situation. Do you realize you have imprisoned the citizens of neutral nations who are not at war with Hungary or Germany? That is a very serious offense. I'd hate to make an issue of it with my friend, Colonel László Ferenczy." Wallenberg knew Ferenczy was the head of police.

Chief Andros took a step back, releasing Wallenberg's arm. "But I didn't know there were such citizens in this group. I was told by the Interior Ministry that the passes were no longer to be recognized."

Wallenberg pulled the police chief off to the side, leading him out of the building. In a low voice he whispered, "The passports are valid under the authority of King Gustav of Sweden. I can understand your mistake in the chaos of the past few weeks. Your lapse will not be reported if it is not repeated." He pressed several hundred dollars worth of Hungarian *pengös* in Andros's palm. The surprised officer's eyes widened.

Wallenberg smiled. "If you will help me remove some of those who have no passports, I will be most grateful." He paused, patting the chief's arm. "And even more generous later."

Andros nodded. "But don't take any more than a hundred of them."

Wallenberg reasserted his authority. "Have your men open the shutters and windows. Let some light and air in for these poor people."

Andros barked some orders.

Wallenberg walked back into the building. The light, filtering through the now opened windows, gave him a clearer view of the degradation and squalor before him. A woman tapped his pants leg. "Save us, please, they are going to kill us." The room filled with cries of "Save us."

Wallenberg raised his arms. "I can take another hundred back to Budapest. I'm sorry I cannot take all of you now." He walked among them selecting young men and women. He looked at some of the older Jews. With moistened eyes, he kept repeating, "Forgive me, please. I have a mission to save the Jewish nation, and I have so little time. I must take the young first. Forgive me..."

He led one hundred frightened young people out to the waiting Red Cross trucks, which those with passports had already boarded. Then he returned to the brick factory and picked up the megaphone. "The Red Cross is coming with food, water, soap, disinfectants and medical supplies. Doctors and nurses will arrive shortly to help you. We will do everything we can. Please, you mustn't lose hope."

Except for an occasional sob or moan, the group had been quiet. Suddenly, someone started chanting the holy *Shema* prayer, the watchword of the Jewish faith. *"Shema Yisraeil Adonai Eloheinu, Adonai echod!"* Wallenberg knew the prayer: "Hear, O Israel, the Lord is our God, the Lord is One!" Others picked up the chant. Soon the room reverberated with the prayer to the one God.

***

A woman looked at the retreating back of the elegantly dressed man as he left the brick factory. She turned to the man hunched next to her. "Who is that gentlemen whose name they were saying? He's like something out of a dream. Everyone else in Budapest hates us and he comes here wanting to save us."

"You haven't heard of Raoul Wallenberg, the diplomat from Sweden? We call him our Savior."

Hegyeshalom, About the Same Time

The SS patrolled the station at Hegyeshalom, where the Hungarians turned the Jews over to the SS for transshipment to the German or Polish borders—and to a death camp. Some of the soldiers held tightly onto the straining leashes of Doberman pinschers, snarling and snapping at the large ragtag group of Jews milling about, who were resisting the pressure to move toward the open maws of the cattle cars.

With dogs, whips and truncheons, the SS shoved the unwilling mass of people forward. Often, the sound of a pistol shot reverberated through the station—another Jew executed for some minor or perceived infraction, the corpse dragged off to a corner of the station waiting room, joining the pile of bodies. No margin of error existed for Jews.

A voice cut through the din. "Where's your superior?" Per Anger barked in German at an SS soldier. The soldier pointed to the German officer sitting at a folding table by the stationmaster's office, examining the pages of a thick manifest.

Anger, followed by his escort, a Hungarian policeman, strode up to the officer. Without an introduction, he shoved forward his diplomatic passport. Annoyed at the interruption, the officer looked up from the manifest and glared.

The Swede took the offensive. "I'm a Swedish diplomat. You must be aware that Germany has good diplomatic relations with Sweden and that we represent German interests in many parts of the world."

"What's your point?" the officer snapped. He unfastened his holster.

Anger wasn't intimidated. "Before this train pulls out, I demand access to the freight cars to search for Swedish-protected citizens."

The officer, eyes narrowed and lips pressed together, stood, leaning his fists on the table. "You *demand*? You'll be fortunate if I don't have you and your driver shot. What you want is totally out of the question. Now get out of here before I lose my patience with you Swedish weaklings."

Anger, still holding his diplomatic passport, slammed it loudly on the table. The officer blinked. "This is one 'weakling,' Captain, that has close connections to Hitler's special envoy in Budapest, Proconsul Veesenmayer. You may have heard of him." The mention of both Hitler and the dreaded Veesenmayer had its intended effect. The officer's look changed from fury to confusion. He sat down. Anger pressed on.

"If you don't allow me on the train, I will report your outrageous conduct to your superior and to Proconsul Veesenmayer. You are creating a diplomatic incident between our two countries. Our ambassador in Berlin, where I served for many years, will be furious, as will your Veesenmayer here in Budapest. Seriously rethink your position, Captain. You are at great risk if I report this incident and your malfeasance."

The captain sighed, then shouted to a soldier standing nearby. "Sergeant, escort this Swede onto the train. Don't take your eyes off

Wallenberg is here!

him for one second. Permit the Swede to take off the train only those with proper Swedish papers. When he is finished, instruct the engineer to get that train out of here, *schnel*."

The captain pointed to the Hungarian policeman. "You—go with the sergeant and make sure the Hungarian documents are what the Swede says they are." The policeman nodded and saluted.

Anger pushed his way onto one of the cattle cars, so packed with people they could only stand. He shouted in German, "All those with protective passes come forward to the door." Only two pushed through the crowd toward him. The sergeant gave a cursory glance at their papers and looked at the Hungarian. The policeman nodded and the sergeant waved them off the train. Frustrated at the meager response, Anger shouted, this time in Hungarian, assuming the German sergeant wouldn't understand. "Show me any papers, any at all. Do you comprehend what I telling you?" The Hungarian policeman, deadpan, looked straight ahead.

The Jews stirred. This time, more started pushing to the door waving driver's licenses, rental receipts, bills and even a bus schedule—anything that they could find in their pockets. The Hungarian policeman nodded as he examined each document and the German sergeant waved them off the train. Forty Jews jumped off that cattle car. The scene repeated itself in the other cars. All told, 180 Jews without any protective passes and 20 with Swedish passes boarded the Red Cross trucks. As each truck filled up, it took off for Budapest and the Swedish safe houses.

It was a successful day for Anger and a profitable one for the Hungarian policeman, who worked secretly for the legation for a few thousand *pengös* and Anger's promise of a personal letter that would permit him and his family to settle in Switzerland after the war.

Pest, Offices of Section C, November 27, 1944

Lars Berg leaned on Wallenberg's desk. "No one who holds our protective passes is safe since the new interior minister announced that the Hungarian government will no longer recognize the *Schutzpass*. If you are going to do anything, Raoul, now would be a good time."

"I'm working on it. I'm meeting with Baroness Kemény tomorrow."

Berg frowned. "But it's the baron who's the foreign minister—and he's a dedicated Hungarian Nazi. Maybe I'm missing something, because he'd seem to be the last person on earth to help you"

"I know, but I think I can get to the baron through the baroness."

Buda, Apartment of Baroness Kemény, the Next Day

Snow flurries, accompanied by below freezing temperatures, warned of the approach of winter. Elisabeth Kemény looked out of her library window and shivered, not from the weather, but from the all too common scene of Jews being led away at gunpoint by the Arrow Cross. It plagued her dreams. Her husband assured her that the Jews were only being deported. She knew better and it was hard to be civil to him about the topic. Her attempts to broach the subject were met with stony silence. The baron steadfastly refused to discuss the plight of the Jews, saying he had enough to do as foreign minister of Hungary, without delving into the affairs of other government ministries. She tried desperately to understand, but could not. That she was well into her first pregnancy only added to her distress. Into what type of world was she ushering her baby? How could she explain to her child that its parents stood by while thousands of helpless people were slaughtered?

The baroness, ignorant of the baron's political views when they married, had never agreed with them. Indeed, they appalled her and she doubted she would have gone through with the marriage had she known. The attraction to him, she now realized, had been mostly physical. The baron, whose family had been proud feudal landowners in Transylvania, was only concerned about Hungary—the rest of the world be damned. His single-track mind saw Bolshevism and the Soviets as the greatest evil facing Hungary—an evil that had to be stopped at all costs. For the baron, the Arrow Cross, despite its largely lower-class members and dependence on Germany, represented Hungary's last chance to resist that evil. It had appointed him foreign minister. That he was allying himself with Jew-hating fanatics was of little concern to him. He did not share his wife's much more liberal concerns about the carnage in Europe.

She looked at her watch. Wallenberg was due any minute. He had called last night asking to see her in private at her apartment because of the nature of what he had to say. She wasn't looking forward to this meeting. She had strong suspicions of what he wanted.

***

The butler took Wallenberg's overcoat and hat, carefully brushing off the small amount of accumulated snow. He ushered the visitor into the library where the baroness waited.

From their long conversations, Wallenberg knew of her anti-Fascist feelings. He'd confronted her earlier on her Jewish heritage. Surely, she must be concerned about the fate of the Jews and sympathetic to his mission. He plunged in.

"Elisabeth, I'll come straight to the point. The Hungarian government has nullified all the *Schutzpasses*. I'm asking you to talk to the baron. If he does not honor those passes, he'll be responsible for the deaths of tens of thousands of people. Then, after the war, he and the other ranking members of the Arrow Cross government will be hanged for crimes against humanity. The Russians will not, however, hang those who obtain the support of the international community for leniency. If your husband honors the passes, I promise to testify on his behalf."

The baroness wrung her delicate white hands. She paced around the paneled room. "Why do you come to me? I can't help you. What do you want of me?"

Wallenberg looked into her sad blue eyes. Even in despair, they retained the bottomless quality that had fascinated him these past months. "Even though you don't consider yourself Jewish, you must have sympathy for their plight."

Her eyes glistened. "I would have anyway, Raoul, without your rubbing my face in it."

Wallenberg nodded slowly. "You're right, I should have known better."

This time, it was Wallenberg's turn to pace. He stabbed the air with his finger. "Unless your husband honors those passports, I cannot save the Jews of Budapest. I'm only one diplomat, not an entire underground partisan organization. I must operate under the rule of law, and that means the baron will have to restore the legal basis for the protective passes. Otherwise, these people will be put to death in a most horrifying way. Tell your husband if he does this, I will also do everything I can to gain international recognition for his administration. Please, Elisabeth, I beg of you, do what you can."

She twisted a strand of hair. "You're placing an impossible burden on me. It's so unfair."

***

Some hours later, nearly finished with dinner, the baron poured himself a cordial. His wife left her place to lay a hand on his arm. "Gábor, I must speak to you."

He looked at her. "I hate it when you start a conversation with those words. It usually spells nothing but trouble for me."

She walked over to the window and stared out into the night, where the street lamps were darkened as a precaution against the British night bombing raids. With a deep breath she began, "Gábor, you must reinstate the protective passes of the neutrals, or else many people will die needlessly and horribly."

The baron put down his glass. "What did you say? No, don't repeat it, I heard you very clearly. Are you talking about saving the Jews?"

She nodded.

"It's none of your business. Besides, they deserve it."

"You can't mean that. I am not married to a beast that kills mercilessly, am I?"

"What are you talking about? I haven't killed anyone."

"The Arrow Cross has, and they've also delivered Jews to the Germans, who have, with Arrow Cross knowledge, slaughtered them—and you're part of the Arrow Cross government, so you can't absolve yourself. At the end of the war, you will bear as much responsibility as those who pulled the triggers."

The baron gripped the table hard. "It's that damn Wallenberg. He's put you up to this, hasn't he? I've been hearing the same thing from that persistent little bastard for a month now. I forbid you to see him again."

She ignored his outburst. "Gábor, you must do this thing for me."

"I have no such intention," he shouted. "It's not up to me, anyway, I run the Foreign Office, not the Interior Ministry."

She sat down again at the table, facing him. "It affects the Foreign Office. Wallenberg said he would fight for international recognition of the regime if you do this. This is what you have been striving for since you've been in office."

"So it *was* Wallenberg. Well, I won't do it—and that ends the discussion."

Her eyes met his and held them. "It certainly does not. I cannot live with a mass murderer. You must do what I asked or this will be the end of our marriage."

The baron stood and with one arm jerked the large linen cloth, sweeping all the dishes off the table in a loud, shattering crash. The butler rushed in. The baron waved him away. "Get the hell out of here!" He stomped a plate that had survived the crash. It crumbled and he kicked away the shards. "You have betrayed me. I cannot and will not change these policies." He stormed out of the dining room and into his study, slamming the door behind him.

The baroness moved into the library and picked up a book, but she couldn't concentrate. So she waited.

An hour later, the baron entered the library and poured himself a snifter of cognac. "Would you like some?"

She shook her head. He sat down in deep red leather chair. She smiled. He was a proud man. Walking behind his chair, she began rubbing his shoulders and the back of his neck.

He turned his head to look at her and sighed. "You are a most difficult person, Elisabeth, most difficult. You must have inherited your stubbornness from the Austrian parliamentarian in your family." He shrugged. "I will see what I can do."

Buda, Apartment of Baroness Kemény, a Day Later

Baron Kemény, blowing on and briskly rubbing his hands, entered the library and headed directly to the fireplace, where he stretched his frozen fingers toward the blaze. "Winter's arrived with vengeance. A few months in southern France would do us a world of good. That luxury, unfortunately, is another casualty of this damn war."

The baroness put down her book and looked at him, waiting.

Her husband smiled. "You want to know what happened? Well, you should be very happy. I convinced the prime minister to revalidate the protective passes. I will announce it on the air tomorrow."

She got up out of the chair and kissed him on the cheek. "I knew you could do it. How did you convince Szálasi to rescind Vajna's order?"

"I told him it was the quickest way to win recognition from the neutrals, especially Sweden. He desperately wants some form of legitimization for the new government. I said we could limit the passes to three thousand each for the Swedes, Swiss and the papal nuncio, and demand that they remove these Jews from Budapest or they will be treated like the rest. He bought the idea."

The baroness frowned. "But only three thousand each? That's not much—many more than that are in danger."

"I know, but there's no way we can keep track of the number of passes issued. Wallenberg knows that. They could issue ten thousand, for all we know. It's a face-saving device for Szálasi and won't hamper the rescue efforts in the least."

"But the neutrals can't ship out their Jews now. The city is practically surrounded by the Soviets."

"That's why it doesn't mean a thing, but it'll sound as if we are taking a tough stance. Believe me, your Wallenberg will be happy—for the moment."

She took his hand in hers. "You did the right thing, Gábor, I'm proud of you. I'm sure Wallenberg will come to your defense after the war."

The baron shook his head. "Ah, that Wallenberg's never satisfied. He bombards me daily with memos about his Jewish problems. Does he think I have nothing else to do but look after his pass holders? And I'll tell you something else. His antics are worrying his fellow diplomats at the Swedish Legation. They think he'll get them all in trouble."

His wife remained silent while he blew off steam. He poured himself whiskey and holding the bottle up, looked at her refracted image through it. He sat down and faced her across a small table.

"The doctor said you should leave Budapest soon because most of the medical facilities here have been destroyed. He said you need prenatal care, so I'm sending you to Switzerland for a checkup. You'll be able to relax—no bombings, no killings and no Wallenberg." He smiled and grasped her hand across the table. "Do it for our son."

Her eyes narrowed.

He shrugged. "Or daughter—whichever."

CHAPTER 14

Washington, WRB Offices, November 30, 1944

Waving a paper at Henry Morgenthau, John Pehle announced, "I just heard from Ivar Olsen. Wallenberg has gotten the Hungarian government to reverse itself. Foreign Minister Kemény has announced that the order invalidating the protective passes has been rescinded and they will be honored by the Arrow Cross government."

Morgenthau shook his head. "How'd he accomplish that?"

"Who knows?" Pehle replied. "But he did it. Our intelligence monitored the broadcasts from Budapest and verified the action. This Wallenberg's just amazing. Somehow, he uses the passes and the fiction of special immunity for his Jews to forestall the death marches. All the more miraculous in the face of the German and Arrow Cross determination to annihilate all of Budapest's Jewry."

Morgenthau pursed his lips. "We owe that man more than we could ever pay back. We were very lucky to find him."

Pehle nodded. "I've been in the Foreign Service a long time. I can say, without reservation, that his achievements are beyond precedent. I can't recall another instance where a junior legation secretary from a neutral country was so influential dealing with a foreign sovereign nation."

"We're not out of the woods yet," Morgenthau warned.

Pehle sighed. "I know. The Germans still have the capability to exterminate the Jewish community before they're pushed out of Budapest by the Soviets. Quite frankly, I don't know how our miracle worker can prevent a Nazi determination to go ahead with the liquidation."

Buda, a Coffee Shop, December 2, 1944

As she sipped a cup of hot tea, the baroness glanced at Wallenberg across the small round table. He was staring vacantly at the steam rising lazily from his coffee. "Raoul, thanks for getting *Schutzpasses* for some of my friends."

"That's the least I could do," he said smilingly. "I'm forever in your debt for getting the baron to re-validate the passes. I could have never protected the Jews without them."

"In the end," she said, curling some strands of her dark hair around her finger, "my husband acted because it was the right thing to do. I just had to jar his conscience a little."

Wallenberg took her hand. "I'd like to have met you at another time, another place and under different circumstances—to have had the opportunity to take you to the theater, the opera, sailing... I'm sorry," he sighed. "That was a stupid thing to say."

"Don't be," she replied, not removing her hand from his. "It was a lovely thing to say and I agree, such an opportunity would have been marvelous." She looked into his eyes, searching for the right words. He cocked his head curiously, waiting for her to speak.

"I hope you won't take this the wrong way, but I think you and my husband are not so different."

He frowned. "How so?"

"You stay in Budapest fighting the hopeless fight for Jews whom everyone else has written off. The baron stays in Budapest to fight for a Hungary everyone else knows is doomed. Perhaps you're not exactly peas from the same pod, but you are both idealists who don't know the meaning of the word *quit*."

Wallenberg briefly closed his eyes. "Or is it perhaps that I'm just not smart enough to come in out of the rain? If we ever get through this chaos in one piece, I would dearly hope we could continue our friendship. It means a lot to me."

"And to me." The baroness dropped her eyes, removed her hand and examined it. "I have some news. I won't be seeing you for a few weeks. The baron insists I take care of our future child by going to Switzerland for a medical checkup."

"He's right about that. I would add that you shouldn't come back until this is all over."

"But this is my home now," she sighed.

Reaching for her hand again he urged, "Protect your child, that's the most important thing. In a way, I envy you. Someday, perhaps, I'd like to have many children."

Now she smiled. "As well you should. You are wonderful with children, especially your animal imitations." Suddenly, her eyes sparkled and she grinned.

Wallenberg is here!

"What is it?" he asked, perplexed. "You look as if you were up to something."

"Would you do one for me?"

"Do one what?"

"An animal imitation."

"Here?"

She grinned mischievously. "Please."

Without hesitating, he let loose with the sound of a crowing rooster. Patrons of the coffeehouse turned to look at them. The baroness laughed, holding her sides. "Please, no more, or I'll have the baby right here." Then, as her laughter subsided, "That was so realistic. If I hadn't had my eyes open I would swear I was having afternoon tea with a rooster!"

"Or more likely, a chicken."

He paid the bill and they left the coffeehouse, heading for her home.

Reaching her front door, Wallenberg took her hand. "I'm glad you and your unborn child will be out of harm's way. But I must confess, it saddens me to lose your companionship. It's been a great source of joy to me." Kissing her hand quickly, he disappeared down the street.

The baroness wiped away two tears making their way down her cheek. She would have been even more distressed had she known she would never see him again.

Pest, Offices of Section C, An Hour Later

Wallenberg had little time to savor the pleasant interlude with the baroness. On his return to the office, an aide handed him a closed envelope bearing the seal of Prime Minister Szálasi. Two days before, Wallenberg, as head of the newly formed Diplomatic Humanitarian Committee, had sent a strong note to Szálasi protesting the cruel treatment of the Jews, the death marches and conditions in the ghetto. "These," he warned, "are acts of inhumanity the whole world is witnessing."

He ripped open the envelope to find his own note. Scrawled on the bottom: "I do not wish to discuss the subject with anyone else again!" It was signed "Szálasi."

Wallenberg sighed and began drafting yet another note, this time, to Baron Kemény. His aide interrupted him.

"Sir, you must come immediately. The Arrow Cross bandits have uncovered the bunker hiding the twenty children. They are threatening to march them to the Danube and shoot them!" the aide cried.

***

Minutes later, Langfelder swerved the Studebaker through the rubble-strewn Budapest streets. Wallenberg held on for dear life, sure that Langfelder would get him killed ahead of the Jews he was striving to protect.

The safe house sheltering the children had been badly damaged by an Allied bombing raid. Part of it had collapsed into the basement where they huddled. Fortunately, none of the children had been killed, but Wallenberg immediately had been faced with finding another hiding place for them. Roving bands of Arrow Cross, without second thoughts, shot any Jewish children they encountered. A Wallenberg aide had found a bunker well hidden from the street. It seemed as secure a place as they could find on short notice. But somehow—perhaps from a snooping or nosy neighbor—the Arrow Cross had discovered the children. If he didn't get to them in time.... He shuddered at the thought.

The Studebaker pulled up to the curb just as a group of armed Arrow Cross ruffians were prodding and shoving children out of the bunker with their rifle barrels. They lined the children up against a brick wall with all-too clear intentions.

Interposing himself between the children and the hastily formed firing squad, Wallenberg thundered, "I am a Swedish diplomat" and waved his diplomatic passport at them. "These children are under the protection of the Swedish nation. How dare you ignore the Swedish flag displayed in the bunker? Are you blind?"

An armed youth snarled, "This is none of your business. These are Hungarian Jews. Now, get out of the way."

Wallenberg did not budge. "You forgot to add one thing—these Hungarian Jews are children. Have you lost all sense of decency?"

While he talked, Wallenberg, behind his back, signaled with his hands. The children understood immediately and started slowly moving behind him.

"Before God, if you want to kill these innocent children, you will have to shoot me first!"

Seeing doubt flicker in the Arrow Cross boys' eyes, he pressed on. "Look around you. See all the witnesses? I doubt that you'll survive the wrath of the prime minister for the cold-blooded murder of a diplomat of one of the few countries still friendly to Hungary."

One fellow lowered his rifle and started arguing with the others. Soon the entire group was engaged in an animated debate for two long minutes. Suddenly, without a word, the squad dispersed and disappeared down the street.

Wallenberg felt his knees buckle. *I can't take much more of this*, he thought. Recovering, he ordered all twenty children into the Studebaker, a car designed for five, maybe six, people. He gave Langfelder the address of another safe house and told him, "Take the children there, I will walk back to the office."

"But the streets are too dangerous," Langfelder protested.

"So what do you suggest? I leave a few of the children here, unprotected? I don't think so. Besides, after facing down a firing squad, the street seems a relatively safe place."

Langfelder relented. "I will look for you after I drop off the children."

Wallenberg started walking as the heavily loaded Studebaker pulled away, bottoming on its springs.

The Road to Hegyeshalom, Early December 1944

Soviet troops tightened the ring around Budapest. But their advance was much too slow for the thousands of Jews that Eichmann, in a frenzy of activity, marched to the border for transport to the death camps.

The safe houses set up by the neutral nations in Pest, an area that became known as the International Ghetto, crammed 33,000 Jews into living space meant to hold 17,000. The Hungarian authorities largely respected the protection of Jews in these houses. It was a different story, however, for the unfortunate ones caught on the street by the Arrow Cross, who preferred to shoot first and examine papers later.

Jews found without protective passes, if not shot on the spot, were marched immediately the seventy miles to Hegyeshalom. On the three-day march, they were given neither food nor water. Since

Eichmann had returned to Budapest, thousands of Jews had died of hunger, thirst and exhaustion on the road. If, for any reason during the march, Jews faltered, they were beaten with whips and rifle butts, and those who could not thereafter continue were shot. A few marchers opted to commit suicide by deliberately stepping out of line and dropping to the ground. The Hungarian or SS guards executed them summarily. It was that simple.

Desperate Jews found alternative methods of suicide at the midway point of the march. In the village of Gönyö, the road ran alongside the banks of the Danube. Some Jews seized the opportunity to die by leaping into the icy river. The Arrow Cross didn't stop them because shooting at heads bobbing in the water provided great sport. Indeed, they enjoyed it so much, they threw other Jews in the river just to have more targets.

The road to Hegyeshalom resembled one long, narrow cemetery with bodies filling the ditches along the entire route. So inhumane were the conditions that General Hans Jüttner of the SS Operational Head Office, on an inspection tour, recoiled at the sight of hundreds of bodies of women and children in ditches. Outraged, he confronted the SS lieutenant leading the march, demanding to know who was responsible for these atrocities. The young officer blanched and stuttered, "C-Colonel Eichmann, Sir." Jüttner ordered the marches stopped. The lieutenant turned the Jews around and led them back to Budapest.

When Eichmann returned from a field trip, Jüttner had already left Budapest. Eichmann simply ordered the resumption of the marches, insisting that his orders came from a higher authority than Jüttner, from the *Reichsführer* himself. In Berlin, Jüttner, furious when he found out, appealed directly to Himmler. Colonel Kurt Becher, who had clashed with Eichmann before about his methods, supported the general, calling Eichmann's activities a clear case of murder. Moreover, Becher argued, they were interfering with his blood-for-money negotiations with the Jews. Himmler dispatched Becher to Budapest to talk to Eichmann.

***

Eichmann's dislike of Becher was mutual. He hadn't forgotten that it was Becher who had stopped the deportations in August that resulted in Eichmann's exile from Budapest. Despite Becher's blistering accusations, Eichmann had blandly denied the atrocities, placing the blame squarely on the rumor mongering of Wallenberg and Swiss Envoy Charles Lutz. After Becher left, the marches had resumed in full force, as inhumane as before.

If Wallenberg thought he had as much as he could handle, he was wrong. Every day, he set out in his Studebaker, the portable typewriter in his lap and the car filled with water and food. Red Cross trucks followed him. The road to Hegyeshalom presented scenes so grotesque, so bizarre, so death-filled and so seemingly hopeless that it sorely tempted the sickened diplomat to throw up his hands and return to the comforts of Stockholm.

Lars Berg, Per Anger and other Swedish diplomats assisted him in his efforts. The diplomats spread out along the route, giving Jews food and water at considerable risk from the often-infuriated Arrow Cross. Relying on their own authoritative demeanors or, failing that, on bribes of food, drink or *pengös*, the persistent Swedes managed to give sustenance to thousands of starving Jews. Wallenberg, a whirling dervish, leaped out of his car every few miles, handing out *Schutzpasses* and shouting at the startled and befuddled Arrow Cross guards that they were acting illegally by imprisoning and killing Swedish citizens. In this manner, hundreds of marchers were bundled onto the Red Cross trucks and taken back to Budapest's International Ghetto.

But thousands were still reaching the assembly point at the border and turned over to the SS, who supervised loading them onto freight trains bound for the extermination camps. Then Wallenberg decided on a change in tactics. He'd focus now on the assembly points at the border.

Hegyeshalom, December 1944

Viktor, an engineer, was hard at work in the factory of a Swedish machine tools company in Budapest; suddenly, the Arrow Cross stormed onto the factory floor and pulled him and all the other Jewish workers out of the plant. Viktor stumbled into the street, clubbed over the shoulders by uniformed thugs for not moving fast enough. Jewish workers from other factories joined them.

The collected Jews, now numbering in the hundreds, were marched, without food or water, the seventy miles to the border. On reaching Hegyeshalom, the SS took charge and were no less brutal. SS guards opened the doors to the cattle cars as the exhausted Jews were pushed and beaten into two lines in front of each car, Doberman pinschers snapping at their heels.

Word about the roundup had spread through Budapest. Dozens of wives had come to Hegyeshalom to plead for their husbands or to say last good-byes. The SS berated them with shouts of "Jew sluts." Many were grabbed and thrown in the cars ahead of the men. Viktor did not see his wife. He prayed she had had enough sense not come to Hegyeshalom.

A commotion farther down the platform attracted Viktor's attention. A whisper raced through the line of Jews, "Wallenberg is here! Wallenberg is here!" Viktor chanced looking around. The guards didn't notice. A gentleman in the trench coat and homburg was engaged in a heated debate with an SS captain. Viktor heard snatches of the argument. "Everyone with a *Schutzpass* must be disembarked and permitted to leave for Swedish safe houses." The civilian's voice and tone sounded like the Gestapo.

An SS colonel approached the arguing parties. Someone whispered, "Colonel Eichmann." In a moment, Wallenberg and Eichmann disappeared into the stationmaster's office. The loading came to a halt. A few minutes later the two men emerged. An aide set up a folding table and two chairs on the platform. Eichmann asserted his authority by sitting down first. Wallenberg shouted to the line of Jews, "Anyone with a protective pass may step forward," then sat down next to Eichmann.

Eichmann whispered something to the SS officer. The officer walked up to the Jews, some of whom were stepping out of line and moving forward, pulling out their precious documents. "Colonel Eichmann has ordered that anyone who presents a forged or invalid pass will be taken out immediately and shot." The officer returned to stand near Eichmann. For emphasis, he placed his pistol on the table.

Viktor looked at his two-line pass with the purported signature of a diplomat from the Swedish Legation. He chewed his lip. He wasn't even sure of the source of the forged pass. A legation aide? A Jewish partisan? They would never accept this paper, he was sure. He'd be

Wallenberg is here!

shot right here. But hell, if they got him on that train, he'd dead anyway. He took a deep breath and stepped forward.

The SS guards examined each document individually and meticulously. Some passes they declared invalid, but Wallenberg argued furiously that he should know if his passes were genuine or not. An SS officer grabbed Viktor's piece of paper and snorted, "Just a scrap of paper, not relevant. Take this dog away!"

Wallenberg jumped up. "Just a moment. Here, let me see that document." He pulled the paper out of the officer's hand and took it over to Eichmann. "Look here, in the lower right hand corner," he said loudly, pointing to two small letters. "Those are my initials." Wallenberg knew Eichmann hated public confrontations. He was right. Eichmann frowned. He'd obviously decided it wasn't worth a scene with the difficult diplomat. Eichmann nodded and the SS officer shoved Viktor toward the Red Cross truck. "Get out of here, before we change our minds."

Viktor ran to the truck and jumped in the back to join the others as the truck's engine roared to life. He could still see Wallenberg arguing for yet other Jews as the Hegyeshalom rail station receded from view.

Pest, the Central Synagogue, December 1944

The Arrow Cross, without warning, had descended on the Jewish Quarter in Pest and rounded up thousands of Jews, including Rabbi Hevesi. They were herded into the Central Synagogue and a smaller one on Rumbach Sebestyén Street. More were crammed in the Central Synagogue until there was no room to sit. Then the doors were slammed shut and padlocked. That had been three days ago, without food or water. Rabbi Ferenc Hevesi pulled on his white beard. His swollen tongue felt like sandpaper. He knew they couldn't survive much longer like this.

The large and magnificent sanctuary mocked the rabbi. All the money that had been poured into this marvelous edifice couldn't now feed its current occupants; it couldn't now silence the moans and cries of his suffering congregation and it couldn't now buy off the Nazis. The rabbi sighed. *Was there no end to German and Arrow Cross cruelty?* Their capacity and innovation for torture and degradation seemed limitless.

A tug on his sleeve interrupted his musings. "Rabbi?"

The old man looked down at a boy, perhaps ten, maybe eleven. Before the rabbi could speak, the youngster pointed to the back of the sanctuary. "I can get out of here, Rabbi, through the small window in the men's toilet."

"It's too small, no one could get out that window."

The boy smiled, "I can."

The Rabbi shook his head sadly.

The boy said with an embarrassed grin, "We used to sneak out of services and Sunday school through that window." He spread his arms in supplication. "Sorry, Rabbi."

The Rabbi patted the boy's head. "Under the circumstances, no apologies are necessary. It seems, young man, the ways of the Lord are infinite, mysterious and sometimes, devious. But enough talk. You must be careful of Arrow Cross patrols on the streets around the synagogue. You know the public phone down the street?"

The boy nodded.

"Good." The rabbi took a fountain pen out of his breast pocket and ripped off the corner of a receipt he found in another pocket. He scribbled a number and handed it to the boy. "Here, this is the number for Herr Wallenberg's office. Ask anyone who answers to give him an urgent message: we're being held prisoner here and can't last much longer." He put some coins in the boy's hand.

The rabbi watched him work his way down the center aisle through the crowd of Jews to the rear of the synagogue.

Already out of earshot, the boy never heard the rabbi whisper, "God go with you, my brave young man—whose name I don't even know."

***

An hour later, Langfelder brought the tan Studebaker to a screeching halt in front of the Central Synagogue. It captured the attention of the Arrow Cross guards ringing the building. The rear doors of the sedan flew open. Wallenberg and Swiss Envoy Charles Lutz jumped out, strode up the steps to the large wrought iron gate and opened it. The guards, who had parted to let them through, did not try to stop them. Just inside, another guard stood impassively in front of the imposing double doors of the main entrance. With

Prussian authority, Wallenberg growled in German, "Open this door immediately or we will hold you personally responsible for any harm to the Swedish and Swiss citizens being held in there illegally and under inhumane conditions!"

Dismayed, the guard glanced at the other Arrow Cross men, who looked away. Wallenberg had anticipated that none of them were about to take responsibility for standing up to well-dressed, important-sounding officials. Lutz turned to the guard. "The key to the padlock" he ordered and stuck out his hand, palm up.

The guard fished around in his pockets for the key and dropped it into Lutz's hand. Lutz turned the lock and swung open the heavy doors. The smell of suffering humanity, incarcerated without adequate sanitary facilities, hit him.

"Anyone here with a *Schutzpass* step forward," boomed Wallenberg.

People in the crowded synagogue surged toward him, whispering, "Wallenberg is here!"

"Everyone with papers form an orderly line outside," Wallenberg shouted out.

Pass holders pushed their way through the milling throng, holding up the precious passes from Sweden, Switzerland, Portugal and the Vatican. Wallenberg took the paper from the holder of a Swedish *Schutzpass* because these were the most impressive with their numerous official seals and signatures. He shoved the paper under the nose of the guard.

"Can you see? This is a Swedish citizen! Didn't you even bother to check?"

The guard fingered the large yellow *Schutzpass* with three blue crowns of the Swedish king emblazoned across the document, stamped and signed by the Royal Swedish Legation. He handed it back to Wallenberg, shrugged and shuffled back, away from this crazy and outraged diplomat.

"You had no right to detain Swedish and other foreign citizens in the first place." Wallenberg followed after the retreating guard. "I order you to release them at once."

The guard finally found his voice. "I-I have no authority to do that without approval of a superior."

Wallenberg copied down the name on the guard's tag. "Young man, if you want to be punished severely, just keep telling me what you cannot do." Ripping a sheet of paper from a pad in his pocket, he wrote rapidly, handing it to Lutz, who also scribbled on the paper. Wallenberg took the sheet of paper and shoved it at the Arrow Cross youth.

"Here is your authority, a receipt for all those citizens, signed by the official representatives of the Swedish and Swiss governments."

Wallenberg turned to the exiting Jews. "All those on line, follow Herr Lutz." Lutz started down the steps of the synagogue to Dohány Street. The sullen Arrow Cross grudgingly stepped aside. The long line of Jews followed him down the street and away from the synagogue.

Cries of "Herr Wallenberg" from the remaining Jews brought him back into the sanctuary. "The Swedish Red Cross is on the way with food, water and soap. You will be released shortly, I will see to it."

Rabbi Hevesi came up to Wallenberg and squeezed his arm. "Once again, thank you, Herr Wallenberg."

The diplomat smiled. "Come with me. I'll drive you home. You look as if you could do with some food and a bath."

The rabbi shook his head. "I'd better stay with those remaining in the synagogue."

***

Within several hours, combined protests of outrage from the neutral nations, from the Papal Nuncio Rotta and from prominent Hungarians, orchestrated by Wallenberg, successfully obtained the release of the remaining hostages and Rabbi Hevesi.

Pest, Offices of Section C, December 10, 1944

Per Anger, with a young man in tow, entered the office. "This is Tom Veres. He's a professional photographer and he needs your help."

Veres stepped forward and shook Wallenberg's hand a little too vigorously. Wallenberg winced. He looked at the tall young man in his mid-twenties with a full head of wavy brown hair. "You need a *Schutzpass?*"

Veres nodded. "I converted to Christianity a few years ago, but the Nazis want to deport me anyway."

Anger patted Veres on the shoulder. "He's the son of Paul Veres, formerly court photographer for the Hapsburgs and later for Regent Horthy."

"Yes, I've heard of your father," said Wallenberg, locking eyes with Veres. "I can use a photographer here. Working here will give you the greatest protection. I need a documentary record of the German and Arrow Cross horrors. I warn you, though, it's risky."

"I'll do it, gladly."

"Can you take pictures surreptitiously?"

"Of course, that's the only way I could get candids of the rich and famous. I've had plenty of experience."

"Well, I hope so," said Wallenberg, stroking his chin. "You'll be deported or shot if they catch you."

"When do I start?"

"Patience—you'll get all the opportunities and trouble you can handle if you work with me." Wallenberg's smile vanished. "The world must not only be told but must believe what happened here—and must never forget it. That's where you come in because mere words can't do it. These horror stories will not be credible without photographs."

So began the unusual working relationship between the young baptized Jewish photographer and the fearlessly unconventional Gentile diplomat. Veres accompanied Wallenberg everywhere, his camera hidden under a scarf, slit just enough for the lens to record a history of the atrocities committed by the Arrow Cross and the SS on the streets, during the marches and at the railway assembly points. Wallenberg took the photos developed in Veres's darkroom and sent them in the diplomatic pouch to Stockholm.

Pest, Jozsefvárosi Railway Station, a Few Days Later

Pressure by General Jüttner and Colonel Becher to suspend the death marches did not faze Eichmann. He brought trains directly to the Jozsefvárosi Railway Station in Pest. Unlike many of the railway terminals in the city, Jozsefvárosi was neither impressive nor opulent, simply a plain one-story building of white brick used for freight, not passengers.

Wallenberg had called Veres to meet him with his camera so that he could photograph, as best he could, the loading of the Jews onto the cattle cars.

The two men found the station ringed with Hungarian gendarmes and SS troops. Wallenberg spotted Ferenczy, head of the gendarmes, conferring with an SS officer over a long wooden table. He marched up to the table, a black ledger book containing the names of his protected Jews, tucked under his arm.

An endless gray mass of men and women were lined up waiting for the loading to begin. Despite his fright, Veres positioned himself to obtain the best shots of the loading process, his camera held steady under the slit scarf while the SS counted out batches of a hundred Jews for each car. When a commotion at the other end of the platform drew all eyes in that direction and he heard murmurs of "Wallenberg is here," Veres began snapping pictures.

Wallenberg slammed his black book down on the table. "You know who I am. You are holding my people. They must be released—now." His voice rang out, aggressively and in German. Veres could hear him clearly. Even the SS stopped counting and loading to watch this strange man in a well-worn trench coat and homburg hat, taking charge as if he were the ranking SS officer.

Colonel Ferenczy eyed the strident diplomat. "Yes, Herr Wallenberg, I know who you are. Can we please dispense with the dramatics?"

Wallenberg sat down between Ferenczy and the SS officer, ignoring the comment. He slapped open his ledger. "Shall we begin before you load any more Jews on the train? It will save you the time and trouble of unloading them."

The SS officer looked at Ferenczy, who said nothing. Previously, Wallenberg had held out to Ferenczy the prospect of testifying on his behalf after the war. Wallenberg knew that Ferenczy sought to cover both flanks by trying to accommodate both the Germans and Wallenberg. The SS officer, trained to obey authority, hesitated to confront this strange Swede barking orders in flawless German and sounding like an *Obergruppenführer*.

Wallenberg rose to his feet, facing the platform, and shouted, "My people, form a line in front of this table." By now, every Jew on the platform knew the identity of this shouting man and, what was more important, what he meant by "my people."

Wallenberg is here!

Several hundred stepped forward. He checked off each name in his black ledger. It didn't matter that half the names weren't in the book. Those who realized the game afoot stepped forward to save themselves. They were directed toward onto waiting Red Cross trucks. While Wallenberg held center stage, Veres snapped dozens of photos.

Wallenberg repeated the process for each of the already loaded freight cars. Spotting a young girl in one car, he said, "Don't I know you? Of course, I gave you a passport myself. Give it to me." She pulled out a crumpled bus pass. He pocketed the useless paper and grabbed her arm, propelling her down the loading ramp. "Get over to my car, and hurry, we haven't much time," he whispered. Langfelder directed the girl to the waiting Studebaker.

After taking as many pictures as he dared, Veres spotted a friend still in line to be loaded onto the waiting train. "Stupid Jew, why do you wait so long to show us your passport? You think we have time to waste on you?" He grabbed the man's shoulder and shoved him roughly out of line kicking him towards the waiting car. The SS guard laughed. "Give it to the dirty Yid!" But the "dirty Yid" had the last laugh—his life was saved.

Pest, Jozsefvárosi Railway Station, the Next Day

The scene at Jozsefvárosi Railway Station the following day was more of the same thing. Veres, inspired by Wallenberg's commanding performance, became bolder. While the diplomat held everyone's attention, the photographer sneaked to the far side of the train, away from the loading area. He began unlocking the car doors on that side, handing out *Schutzpasses* and pencils and whispering to the Jews to fill in their name, get off and head for the waiting Red Cross trucks.

On the near side, Wallenberg worked the loading area, shouting for Jews to step forward with their papers, pushing them toward the waiting trucks. Before long one of Eichmann's assistants, SS Captain Theodor Dannecker, arrived. "*Nein*," he screamed, running over to Wallenberg. "What the hell are you doing, Jew-loving dog?" He drew his pistol.

Wallenberg realized he'd pushed to the limit. He slammed his ledger book shut and bounded to his car. An Arrow Cross guard challenged Veres, who was just emerging from the other side of the train. Wallenberg yelled to him. Veres sprinted past the surprised guard and dove through the open rear door of the Studebaker. The car roared away past a still screaming Dannecker. Frustrated, Dannecker climbed inside his armored car, slamming the green metal door shut. "Damn that Wallenberg to hell," he said to the driver. "It's too bad I couldn't shoot him where he stood. But I'm not done yet. I will see that Jew-loving Swede in his grave before long. You can count on it!"

Pest, Jozsefvárosi Rail Railway Station, Two Days Later

The forays to the Jozsefvárosi Railway Station had become more exciting than Veres had bargained for. But Wallenberg would not be deterred. He was back again two days later. Approaching the cattle cars, he was stopped this time not by the SS but by Arrow Cross guards jabbing bayonets at him. The rules had changed. Wallenberg sensed the direct approach would not work today. He backed off and moved around the back of the train, climbed atop one of the cattle cars and shouted to the Jews through the slats, "Are there any Swedish protected Jews in there who have lost their passports?" There were affirmative cries, so he shoved passes through openings in the roof, jumping to the next car, leaping from roof to roof. Veres recorded his progress on film.

When an Arrow Cross guard fired a volley of shots over Wallenberg's head, he leaped off the train and sprinted with Veres for the Studebaker. "What, exactly, did that accomplish?" asked Veres. "They're still on the train."

Wallenberg smiled. "Just wait and you'll see."

Suddenly, a truck pulled up alongside Wallenberg's car. A squad of Hungarian soldiers leaped out. "Who are they?" Veres asked in astonishment.

"Friends. Jews and partisans dressed as Hungarian soldiers. There's Pista." Wallenberg pointed to a Hungarian officer, "and Joni Moser, over there."

Veres shook his head. "I'd never recognized them."

Wallenberg smiled. "Well, I certainly hope not!"

Under the protection of the ersatz Hungarian Army, Wallenberg set up a folding table on the platform in front of the sullen Arrow Cross. He whispered something to Pista, disguised as the Hungarian Army officer.

Wallenberg is here!

On Pista's signal, several soldiers, led by Joni Moser, slid open the doors to the cattle cars while the rest trained their automatic weapons on the Arrow Cross, whose bravery seemed to extend only to confronting unarmed Jews.

Jews streamed out of the cars waving their *Schutzpasses*. One of the leaders of the Arrow Cross protested to the Hungarian Army officer that the Jews hadn't had those passes when they'd been loaded on the train.

"Well, they have them now," said the officer, "and we've been instructed by Baron Kemény to honor the *Schutzpasses*. So we will. Now, step out of the way."

Wallenberg looked over the line of Jews waiting to be herded on the train—he hadn't had the opportunity to hand passes out to them. He opened his big black ledger and began shouting out the most common Jewish surnames. Veres circulated among the line of Jews whispering, "Raise your hand." Wallenberg "recognized" each one that stepped forward, vouching personally for him and issuing a pass.

An SS officer finally arrived on the platform and strode up to Wallenberg. "What's going on here?"

Without looking up from his ledger, Wallenberg replied in a matter-of-fact voice, "Just retrieving Swedish citizens illegally detained."

"I will take over checking these supposed protective passes. Anyone without proper papers will be shot."

"Very well," shrugged Wallenberg.

A Jew stepped forward and said softly to Veres, "My papers are forged. I'm a doctor." When the doctor reached the table, Veres bent over and whispered into Wallenberg's ear.

Wallenberg took the forged passport, then looked at the Jew. "Doctor, I remember you!" He turned to the SS officer. "I personally issued his *Schutzpass*. We need him at the Swedish Legation infirmary, so let's move on."

The Nazi officer waved the doctor by, "You're wasting our time. Next!" On that day at Jozsefvárosi Railway Station, a few hundred more Jews were saved.

CHAPTER 15

A Train near Triberg, Field Headquarters of the Reichsführer SS, December 15, 1944

As the Allied forces pressed closer, Himmler had, earlier in the month, assumed command of the German defense positions in the southwest quadrant, that is, from the Swiss border through Alsace to the Palatinate. Commanders in the field despaired of their flanks being protected by the likes of generals such as Himmler in the West and Hitler on the Eastern front, with no more wartime field experience than that of a uniformed trolley conductor.

Himmler's field headquarters was a parlor car on a train halted near Triberg, adjacent to the Rhine Valley, on the tracks of the Black Forest Railway. When enemy bombers came over, the car would disappear into one of the tunnels in that mountainous area.

In his rolling-stock office, Himmler once again looked at the damning photographs taken by Tom Veres. Von Ribbentrop had received them from the Swedish ambassador in Berlin. Eichmann, the damn fool, let things get out of hand, thought Himmler. "With these pictures in circulation, I can't let the deportations continue or the Allies will never negotiate with me," he muttered.

Since the beginning of the month Hungarian Prime Minister Szálasi had been pleading with Himmler to halt the killing. Himmler knew it was not that the Hungarian Nazi had qualms about killing Jews. It was rather that Szálasi didn't want to stand shoulder to shoulder with Eichmann on the gallows after the war. Himmler had similar concerns. He had been preparing the groundwork for peace feelers to the Allies, but Eichmann's single-minded determination to complete the Final Solution could scuttle everything. By giving orders to stop the extermination program and Eichmann's genocidal frenzy in Budapest, Himmler saw the opportunity to present himself to the Allies as the trusted elder statesman bringing reason back to the Reich. He deluded himself with the hope that such a characterization would make him the logical choice of the Allies to assist in the formation of a new German government, possibly with him at its head. Carrying his rationale to its logical extreme, he decided that first, he must stop Eichmann's activities. He knew, however, that he would be walking a tightrope in making such a move. If Hitler ever found out…

A light rap on the door brought Himmler out of his musings. "Come in." The two antagonists, Kurt Becher and Adolph Eichmann, entered. He motioned them to the overstuffed red velvet chairs that matched the wall coverings in this private club car. Crossing the red-carpeted floor to the carved wood and cut glass bar, he poured three glasses of whiskey. No bombers threatened at the moment, so the train rested quietly on its siding. Another type of explosion was imminent, however.

Himmler eyed Eichmann through his pince-nez and tried, uncharacteristically for him, an informal, friendly first-name approach. "Adolph, you have done a fine job as head of the Gestapo's Jewish Department, but now you must stop."

Eichmann's looked affronted. "What do you mean stop? Stop what, *Reichsführer?*"

Himmler could see the friendly approach would not work. His tone became more strident. "Stop rounding up Jews, stop deporting Jews, and stop all programs directed against them. I forbid any further annihilation of the Jews."

Eichmann squared his jaw. "But that's quite impossible, *Reichsführer*. I am on the threshold of achieving a *Judenfrei* Hungary."

"Colonel, you'll have no place to ship them. The gas chambers and crematoria are being leveled as we speak."

Eichmann shook his head in disbelief. "You can't be serious! I find that impossible to believe."

Himmler, losing patience, stood up. "I'm deadly serious. Believe this, Colonel, you are being ordered to desist."

Eichmann sat there, defiant.

Himmler turned livid and shouted, "Until now you have murdered Jews under my authority. Now, I order you to protect the Jews."

Eichmann remained silent, chewing on his lip.

Himmler walked around the desk to Eichmann's chair and stood over him, hands on his hips. "Tell me right now, Colonel. Are or are you not going to carry out my orders?"

Eichmann did not look up. Clasping his hands to together, he gave a slight nod. Then he stood up, saluted and stomped out of the office.

Becher looked at Himmler. "*Reichsführer*, you'd better straighten things out with Eichmann before he leaves or, mark my words, he'll continue on his mad path. Killing Jews is an obsession with him. He will bring us all down unless he is reined in."

"Don't worry, Colonel, I'll handle him. Please ask him to come back in. That will be all."

Becher saluted and left.

When Eichmann reappeared, Himmler addressed him, returning to a first-name basis. "Adolph, I know this must be a shock to you, but you must be realistic. We cannot continue as if we were on the verge of victory. For your past service, I am awarding you the Iron Distinguished Service Cross, First Class, with swords."

Tip lipped, Eichmann mumbled, "Thank you, *Reichsführer*."

Himmler was satisfied that Eichmann had been placated. Appearances, however, could be deceiving. He would later learn that Eichmann had circumvented his orders simply by changing tactics.

Pest, Offices of Section C, the Next Day

Per Anger shook the snow off his hat and tossed it on the rack. "Danielsson just heard from Prime Minister Szálasi. Szálasi says he convinced Himmler to stop the forced marches. He told Danielsson quite pointedly that he expects him to live up to his promise to support Szálasi after the war."

Wallenberg nodded. "But he hasn't done anything about his own Arrow Cross that are running wild in the streets killing people at random. Those toughs have a new game now. They march Jews down to the quays and bridges on the edge of the Danube, tie three of them together and shoot the middle one so they all fall into the river and drown. As far as I'm concerned, the prime minister hasn't quite exonerated himself."

"But surely that must be an exaggeration," protested Anger, running his hand through his hair. "It's too ghastly even to contemplate."

"I only wish it were," Wallenberg grumbled. "These are firsthand accounts—some of the victims escaped, cutting themselves loose and swimming to safety. They reported what happened. If you can believe it," he sighed, "the Germans are easier to deal with. They're just as vicious, but at least they're organized, methodical and bureaucratic—and therefore, predictable. These Arrow Cross boys, however, they kill as the spirit moves them, which is most of the time."

"Some of our informants say the word is out among the Arrow Cross to assassinate you," worried Anger. "It's not safe for you in Pest. Danielsson wants you back in Buda at the legation immediately."

Wallenberg, eyes narrowing, spoke with determination. "Tell Danielsson I've come too far to be scared off now. Don't worry, I'll be careful."

Anger frowned. "The streets are a war zone. Let someone else take over Section C."

"I can't. They will all die if I pull back. It's out of the question."

Pest, the Streets, and Buda, Majestic Hotel, Eichmann's Office, December 17, 1944

Two cars sped through the streets of Pest. A black Mercedes with Nazi flags was following so closely behind the tan Studebaker that an observer might justifiably have concluded that the Gestapo was chasing it. In fact, Pista, Joni Moser and two others from Section C rode in the Mercedes. They had one thing in common—blue-eyed and blond, they looked like Aryans and were dressed in Gestapo uniforms.

Langfelder, at the wheel of the Studebaker, carrying Wallenberg, was the first to spot the ragged group of marchers, escorted by armed Arrow Cross guards. Six hundred men, part of a compulsory labor battalion from a nearby work camp assigned to clear away rubble and dig anti-tank ditches, had been taken away from their work by the Arrow Cross and shoved into line to march toward the border. Before they left the city, one worker had managed to slip away to alert Section C. Wallenberg had hastily put together his Jewish Gestapo and taken off to find the rest of the marchers.

"Cut in front of the line," he ordered. The Studebaker screeched to a halt, blocking the marchers. The Mercedes stopped a discreet distance further back. Wallenberg grabbed his black ledger and leaped out. "These are Swedish citizens. Release them immediately!" he demanded of the guards at the front of the line.

Then he shouted for the marchers to produce their passports. As Wallenberg collected their *Schutzpasses*, he put them down near Langfelder, who picked them up and slipped them to the laborers who did not have them. Thus, six hundred people were protected with one hundred passes. But they weren't out of danger yet.

"That's Wallenberg," yelled an Arrow Cross guard, pointing excitedly at the Swedish diplomat.

"Kill them both," another guard shouted. The first guard leveled his rifle at Wallenberg's stomach.

"Halt!" came a voice from behind. The Arrow Cross guard whirled around and found himself facing four Gestapo troopers holding Wehrmacht-issue MP-38 rapid-fire machine pistols. "Where do you think you're taking these scarce able-bodied laborers? There's a war on. The Reich needs these men. We will take over. Now hand over your weapons."

"But we've been ordered…"

"Enough," Pista shouted. He pointed the machine pistol against the guard's chest. "Now all of you do as I say or I will kill this man where he stands."

"Can we at least kill the foreign troublemakers?" one guard whined. Pista answered by jamming the pistol hard into the guard's ribs. They'd had enough. The Arrow Cross guards laid down their rifles and drifted away.

Pista turned to Wallenberg. "You'd better travel with an armed guard from now on. The Arrow Cross is under orders to kill you. We'll escort you back to Ullöi Street."

Wallenberg, annoyed, shook his head. "No, I don't want an escort. Just see that these Jews get back to the safe house. I'll be careful."

"We will leave some armed men here to protect the laborers and dispatch trucks to pick them up. Now, please, no arguments, get into the Mercedes," Pista insisted. "Langfelder can follow in the Studebaker." Resigning himself, Wallenberg shrugged and climbed into the back seat of the black sedan.

The ride back to the Ullöi Street offices, less frantic than the wild dash to save the labor battalion, enabled Wallenberg to close his eyes. He nodded off, dreaming of the idyllic days of the pampered existence at his grandparents' summer home in Kapptsta, an island near Stockholm. This little piece of land in the Baltic had, for many years, been a refuge and retreat for him. He could use such a place right now.

A scream, "Watch out!" jerked Wallenberg out of his dream state. It was followed by the sounds of metal rending and glass shattering behind him. Swiveling his head to look out the rear window, he saw the driver of a large German military truck back it off the shattered Studebaker. The gunned engine shrieked in protest as the truck sped past the Mercedes and disappeared down the street ahead.

"Langfelder," Wallenberg shouted. Even before the black sedan stopped, he grabbed the door handle and jumped out of the car. There was nothing recognizable as a Studebaker from the rear bumper to the back of the front seat, only a twisted tangle of tortured metal. No one sitting in that back seat could have survived.

Langfelder was conscious. Wallenberg tried the driver's door, but the warped frame held both front doors securely closed. Pista locked the metal shoulder stock of the machine pistol in place and smashed the driver's window with it.

"I think I'm all right," the stunned Langfelder croaked, as Pista helped him crawl out the shattered window.

Pista examined him. "You're lucky, that crash could have broken your neck. We'll take you to a doctor. You may have some internal injuries, even though you don't feel it now."

Langfelder looked at the rear of the Studebaker. "What the devil happened?"

Pista frowned. "This much is clear. The German who drove that truck must have assumed Wallenberg occupied the back seat of the Studebaker. He tried to kill him."

Wallenberg couldn't suppress a shudder. Twice in a day. Once, almost shot by the Hungarian Nazis and now, almost crushed to death by the German Nazis. "This is Eichmann's work," he declared. "I'm sure of it." He gestured to Pista. "Let's get back to the office. We've got work to do. But first I'd like to make a brief stop at Gestapo headquarters. You'd better get out of those SS uniforms before we get there."

Pista dropped Moser and the German uniforms at Section C offices and proceeded directly to Gestapo headquarters. Wallenberg leaped out of the car, bounded into the building and demanded to see Eichmann. The desk sergeant advised him that without an appointment, it was quite impossible.

"Then just give the colonel this message: 'Wallenberg is still alive and demands to see him.'" He sat down and waited, but not for long. Before five minutes passed, an aide appeared and ushered him into Eichmann's office.

Eichmann smiled. "Good day, Herr Wallenberg. Now, what's this about your still being alive?"

"You tell me, since you sent that truck out to ram my car and kill me."

Eichmann spread his hands. "I can assure you, I know nothing about your accident."

"It was no accident, but I don't have to tell you that. Veesenmayer will hear about your attempts on a Swedish diplomat's life."

"Please accept my apologies on your brush with disaster. Would you like a drink?"

Wallenberg shook his head. "Just keep your hoodlums away from me." He turned and walked out.

Eichmann shouted after him, "Again, I apologize. But don't worry, someone will try again." He gave a lusty laugh.

CHAPTER 16

Pest, Offices of Section C, December 18, 1944

A woman, sitting on the curb in front of the Section C building, sobbed bitterly and rocked a young child in her arms. The passing bicycle rider, pressing back on the pedals, glided to a smooth stop in front of her. Dismounting, he squatted down besides her, gently touching her shoulder. "Can I help you?" He handed her his handkerchief.

Between sobs and gasps for air, she blurted out that she'd waited in line every day for a week hoping for a Schutzpass but had never been able to reach the front of the line before the office closed.

"Get up and come with me. It isn't safe in the streets in the evening." Taking a firm grip on her arm, he helped her up. Inside, he took her name and that of her child and told her to wait in the reception area. Fifteen minutes later, he returned holding two Schutzpasses. Placing them in a manila envelope, he handed it to her. "The streets are too dangerous after dark. You must stay here tonight. We'll escort you home tomorrow morning."

She removed the Schutzpasses from the envelope and examined the names on them. Her hand went up to her mouth and she started crying again, this time more softly. "You've saved our lives, how can I ever repay you, Herr…?"

He squeezed her hand gently. "Wallenberg, Raoul Wallenberg. I'm happy to be of service."

***

By mid-December, Budapest was under Soviet siege and most Nazis knew the hopelessness of their cause. The most recent manifestation of their disillusion was the suspension of deportations to the death camps. German fears for the future became Wallenberg's most effective tool to protect the Jews from lingering German malevolence. He promised wavering Nazis postwar support before war-crime tribunals.

But two dangers still confronted the Jews of Budapest and Wallenberg himself. One was Colonel Eichmann, who seemed impervious to, and even scornful of, postwar retribution. The other was the marauding bands of Arrow Cross. One fed on the other. Specifically, Eichmann encouraged the acts of bestiality and terror against Jews by these Hungarian thugs.

Dangling prospects of diplomatic recognition by Sweden had obtained cooperation from some Arrow Cross leaders, but the approach had worn thin because there had been no movement whatsoever in the direction of recognition by Sweden and other neutrals. Wallenberg had had to fall back on his other approach, namely, bribery with money or stockpiled food. As it turned out, he was feeding both the Jews and Arrow Cross.

Despite Wallenberg's deals with Arrow Cross leaders, nothing seemed to deter roving bands of hoodlums from looting, torturing and killing. Now, they had added a new target to their list—Wallenberg. And then there was Eichmann, who ordered the Jews herded into an area of Pest known as the Central Ghetto and did not permit them to leave for any reason, even to obtain food or medicine. He had 12,000 Christians moved out of the ghetto area to make room for 63,000 more Jews. It was not difficult to divine the colonel's intentions—the large concentration of Jews in a small area made mass extermination more manageable and, therefore, more likely. Things took an ominous turn when the Arrow Cross erected six-foot-high wooden walls, fencing in the entire ghetto, blocking all means of access and egress. The similarities to what had occurred in the Warsaw Ghetto massacre were, to say the least, unsettling. Another concern was the Jews in the safe houses in the International Ghetto. Would they be forced into the Central Ghetto as well?

The key, of course, was Eichmann, and this gave Wallenberg an idea—he dialed Eichmann's number. To his surprise, the colonel himself answered the telephone. After making Eichmann an offer he couldn't turn down, Wallenberg turned his attention to the protection of his workers in Section C.

You are fair game now for the Arrow Cross," Wallenberg told them one day. "The safe houses no longer provide adequate protection. Raids on them are daily occurrences, and with so many summary executions, we don't have the time to mount rescue attempts." At his words, looks of concern appeared on the faces of the assembled Section C workers. "For now, you must not return to your safe houses. Bed down here instead. It is too dangerous to be on the streets."

"But you go in the street, and on a bike, no less!" a voice in the group interjected.

Since his car had been demolished, Wallenberg had taken to riding a woman's bicycle around Pest. Although he was exposed, he felt less conspicuous than in his large American Studebaker.

"I have to venture out to be of any use," he explained, "but for most of you, your work can be effectively accomplished staying here."

"How are we safer here?" another voice queried.

"We have arms in the office and some of our group will be guarding this building around the clock. I have also persuaded our friends in the Budapest Police to provide some protection outside the building. If you must go out in the street, wear good walking shoes in case you're caught and forced to march. It's the ones with good shoes that survive. And those of you still wearing yellow stars, take them off. There's no sense making it easier for them to identify you."

Hugo Wohl, a short, stocky, powerfully built man, and one of Wallenberg's chief lieutenants, stood up and cleared his throat to catch Wallenberg's attention. "I assume the Schutzling-Protocoll group will continue with its rescue efforts on the streets."

Wallenberg nodded. "Yes, and I also think it's a good idea for your people to sleep here for their own protection and to provide more security for the building."

The Schutzling-Protocoll, headed by Wohl, was the part of Section C responsible for carrying out rescue missions to save Jewish lives. Wohl, a Hungarian Jewish businessman with connections to Sweden, had become acquainted with Per Anger on Wohl's trips to Scandinavia before the war. Stripped of his business by the SS and threatened with deportation, Wohl had come to Per Anger in desperation. Anger, against all diplomatic rules, had saved Wohl and his family by issuing the first provisional passport, the forerunner of the now indispensable *Schutzpass*. Now, Wohl himself was indispensable to the rescue program. Next to Wallenberg himself, no one had more responsibility for rescue efforts. He'd collected uniforms of doctors, nurses, priests, nuns, the Arrow Cross and the SS as well as German weapons for use of his group as needed. He developed and supervised the actions to impersonate SS and Hungarian troops that worked so successfully at the railway stations and on the marches.

Another voice cried out, "How will we eat if we can't go out for food?"

"Lars Berg's section has taken over the abandoned Finnish Legation, where we have two large rooms filled with potatoes, rice, canned food and other items. Consul Yngve Ekmark, who joined us this summer, has organized supplies of food and medicine to be delivered to the legation, this annex, the safe houses and the ghetto, as needed. So we won't be wanting for sustenance."

Ekmark had passed through Budapest on his way home from a harrowing few years in the Swedish Embassy in Belgrade, where active resistance caused the Germans to be merciless to the general population of Yugoslavia. When Ekmark saw he was needed in Budapest, he had stayed on to take over the economic section of Wallenberg's operation, giving up a well-deserved home leave. He had combed the countryside, buying up enormous quantities of tinned meat, potatoes and other foods, much of which was now hidden away. A grateful Wallenberg had welcomed the help of this selfless diplomat.

Budapest, December 19, 1944

Wallenberg despaired at his failure to work his magic on Hungary's deputy foreign minister, Zoltan Bogossy. Bogossy, an unrepentant Hungarian Nazi with a sadistic and unrelenting hatred for Jews, seemed impervious to persuasion, bribes or threats of later retribution. He urged his Arrow Cross troops to kill Jews, including those with Swedish *Schutzpasses*. He effectively undercut Kemény's order to honor the *Schutzpasses* and the baron was too busy with other matters of state to care much about the Jews, especially with the baroness out of Budapest. Besides, Kemény had fallen out of favor with both the Germans and the Arrow Cross government. They considered him too soft on Jews.

The German struggle to defend Budapest from the Soviet siege that began on December 8 was one of the bloodiest of the war. Over the objections of General August Schmidthuber, the commander of the German garrison in Budapest, Hitler had ordered Budapest to be defended to the death. The general had begged the Führer to permit him to pull back his troops in order to defend the fatherland. Budapest, after all, he argued, wasn't Berlin. His entreaties had fallen on deaf ears, earning him only threats of court martial if he gave up so much as an inch of territory in Budapest.

The siege and the daily Allied bombing raids took their toll on the infrastructure of the city government, particularly the food supply. Food was scarce not only for the Jews but also for all the citizens, including the Arrow Cross. Bogossy ordered raids on Swedish-protected storehouses to seize provisions.

In one such raid, members of the Swedish Legation, including Wallenberg, rushed to a factory, one of the places where Swedish supplies were stored. The Arrow Cross had already occupied the factory and refused to leave, showing Anger and Wallenberg written orders from Bogossy to seize the food. Wallenberg angrily telephoned Bogossy, who warned him not to interfere with or obstruct Hungarian authorities in what he characterized as "their lawful actions." The raids on the food stocks continued, and a frustrated Wallenberg found himself powerless to prevent them. He derived some solace from the Arrow Cross's failure to find much larger stores hidden elsewhere.

In was in this maelstrom that Wallenberg received a call from a dentist he knew, Dr. István Szondy. The call sent him scurrying for his hat and coat.

Buda, Dental Office of Dr. István Szondy, an Hour Later

Like everyone else in Budapest, Dr. Szondy kept his door locked. The receptionist admitted Wallenberg but only after looking through the peephole in the door and checking his identity. She led him to one of the treatment rooms where Dr. Szondy was leaning over a patient. "Please have a seat, I'll be with you in a few minutes," the dentist said, still concentrating on his work.

Two minutes later, Dr. Szondy straightened up. "There, that should hold you until next week," he advised his patient. He turned around, smiling, and extended his hand to his visitor, who shook it. The dentist was a short man with a thin neck, a large Adam's apple and a receding hairline. "Thank you for coming," he said. Turning to his patient just climbing out of the dental chair, he announced, "This is Zoltan Bogossy. I understand both of you have talked but never met."

Bogossy nodded in Wallenberg's direction. Wallenberg fixed the deputy foreign minister with a malevolent stare.

Dr. Szondy broke the frosty silence. "Minister Bogossy knows the war is lost. He's reconsidered his position. I suggested to him, therefore, that he speak to you about Swedish passport protection."

Bogossy stepped around the dentist. "I think I can speak for myself, Doctor. Herr Wallenberg, in several of our telephone conversations, you suggested that I could help myself to avoid retribution from the Allies after the war. I am interested in taking up your offer for my son and myself."

Wallenberg glared at the minister. "There have been a lot of deaths and suffering that you could have prevented since I first offered you protection. It's a little late now."

Bogossy pulled on his ear lobe. "There's still a lot I can do," he said. "Also, I can be your eyes and ears within the Hungarian administration, though it will be safer if we communicate through Dr. Szondy rather than directly."

Wallenberg intensely disliked this brutal Nazi, but he needed all the help he could get from any quarter of the Hungarian government. "Very well. If you will protect my Jews and warn me of any plans by your government to move against them, I will issue you and your son Swedish protective passports."

Bogossy put out his right hand. "Agreed." Wallenberg shook it, reluctantly. Dr. Szondy beamed with satisfaction.

***

A few days later, Wallenberg tested Bogossy's good faith. The Arrow Cross had raided a Swedish safe house and marched its 250 inhabitants to party headquarters. Wallenberg's call to the go-between, Dr. Szondy, resulted in all the Jews being returned to the safe house within the hour.

Neither Bogossy nor Szálasi, however, could stem the tide of violence and terrorism sweeping the streets of Budapest. Father Kun still rampaged through the streets with his crucifix and his gangs, torturing and killing. Another Arrow Cross killer, known only as Frau Salzer, engaged in her own torturous games. Cradling a Thompson sub-machine gun in her arms, she took particular delight in burning the genitals of her female victims with lit candles before shooting them.

The Jews were not the only ones caught in the crosshairs of the Arrow Cross and other murderous gangs. Father Kun handed out "wanted" posters of Wallenberg to his men with instructions to shoot him on sight. Kun posted a reward for Wallenberg's capture, dead or alive.

Wallenberg, undeterred, continued to line up Arrow Cross officials to protect him and his Jews, promising to intercede for them after the war. He enlisted not only Bogossy but also Pál Szálai, a high-ranking government police officer. Szálai, sickened by the excesses of the Arrow Cross, approached Wallenberg on his own. Their alliance turned out to be particularly beneficial because Szálai was generally well informed of Arrow Cross plans. He not only willingly offered information but also provided armed protection for Wallenberg and many of his Jews.

CHAPTER 17

Budapest, Eichmann's Staff Car and Wallenberg's Apartment, December 22, 1944

The Allied bombings increased in intensity and the rumble of Soviet artillery continued almost nonstop. The ring tightened around the city as Marshal Rodion Malinovsky's forces moved in from the east and Marshal Fyodor Tolbukhin's approached from the south. The only open roads out of Budapest were to the west. Most civilians had fled, except for the Jews, most of whom had been herded by the SS and Arrow Cross into the Central Ghetto. The stockade-like fence erected around the entire area effectively sealed them off. Those aware of the fate of the ghettos of Warsaw and Kraków felt sure that the final phase, the annihilation of the Central Ghetto, was near. That decision rested with *Der Bluthund,* Colonel Adolph Eichmann, who, at this moment in the early evening, sat relaxed, smoking in the back of his staff car, headed for Wallenberg's apartment.

Major Krumey, sitting next to Eichmann, fidgeted. "I don't like the feel of this, Sir. What if it's a trap?"

"I doubt that." Eichmann fingered the miniature Walther pistol, sitting securely under his jacket. "Besides, there's no cause for concern. A detachment of SS will watch the place while we're there."

"I still don't understand what we will accomplish."

Eichmann rubbed his freshly shaved chin. "Satisfying my curiosity. For some time, this strange and mysterious Swede has fascinated me. Remember when we first met him early last summer at the Arizona Nightclub?"

Krumey nodded with a sardonic smile. "I do. I also remember that you dismissed him as just another weak-kneed aristocrat playboy—another soft and effete diplomat from the neutrals."

"I admit it—I underestimated this Wallenberg. Now, while we fight each other, we both wrestle with a common enemy—time. But in the end, I shall prevail. I will wipe out the Jews before the Soviets take Budapest. Wallenberg can't stop me."

Wallenberg is here!

***

That day Wallenberg had chanced staying at his apartment. As he lifted the blackout shades and looked down, he saw a black Mercedes, flying swastika flags, pull up to the building. Frowning, he watched two Gestapo officers, dressed in formal black uniforms, emerge from the car. Wallenberg slapped his head. Eichmann! Damn, he had asked him to dinner tonight! In all the excitement of the past few days, he had forgotten. Wallenberg had hoped to use the indulgence of good food and wine to soften Eichmann to his proposals that the colonel abandon further efforts towards the Final Solution. Now, everything could be ruined by his own stupidity!

While the Gestapo officers climbed the stairs to his door, Wallenberg dialed his one hope—Lars Berg. Berg and a colleague, Göte Carlsson, shared a house lent to them by a wealthy Jewish count so that it and its contents would be protected from Nazi looting and confiscation. The house came with a full complement of servants, including a master Hungarian chef. Please be there, Wallenberg prayed.

"Lars? Raoul here. Thank God you're home. I have an emergency. I invited Eichmann and Krumey to dinner for tonight. It totally slipped my mind. I don't even have food in my apartment. Can I bring them over to your house?"

A knock sounded. "They're here! I have to go." Wallenberg hung up without waiting for an answer and opened the door. Eichmann and Krumey stood there in full black regalia, Eichmann's hand leaned on the SS dagger chained to his black Sam Browne belt, his polished knee-high jackboots reflected the light coming from the hallway.

Wallenberg smiled. "Come in gentleman. Welcome. Can I offer you a drink?"

Eichmann nodded. Wallenberg could see the colonel was puzzled as he looked around—no places set on the dinner table and no one but Wallenberg in the apartment. "Have we come on the wrong evening?"

Wallenberg laughed. "No, Colonel, I should have warned you. We are having dinner in far more comfortable and sumptuous surroundings than my humble apartment—and a wonderful Hungarian cook is preparing the meal. As I told you last week, it would be an offer you could not refuse and I assure you, you won't be disappointed. My apologies though, it would've been smarter if I had you go directly to Lars Berg's house."

A flicker of irritation flashed across Eichmann's face, then just as quickly, vanished. He shrugged and accepted a glass of scotch, neat.

Buda, Berg's House, a Few Minutes Later

The staff car, followed by an SS armored personnel carrier, made its way carefully through the blacked out, rubble-strewn streets, eerily illuminated by flashes of the not-too-distant Soviet artillery. They pulled up to a house on Buda's fashionable Hunfalvi Street. The two Gestapo officers and Wallenberg climbed out of the car. They could see that the house, while not large, had been built by someone with taste and money.

A cordial Lars Berg greeted them. He led the visitors to the oak-paneled library, warmed by a robust blaze in the fireplace. Göte Carlsson took drink orders while Berg set down a silver tray of sliced Kolbasz, a Hungarian sausage, and then, a large plate of spreadable Hungarian cheese and small round crackers.

Both the Swedes and the SS officers savored the drinks and the hard-to find gourmet treats. Wallenberg limited himself to small talk, not wanting to broach contentious topics until full stomachs and fine wine mellowed his guests.

After forty minutes of light chatter, they sat down to dinner. The house's best porcelain service and silver graced the table. Royalty would have felt quite at home in this dining room. Eichmann curled his lip and nodded. "I am impressed—such civilized splendor in the midst of all this chaos."

A servant lit the candles sitting in the silver wall sconces behind the diners while a waitress placed a steaming tureen of sweet and sour cabbage soup on a small serving table. She filled their bowls. Thick slices of freshly baked bread accompanied the soup. When the soup dishes were cleared, she served plates of *sorma*, a Hungarian specialty of stuffed cabbage.

Krumey put his hand over his mouth to stifle a belch. "That was a treat, there was actual beef in the stuffed cabbage."

Berg nodded. "Ground beef, ground pork and some Hungarian sausage, mixed together."

Wallenberg is here!

Eichmann laughed. "Thank God—it seems everywhere else I eat they serve me old horse meat." He patted his stomach. "Excellent meal. Is there dessert?"

Berg smiled. "There's still the main course, Colonel."

Eichmann shook his head. "You're not serious? I have to admit it, you Swedes can eat and entertain better than Germans."

Berg was serious. The waitress brought out large platters of chicken paprikash, spaetzle, breaded cauliflower and hot bacon potato salad.

Krumey tasted the potato salad first. He licked his lips. "It tastes like my mother's."

The diners selected from choice vintages of French white and red wines. Eichmann held up his glass. The candlelight flickered and shimmered through the red wine. "Where did you find this vintage? I haven't had any like this since Paris."

Carlsson shrugged. "We inherited a substantial prewar wine cellar."

The meal concluded with apple strudel and Hungarian egg coffee. After the meal, a servant poured glasses of the Hungarian Tokaji Aszú. Carlsson took a sip and raised his glass. "The Hungarians have a saying about this drink, *Vinum regum, rex vinorum,* the wine of kings and the king of wines."

Eichmann chuckled, lifting a bottle of vintage French Burgundy. "I prefer to think of this as the wine of kings."

The group retired to the drawing room. Berg passed out cigars. The men lit up, and Wallenberg made his way to the window through the haze of cigar smoke. Parting the curtains, he opened the window, absent-mindedly watching the smoke being drawn outside. He flicked off the light switch. As he had hoped, the room wasn't plunged into total darkness. Flashes of Soviet artillery periodically bathed the room in an angry red glow. He extended one hand toward the red afterglow on the horizon. "The Soviets, Colonel—at your doorstep. Your position is hopeless. Surely you can see that. You can't seriously be thinking of continuing this frenzied killing."

Eichmann said with determination, "My orders are to exterminate every last Jew in Budapest, and by God, that's just what I intend to do."

Wallenberg's eyes narrowed. "How can you speak of butchery in the same breath you invoke the name of God?"

Eichmann stubbed out the cigar and lit a cigarette. He coughed after he inhaled. He didn't reply.

"Heed my warning, Colonel," Wallenberg said, shaking his head. "Things will go badly for you after the war if you don't stop this senseless killing."

Eichmann blew smoke at the ceiling. "Surely you must know, Herr Wallenberg, that regardless of what I do or don't do now, I'll be given no pardons. I'll be executed by the Soviets without a second thought. So what reason is there to drop my life's work? Besides, the Führer has a secret weapon that he will soon use to save the Reich."

"This late in the war? Don't insult my intelligence. Face it, the war is over and Budapest is about to be overrun. Leave the city while you can."

Eichmann sighed. "You're probably right about the secret weapon. I've been hearing about it for the past two years. But leave Budapest? Not until I complete my mission by dealing with the Jews."

Wallenberg switched on the lights and sat down opposite Eichmann. "Colonel, I know you're an intelligent man. You can't believe the Nazi tripe of the past ten years about Jews being a danger to the mighty Third Reich. You claim to know the Jews. Educate me. How could these unarmed, defenseless people ever have presented any danger to Germany?"

Eichmann took a long drag on his cigarette. "Their scientists are helping our enemies."

"And whose fault is that? Before they were driven out of Germany—or murdered—these loyal Jews had provided Germany with great thinkers and scientists. Hitler lost all that potential for advancement in technology and science when he forced those formidable and innovative minds into the waiting and welcome arms of your enemies."

Eichmann flicked ash off his cuff but said nothing.

"Think, Colonel, of what Hitler could have gained by embracing these people and harnessing their intellect, energy and vitality. Forget those he drove into the arms of Allies. Look at the thousands of doctors, scientists and artists he put to death. Victims who would have aided Germany's short-term war effort and long-term improvement in the quality of life within the country."

Wallenberg is here!

Eichmann stubbed out his cigarette. "The trouble with you Swedes is that you exaggerate."

"Do we now? Let's see whom you have lost—the physicist Albert Einstein, the Nobel laureate Enrico Fermi, Peter Debye of the Max Planck Institute, the geneticist Max Delbrück, the mathematician John van Neumann... Shall I go on?"

Eichmann uncrossed his legs. "I don't know where you think you're going with this conversation, but it amuses me. No one has dared to challenge me in this way for a long time. I find it rather refreshing, but don't push it too far."

Wallenberg held the colonel's gray eyes. "So answer my question then, why do you continue killing the Jews?"

Eichmann shifted in his chair. "I spent time in Palestine, so I'm very familiar with Zionism. The Zionist Chaim Weizmann had declared war on us in 1939 and we just responded in kind. Also, Jewish resistance groups, supported by the Jewish population, had to be dealt with."

Wallenberg frowned. "Engaging in a little revisionist history to justify yourself? I'm familiar with those events. Weizmann merely said, 'The struggle of the Western democracies is our struggle.' After all, Germans were debasing and murdering Jews long before 1939. Are you really surprised that Weizmann felt hostile to the Nazi cause? But war? The Jews were never in a position to wage war."

Eichmann glanced at Krumey, as if to invite his assistance in the debate. Krumey did not meet his gaze. Eichmann turned back to Wallenberg. "It's simple, either the German people or the Jews would survive, there was no room for both."

"I think that what the Germans hate most in themselves, the drive for power that they projected onto the Jews. You are too bright, Colonel, to believe that it is war that Germany is waging against the Jews. After all, the Jews are only civilians, well dispersed among the nations of Europe with no country of their own and no political power base—they have none of the capabilities that even the smallest nation could muster to wage war. 'World Jewry' did not pursue the sinister aims that Hitler, in his flight of fancy, attributed to it. If you're such a student of Jewish culture, you'd know that world Jewry has no common aims and is hopelessly divided along issues of religion, secularism, internationalism and Zionism."

Berg stepped between the protagonists and refilled their glasses.

Wallenberg leaned around Berg to look at Eichmann. "The Jews comprised less than one percent of the German population. So why did Hitler inflate them into a national danger? And the resistance groups? How incredibly weak, pitifully small and basically harmless they were—and how little of the Jewish population they represented. All your premises are clichés built on clichés."

Eichmann coughed again and cleared his smoker's throat. "Do I really believe the Jews were ever a threat to the Third Reich? Not really. But you have to concede the effectiveness of the propaganda about the Jews. Propaganda Minister Goebbels is a genius, don't you agree?"

Wallenberg rolled his eyes. "Then why are you determined to continue the killing? Is it simply slaughter for the sake of glorifying propaganda?"

Eichmann examined his fingernails, then looked up and smiled. "To be honest, Herr Wallenberg, it's a much simpler proposition. Before the Final Solution, I was a low-level functionary and probably would have remained so. But, as the specialist in Zionism, I was presented with the opportunity to carry out the Führer's Final Solution. I jumped at the chance and, by doing it with gusto and without mercy, I amassed power and wealth beyond the dreams of most men. My work and position enabled me to acquire almost anything I wanted—art, women, horses, fine china…"

Wallenberg interrupted. "But surely you must face up to the fact that now it's ending. Give up this killing frenzy!"

"Listen to the Swede beg, Major Krumey," Eichmann chortled. "I'm sorry to disappoint you, but I enjoy my privileges in Budapest. I concede that time is short." He shrugged. "But still, I'm not willing to abandon it all up. So, I'll continue doing what I do best. I will have your Jews, that's a promise." He raised his glass. "So much for your intellectual argument, Herr Wallenberg."

Wallenberg shook his head. "I simply don't understand why you must carry out the orders of that madman. Bring an end to these crimes. You are the only one who can do it!"

Eichmann stood up, hands on his hips, the color rising in his face. "Madman? To my face, you call the Führer a madman? That 'madman,' Herr Wallenberg, has given us back the self-respect taken away by the weak-kneed civilian traitors who stabbed us in the back in the First World War by surrendering when Germany could have won."

Wallenberg waved aside the statement. "That old saw about restoring self-respect to German citizenry won't work with me because I know that your Gestapo, in the calm and quiet of the prewar period, developed and refined its techniques of persecution, torture and murder on its *own German citizens.* They killed countless Germans before unleashing such terror on the rest of Europe. By my way of thinking, that's not restoring the self-respect of Germans."

Eichmann's eyes narrowed. "Are you quite finished?"

"No, Colonel," said Wallenberg, locking eyes with his adversary. "The 'stab in the back' myth is a pathetic lie foisted on the German people by Hitler for his own political gain. I know a little about World War I. The German military covered up its worsening battlefield situation so that when the generals wanted to surrender, the civilian government actually refused. It wasn't until General Ludendorf and Field Marshal von Hindenburg admitted that Germany was about to lose the war if the fighting did not stop immediately, that the civilian government finally accepted an armistice under the Treaty of Versailles. That's something you'd have known if you ever bothered to read Hindenburg's letter to Prince Max, insisting—almost begging—that he sue for peace."

"It's all beside the point, isn't it? The Führer's orders are quite clear and they are the law of the land. Therefore, what I do, I do as a law-abiding German citizen. As SS, I swore an oath of blind obedience to the Führer. By adhering to that oath, I am living my life according to Kant's moral precepts and definition of duty."

Now Wallenberg stood up. "Kant? Is that what you said? You don't understand the teachings of Immanuel Kant. His moral philosophy is based on man's actions undertaken from a sense of duty dictated by *reason,* in other words, man using his faculty of judgment. That, Colonel, rules out your oath of blind obedience—especially the blind obedience to plunder and murder. I happen to know the SS term for it, *Kadavergehorsam,* the 'obedience of corpses.' Quite an appropriate appellation. My God, Kant's beliefs are the very antithesis of everything you and your Führer espouse."

Eichmann rubbed his chin and thought for a moment. "Perhaps Kant's a poor example. All I meant was that my will and my actions are in accordance with the principle of general law and order in the land."

"Colonel, you are talking about the law and order of murder and theft. Think! Even the murderers and thieves in the government would not wish to live under a legal system that gives others the right to rob or kill them. I imagine not even you would want to live under such a system. That, Colonel Eichmann, is not a principle of law and order, that's anarchy."

Eichmann lit another cigarette. Wallenberg could see him struggling for the right words. "You are most difficult, but you must admit we had the support of the German people."

Wallenberg rolled his eyes. "Permit me to be even more difficult." He raised his voice. "The support of the German people? Is that why you kept the Final Solution secret? Is that why you used euphemisms of 'resettlement' and 'deportation' for extermination? No, you know very well that you didn't have popular support for the merciless extermination of unarmed men, women, children and babies."

"The secrecy orders were Himmler's," Eichmann protested, "not mine."

"Then at least Himmler faced up to the fact that the German people did not possess the venality of their leaders. He remembered what happened when Hitler ordered euthanasia for anyone considered mentally or physically deficient—there was such a hue and cry from the citizens that even your Führer was forced to stop the program he had concocted from a twisted melange of nineteenth-century racist and Social Darwinist ideas. I'm sorry, but justifying Nazi actions under the rubric of national support just won't work."

Eichmann began to pace around the room. "The Führer gave us hope for the future by rekindling the principles of the Aryan master race and our great Nordic heritage."

Wallenberg looked first at Eichmann, then at Krumey. "Has either of you ever read *Mein Kampf?*"

Krumey shook his head.

"Only parts of it," Eichmann admitted.

Wallenberg pursed his lips. "Well, *Mein Kampf* was right about one thing—the gullibility of the German people. Putting aside the myth of the Aryan superman for the moment, the thing everyone seems to have recognized but the Nazis, is that most Nazi leaders are not the blue-eyed, blond, tall, fair-skinned, handsome Aryans. Hitler's receding forehead, ugly nose, broad cheekbones, small rat's eyes and dark hair hardly fit the description of the Aryan superman. And what about the flabby, balding, mousy Himmler? Or the dwarfed, club-footed Goebbels, who would have been eligible for extermination under Hitler's euthanasia program?" Wallenberg laughed and touched his face. "And just look at both of us and our own big noses, Colonel. Hardly the stuff of Aryans."

Eichmann's eyes glinted dangerously, making a fist.

This time, Krumey came to his aid. "But through selective breeding, we could have achieved a population of Aryans in a few generations—that's the whole point."

Eichmann nodded his agreement.

"Hitler's babble about the superior Aryan and Nordic race," Wallenberg declared, "is simply the fluff of Wagner's operatic fairy tales and the journalistic rantings of Dietrich Eckart, a vagrant, drunkard and morphine addict, who eventually ended up in a mental institution. None of Hitler's pseudo-scientific cronies has ever presented the slightest proof that millions of members of one particular race of people are all endowed with the same intellectual, physiological and psychological characteristics. You don't have to be a scholar to know that all races or groups have both intelligent and stupid people, lazy and diligent ones, heroes and cowards, great thinkers and dullards. Otherwise, how do you account for so many blue-eyed, blond Jews?"

Eichmann did not answer, focusing on the smoke rings he was patiently forming.

Wallenberg began pacing in his turn. "I'll tell you what I think. Hitler found himself at the bottom of the social ladder and it gave him great satisfaction to imagine himself as belonging to the chosen Aryan master race. So, he found a convenient scapegoat to differentiate—the Jews."

Eichmann abruptly sat down, cupped his chin in his hand, and appeared to be deep in thought. Looking up, he said, "You can't deny he's been a great leader of our armies—armies that conquered most of Europe. The Führer is our Napoleon or Alexander the Great. Those leaders were also branded criminals."

"How can you equate your psychopathic Führer to Napoleon or Alexander? True, many people were killed during their reigns, but neither of them had people put to death for no political or military reason, or simply to satisfy some personal gratification." Wallenberg threw his hands up. "Hitler a great leader? Not likely. He's simply the most effective mass murderer ever, whose legacy is to teach German bureaucrats and the glorious SS to be immune to the slaughter of women and children, who has trained future Nazi leaders to be exploiters and killers without shame, conscience or God."

Eichmann slapped the table with the palm of his hand. "But unlike Hitler, Napoleon did not have to overcome traitorous generals."

"Traitors or realists?" Wallenberg laughed harshly. "Hitler destroyed all power of self-criticism around him, surrounding himself with sycophants. He replaced reality with wishful thinking by firing all the brilliant generals who had conquered Europe for him. Just think about it: Rundstedt, Kluge, Speidel, Leeb, Bock, Guderian and Hopner. And why? Simply out of pique that things weren't going his way. Could all these outstanding officers, trained in warfare in the great Prussian tradition, be wrong? Could they all be 'traitors'?"

Eichmann's smoker's cough flared up. He took a sip of the liqueur and looked to Krumey, who shrugged. He turned to Wallenberg. "Perhaps you're right about some things, but the Wehrmacht was not up to the task. They let the Führer down."

Wallenberg looked up at the ceiling, then stared at Eichmann. "You're not serious? Can't you see the irony of what you're saying? It was Hitler's personal hatreds and psychoses that hurt the German war effort, not the failures of his brave soldiers. He murdered skilled workers and artisans that the armaments industry desperately needed. He withdrew from the war effort millions of men and thousands of scientists and technicians and devoted them to the extermination of a helpless people that were neither a military nor a political threat to Germany, he diverted rolling stock to ship Jews to death camps, trains critically needed by the Wehrmacht to ship materiel and personnel to the front. But you should know that better than anyone."

Eichmann grimaced. But before he could reply, Wallenberg started ticking off points on his fingers. "Without the slightest idea how he could defeat America, Hitler declared war on the powerful United States while he was still fighting the Soviets and British. He accomplished what Roosevelt could not. He overcame isolationist opposition to American entry into the European war."

Wallenberg touched the next outstretched finger. "His mindless order to kill Ukrainians wholesale turned a people who originally looked upon the occupying Germans as liberators and allies into implacable enemies of the Third Reich. That order tied down several panzer divisions sorely needed to fight the Soviets. Your 'great' leader has one unique accomplishment: he has, single-handedly, managed to turn glorious victory into ignominious defeat and destroyed Germany and its people." Wallenberg chuckled. "The Aryan master race, it seems, finds itself bested by the 'racially degenerate' Slavs and the mixed breeds of the Western democracies."

Eichmann wandered over to the window and absently watched the Soviets' pyrotechnic display. He flicked his lighter, put the flame to the tip of a cigarette and inhaled. His eyes followed the drifting smoke.

Wallenberg walked up behind him. "If you had read *Mein Kampf*, you would have found it a half-baked mixture of pseudo-scientific claptrap, racial myth, anti-Semitism and *lebensraum* fantasy. Of course, what can you expect from a man who never held a job until he became Chancellor of the Third Reich?"

Eichmann's face flushed. "You're baiting me—and that is not healthy."

Berg stepped between them with fresh glasses and a bottle of cognac. Eichmann nodded. Berg poured him a glass. Eichmann swirled the golden liquid. He raised the glass towards Wallenberg. "You're quite the intellectual debater, Herr Wallenberg, I have to give you that. I must admit that I don't really believe all the principles of Nazism, but I am deeply attached to everything it has given me—power and wealth. If I continue to eliminate our enemies, I may delay defeat for a few days, and when I go to the gallows, I'll die with the knowledge that I have completed my mission."

Wallenberg lightly grasped Eichmann's arm, softening his tone. "Please, call off your people–leave Budapest while you can. You'll accomplish nothing by continuing to kill."

Eichmann jerked his arm away. He stood stiffly, raising his voice. "Budapest will be held as though it were Berlin. That is the Führer's order and it will be faithfully carried out."

Eichmann asked for his greatcoat. He turned to Wallenberg. "I must thank you for a charming evening of surprisingly fine food and wine, and stimulating conversation." He smiled frostily. "Quite different from the social discourse I have become accustomed to—most interesting. People have been shot for much less than what you have said tonight. But don't interpret my restraint and politeness for friendship—quite the contrary, I intend to do everything I can to keep you from saving your Jews."

Eichmann turned to Berg and Carlsson. "Thank you for hosting this fine dinner. Perhaps you can advise my aides on where to find such delicacies and drink in Budapest?"

He shook himself into his greatcoat. Krumey did likewise. Eichmann carefully placed his peaked black death's head cap on his head. He turned to Wallenberg, smiling. "Your diplomatic passport won't help you if I find it necessary to do away with you. Accidents do happen, even to neutral diplomats. Goodnight, Herr Wallenberg."

CHAPTER 18

Buda, Office of the Hungarian Foreign Minister, December 23, 1944

Prime Minister Szálasi had fired Foreign Minister Baron Kemény. Per Anger knew that Kemény's replacement, Ladislaz Vöczköndy, spelled trouble for the Swedes. Vöczköndy had been Hungary's military attaché to Sweden and had been expelled from Stockholm for his Arrow Cross activities. He had no love for the Swedes and, as soon as he took over the Foreign Ministry, he summoned Anger and Wallenberg to his office.

Upon entering the Royal Palace, the two diplomats were shown into the Baroque anteroom outside of Vöczköndy's office, where they waited. The room, with its parquet floors and marble walls, reflected the tastes of the Austro-Hungarian monarchy. A priceless Persian rug, one of the few not looted earlier by the Nazis, graced the floor.

After a while an aide motioned them into Vöczköndy's office. Chaos reigned in this once elegant domain of the baron. Documents were strewn all over tables, and valuable paintings lay piled haphazardly on the floor. The room looked as if it had just been ransacked.

Without greeting, Vöczköndy came directly to the point. "You must immediately pack up and leave Budapest for Szombathely in western Hungary, where our government has relocated. Otherwise, I cannot guarantee your safety."

Anger shook his head. "That demand is unreasonable, Foreign Minister, and leaving is quite out of the question. We have obligations right here in Budapest to represent Sweden and numerous other nations. You may go on to Szombathely if you wish, but we shall remain here."

Vöczköndy flushed. "How dare you defy the Hungarian government? This continuing insult must stop. You have, with unfailing consistency, ignored all our requests, and, despite your numerous hollow promises, you have never recognized our legitimate government." He stood and glared down on them. "And you say I'm unreasonable? I haven't forgotten how your government expelled me from Sweden on only two hours notice. Well, now I'm the one demanding that you must leave. If you do not, I cannot be responsible for your lives."

Wallenberg leaned forward. "What are you saying? Are you threatening us?"

Vöczköndy sat down. He smiled. "Who knows what can happen in these turbulent times? That's why you'd better leave Budapest."

Anger stood up. "We're staying in Budapest—and you will be held personally responsible for any harm that befalls our representatives." The two diplomats left the office without further conversation.

***

Back in the Swedish staff car, Anger turned to Wallenberg. "I think Vöczköndy's threat is directed at you. With Eichmann and this new foreign minister after your hide, you should leave Budapest. Berg and I will try to take up the slack."

"I can't leave at this critical juncture. There's a lot of work to do. All could be lost if I give up now."

Anger touched his companion's arm. "Dead, you won't be of much help to anyone. At least go underground, you're too tempting a target."

"I know—and I'm frightened. Since Bogossy warned me that the Arrow Cross had orders to kidnap me, I've been sleeping with one eye open." He sighed. "I'll be glad when the Soviets finally get here."

"Stay with me at Uri Street. You can't go back to your apartment."

"I'll stay tonight, but I can't put you in danger. I'll move from place to place—it's better that way."

The air raid sirens wailed. Wallenberg frowned. "It never lets up. It's the bombs that really scare the hell out of me. Another week of this, I'll be a wreck."

The driver pulled up to one of the Swedish safe houses and declared, "We will take cover here. This building has a sturdy cellar."

After one of the residents recognized Wallenberg, the three of them were warmly welcomed. They crowded into the cellar. Twenty minutes later, they heard the muffled blasts of exploding bombs. The military and industrial complexes were the targets, but bombing, an imprecise art at best, destroyed or damaged residential areas in the vicinity, as well.

The house shook from a nearby explosion. Bits of plaster showered down while dust rose from the floor. Wallenberg shut his eyes, his hands clasped tightly together. He shivered. Using his intellectual, acting and debating abilities, he could handle the Arrow Cross and the SS without flinching, but a stray bomb presented the lack of control over one's destiny that scared the wits out of him. Whether you were a coward, hero, genius or moron didn't matter if you crossed paths with a bomb. The prospect of vaporization, the thought of a moment never completed and instant oblivion terrified him. Most of all, he resented the impersonality of the destruction.

Then the all clear sounded.

Pest, Offices of Section C, December 24, 1944

An explosion on the first floor interrupted Hugo Wohl's last-minute instructions to his rescue team. As they started down the stairs to investigate, they met a squad of Arrow Cross charging up. Wohl found himself looking down the barrel of a machine pistol.

"Everyone up the stairs, no exceptions," the Arrow Cross leader screamed. "We have sealed off the building. Anyone who tries to leave will be shot!"

As the Section C group retreated up the stairs, Wohl shook his finger at the Arrow Cross men. "This entire building is part of the Legation of Sweden, Swedish territory. You have no authority here!"

"We no longer recognize your fake passports or your Swedish safe houses. Now shut up or I shoot," the Arrow Cross soldier shouted, spittle flying from his lips.

Arrow Cross men stormed through every room in the house. The officer in charge put his pistol to the head of one of the secretaries, "Where's Wallenberg?" Too terrified to speak, she could only shake her head.

Wohl stepped up to the leader. "He's not here. He left Budapest."

The officer smashed Wohl in the stomach with the butt of the machine pistol, causing him to double over, gasping for breath. "I wasn't talking to you, Jew."

Arrow Cross soldiers checked the identity of everyone in the house. No Wallenberg. Frustrated, the officer smashed a nearby lamp and ordered his men to ransack the offices, spilling files on the floor, overturning furniture and breaking equipment. Finally they left without arresting anyone.

Wohl turned to Pista. "We must get word to Wallenberg. The Arrow Cross people are out in force looking for him, I'm sure with orders to kill."

***

Frustrated, the Arrow Cross officer headed for a second Swedish safe house, on Jokai Street, another Section C office, where he'd earlier dispatched a squad based on rumors that it might be a Wallenberg hiding place.

The squad sergeant saluted the officer, and said, "Wallenberg isn't here."

"Shit, I told you to find him; those were your orders."

"We tore the house apart, Sir, there was no sign of him. What else could we do?"

"Comb the streets, you idiot. He's got to be somewhere in Pest."

"What shall we do with the Jews we found in the house? There are about two hundred of them."

A malicious grin formed on the officer's face. He rubbed his chin. "Take the scum down to the Danube and get rid of them. We'll teach this Wallenberg a lesson through his Jews."

***

Staying in the shadows along Jokai Street, the former ballerina turned underground fighter, Teca Zöldi, followed the Arrow Cross guards as they herded their Jewish prisoners toward the river. Since joining the underground, she spent most of her time in the streets, so she knew the route would lead them to the killing fields on the banks of the Danube. She cradled her machine pistol. God, how she hated those Arrow Cross guards, especially their leader. She imagined the scene was not much different when her daughter and husband were herded to their deaths for no reason other than being Jewish. She no longer had any hesitation using her weapon; she wanted to kill the

Wallenberg is here!

bastards, now. Her finger began to tighten on the trigger, then relaxed. She knew her colleague Solomon would be very unhappy if she acted prematurely. Somewhere, in other shadows he was tracking the same procession. She was not sure what only two of them could accomplish. They would have to play it by ear, but they would do something.

***

Swept up with the rest of Section C from the Jokai Street office, George, who'd escaped from the death march to the brick factory in November, found himself once again in harm's way. Now, however, no possibility of escape presented itself. Arrow Cross hoodlums shot Jews for the least provocation—walking too slowly, wandering out of line—virtually any picayune excuse warranted execution. In the subzero temperatures, both the recently killed and long-frozen corpses littered the streets leading to the river.

George put his arm under that of an older Jew, so that the old man did not lag behind. As they approached the Chain Bridge, he heard the hysterical yells of Father Kun, "In the name of Jesus, fire!" Then a volley of shots.

The presence of the fanatical priest dashed any hopes of rescue. As George and the other Section C Jews approached the Danube, they saw the Jews ahead of them being lined up at the edge of the river and shot, their bodies falling into the Danube. Silhouetted against the gray sky, after each volley, was the crucifix Father Kun raised above him with one arm while cradling his pistol with the other.

A guard prodded George roughly towards the riverbank, the water now tinted red. He could see the floating bodies. It almost seemed as if his mind had shut down: his life did not flash before his eyes and he had no inclination to beg for mercy; he felt just numb as he waited for the end of life. Nevertheless, he managed a mumbled *Shema* prayer as he stood there, looking down at his shoes.

Suddenly something changed. George wasn't sure what. He heard a shout—it was different! As that thought registered on his brain, he also realized that he was still standing; that no shots had been fired.

A familiar voice called out, "Those are Swedish citizens; release them immediately!"

He looked up. Per Anger stood face to face with the Arrow Cross officer. Behind Anger, the Budapest police, Pál Szálai's men, looked on.

"We have our orders," blustered the Arrow Cross leader. "Now, out of our way."

A Budapest police captain stepped between Anger and the Arrow Cross officer. He placed his revolver under the man's nose. "There will be no more murders here tonight. Is that understood?" The captain pressed the weapon into the soft part of the man's cheek until he could feel the resistance of teeth.

A scream from Father Kun diverted the police captain's attention for the moment. "No, we must finish our holy mission. Death to the Jews and anyone who protects them." The priest raised his machine pistol in the direction of the captain and Per Anger, as did the Arrow Cross officer, who had drawn his revolver during the distraction.

Shots were fired. The impact threw the priest backwards, his weapon and crucifix falling onto the promenade that paralleled the Danube, making no sound in the accumulated snow. The priest died before he hit the ground. Ten feet away, the Arrow Cross officer had slumped to the ground, a red stain spreading across the front of his uniform.

***

Teca inserted another ammunition clip in her smoking machine pistol, still staying in the shadows and watching. She was glad she had waited. But there was no elation. The Nazis not only murdered her family, they turned her into a killer. For that, as well, she hated the Germans.

The Arrow Cross guards, no longer having the stomach for their mission, faded into the streets of Pest. Anger and the Hungarian police escorted George and the other Jews to a warm safe house.

Teca joined Solomon, and the two partisans disappeared into the mean streets of the city.

Wallenberg is here!

Buda, Apartment of Alexander and Elizabeth Kasser, Christmas Day, 1944

Elizabeth Kasser extended her hand and squeezed her guest's fingers affectionately. "Welcome, Raoul. I'm awfully glad you got here safely. I worried. How you manage to navigate these streets without getting caught, I can't imagine."

"A good chauffeur and a sturdy Swedish staff car, I guess," he replied and smiled at Langfelder, standing next to him.

She turned, with a bright smile, to the chauffeur. "Thank you for protecting our dear friend." Embarrassed, Langfelder merely looked down.

Alexander Kasser laughed. "At least today, both of you will have a decent meal."

Wallenberg shook his hand. "You and Elizabeth are very brave to remain in Budapest now. I would understand if you left. After all, you have children."

Elizabeth handed Wallenberg a glass of wine, explaining, "The children are safely out of Budapest. But if we left, who would represent the Swedish Red Cross?"

"Your efforts, though, are beyond the call of duty," Wallenberg offered. "I heard about the fifty children you and Alexander saved yesterday."

Elizabeth looked in Wallenberg's eyes. "Can you imagine people so perverted that they slaughter babies? We were very lucky this time. The Arrow Cross came to the Orphans' Home on Munkácsi Mihály Street…"

Wallenberg nodded. "I know the one. I set it up myself for children whose parents had been killed or deported."

Elizabeth stared at her glass of wine for a moment. "Anyway, they took all the children, over fifty of them, and began marching them down to the Danube. I don't have to tell you what that means." Wallenberg looked at her, grim faced. She continued. "Maurice, the home's director, managed to get away to alert us. We raced to the Chain Bridge with a few Red Cross trucks but without much hope because more than an hour had elapsed. But fate, or I should say, Allied bombers, intervened. As the Arrow Cross and the children approached the Danube, bombs started falling. Everyone scattered, including the children. The Arrow Cross men shot some fleeing children, but most of them escaped in the chaos and ran back toward the orphanage. We found them wandering the street, terrified." Tears rolled down her cheek. She brushed them away.

"Those poor children told me about one lame little boy who was shot in the head by one of the Arrow Cross simply because he couldn't keep up." She took out a handkerchief and dabbed her eyes. "For the life of me, Raoul, I cannot imagine such brutality. My mind simply cannot conceive it."

Wallenberg squeezed her arm. "I know, I'm sick to the core about what's happening. But we can't give in to it. There are still 100,000 Jews in Budapest and we must continue to try to protect them."

Elizabeth, sniffling, shook her head. "I don't know how we can, Raoul, I just don't know."

"Enough macabre talk, Elizabeth," Alexander interposed. "Do we have time for more pleasant things before dinner?" She nodded. "Then let's give them their gifts!"

Elizabeth forced a smile. She disappeared into another room. Wallenberg looked puzzled. "Gifts? But how? We have nothing to give you."

Elizabeth came out with brightly wrapped parcels. "Don't worry, you'll have plenty of opportunity to reciprocate when you return to Stockholm."

"*If* I return," Wallenberg muttered.

She shook her finger at him. "I heard that. I forbid any more pessimism tonight. Now open your present."

Wallenberg smiled. "Gifts, Christmas dinner—how do you manage, Elizabeth? You're an amazing woman."

She watched expectantly as Langfelder tore off the wrapping quickly and held up a fine fountain pen. Overcome with emotion, he could only nod his thanks.

Wallenberg was more deliberate, carefully removing the wrapping paper. An impatient Elizabeth, exclaimed, "Oh, just open it, Raoul, it's cheap paper."

Nodding, he ripped off the rest of the wrapping and held a small, beautiful Greek statue up to the light.

"That's Pallas Athena, the goddess of wisdom," Elizabeth announced. The Kassers were noted for their art collection and Wallenberg knew that's where this statue came from.

Wallenberg is here!

"It's exquisite. It will start me on the way to my own collection." He bent over and kissed her cheek. Then he shook Alexander's hand. "Thank you so much."

They sat down to dinner, toasting the coming of the Soviet liberators and the demise of the SS and the Arrow Cross. After dinner, Wallenberg pulled his host aside. "I didn't want to ruin Elizabeth's Christmas party," he whispered, "but last night, Vöczköndy's Arrow Cross men raided the Swedish Legation itself, apparently determined to take the staff to western Hungary. Lars Berg and two other Swedish diplomats were taken away—we haven't heard from them—and Greta Bauer and another secretary were carried to the Central Ghetto."

Alexander nodded. "Let me see what I can do tomorrow through the good offices of the Red Cross."

Elizabeth and Langfelder joined them. "So, Raoul, what are you going to do when Budapest is liberated?"

"Go back to Stockholm and tell the country and the world about the horrors of Budapest. I hope to raise enough money to reunite Hungarian families and care for the Jews in the Central Ghetto. They are going to need food and medical supplies and a great deal of assistance." He smiled. "First, though, I will see my family, especially my mother, sister and brand new niece. Nina had a baby girl right after I arrived in Budapest. Eventually, of course, I must find gainful employment."

"But you're a Wallenberg!" Elizabeth looked perplexed. "You mean to tell me that in your family's vast financial and industrial empire…"

Wallenberg cut her off. "Wrong side of the family, I'm afraid. The fathers and grandfathers of my cousins Marcus and Jacob were the industrialists. My ancestors were only diplomats, naval officers and advisers to kings."

"But surely…"

"That, dear Elizabeth, is why they have so much money." Wallenberg chuckled. "They know how to protect it, especially from their poorer relatives."

As evening approached, Wallenberg and Langfelder took their leave. Langfelder dropped Wallenberg off in front of Anger's apartment on Uri Street. Wallenberg moved every night in his effort to remain elusive. Tonight, Anger would be his host.

Buda, Apartment of Per Anger, Several Hours Later

Anger and his guest heard a light rap on the door. They picked up their pistols and silently approached the entrance, barricaded with a heavy chair wedged under the door handle. Another rap.

"Per, it's me, Raoul. Open up," a voice said, just loud enough to be heard through the panels.

Anger nodded to the other man, who removed the chair and unbolted the door.

Wallenberg, in his black winter coat and homburg, with a red scarf wound several times around his neck, swept apparition-like, into the room. He looked at the stranger and then at Anger, his face registering concern.

Anger smiled. "It's all right. This is George Libik, a resistance fighter. Like you, he needs shelter this evening."

Wallenberg looked at his colleague. "What little diplomatic immunity you possess, you may lose by hiding resistance fighters."

Anger shrugged. "Like you, I must do what I must do." He held up the machine pistol. "Besides, he's familiar with these playthings."

The three men spent the night barricaded in the apartment, automatic pistols within easy reach. With Lars Berg and several other diplomats missing, the weapons that Berg had had the foresight to stockpile here and at various other locations were now being used for their own protection.

Anger told Wallenberg of the Arrow Cross raids on Section C offices. "They were looking for you, Raoul, and took out their frustrations on the Jews. It was only through Pál Szálai's intervention and that of some unidentified partisans that I was able to avert a wholesale slaughter of hundreds of our workers."

Wallenberg looked grim. "Budapest's turned into a continuing nightmare. Now they are raiding children's homes. Today—Christmas day, the day of Our Lord—they broke into a protected house and killed two elderly ladies and three small children. Just shot them, right in the house. These animals take children down to the Danube and throw them in—mere children for God's sake," he growled. "Is there no decency or humanity left in this city?"

Anger grasped his friend's shoulder. "You've done more than enough, Raoul. Get the hell out of Budapest now, before they catch you. They'll kill you, you know."

Wallenberg shook his head. "That's what they want me to do, flee with my tail between my legs. We're the only thing standing between them and a free reign of terror. No, there's still too much to be done. We have tens of thousands of Jews in both ghettos to protect from Eichmann. I have to hang on until the Soviets get here. I'm too close and have come too far to abandon these people now."

Anger squeezed Wallenberg's shoulder harder. "My dear friend, what can you possibly do if Eichmann persuades the Wehrmacht to level the Central Ghetto, the way they did in Warsaw?"

Wallenberg examined his fingernails, then looked up. "Something will come to me—but only if I stay."

Pest, A Safe House, December 26, 1944

The day after Christmas a combined SS and Arrow Cross force raided a Swedish safe house on Üllöi Street, a block from Section C offices. Arrow Cross men herded three hundred inhabitants into the street. Many of the Jews were waving their *Schutzpasses* at the guards.

An SS officer grabbed one of the passports and tore it into several pieces, dropping it in the gutter. "That's what Swedish protection means today—nothing—and Wallenberg is not here to protect you."

One Jew emerged from the building with a suitcase. The Arrow Cross leader grabbed it out of his hands and threw it against the brick wall of the building. It split open, spilling clothes and personal effects on the sidewalk. "You don't need luggage because soon you will be dead."

***

Word of the raid came to Wallenberg and Anger at Anger's apartment by way of a runner from Section C. Out of breath, he could barely get the words out. "They were marched to the local SS headquarters, not far from Üllöi Street."

Wallenberg grabbed his coat. "Langfelder and the legation car, where are they?"

"He never returned last night," was the reply. "He's missing."

Anger fetched his own coat. "Come on, we'll use my car." He turned to the resistance fighter. "Libik, can you drive?"

"I'll be glad to," Libik said, "but what can only two of you do? They're already at SS headquarters."

"Leave that to us. You just stay in the car." Wallenberg was out the door.

It was early, the streets were empty and no bombers appeared overhead. They made good time, even while dodging the debris from last night's bombing raid.

In the back of the sedan, Anger turned to Wallenberg. "If Eichmann is out to get you, you shouldn't be marching into SS headquarters."

"I'm not too worried about that. The Germans won't openly harm me. They'd arrange an 'accident.'" He smiled and patted Anger's hand. "I'm as safe at SS headquarters as anywhere."

The two diplomats climbed out of the car while Libik was still rolling to a stop in front of the SS headquarters. Anger turned to the driver. "Look, since the SS is looking for you, if you feel in any danger, take off. We'll find our way back." Libik nodded, cradling the submachine gun in his lap as Wallenberg and Anger disappeared into the building.

A captain met them on Anger's demand to see the officer in charge.

"You must release citizens under the protection of the Royal Swedish Legation, seized illegally on Swedish territory. You've violated our sovereignty," declared Anger.

The captain shook his head. "These are Hungarian citizens and you have no jurisdiction. We are assisting the Hungarian government. You have no right to interfere in its internal affairs."

Wallenberg stepped forward to confront the captain, the diplomat's face inches from the officer's. He barked, "Do you know who we are? You were just addressing—and insulting—Secretary of the Swedish Legation, Per Anger. Don't you know that our Foreign Ministry represents German interests in important countries around the world? And this is how you treat us? It will not bode well for you to ignore our legal and reasonable demands." The captain took a step back. Wallenberg immediately closed the gap. "Do I have to get Proconsul Veesenmayer here or have our ambassador in Berlin complain to Hitler to resolve the serious diplomatic breach you caused?"

"I-I need authority to release the prisoners."

Wallenberg nodded his understanding. He pointed to a clerk. "You, give me a sheet of blank paper."

He took the paper and looked at the captain. "How many people do you have imprisoned in there?"

"We counted 301."

Wallenberg scribbled on the sheet of paper and signed it. He handed it to Anger for his signature. Then Wallenberg shoved the paper at the captain. "There, a receipt by two Swedish diplomats for all 301 people—your written authority."

The SS captain looked at the paper for several seconds. "I just don't know…"

"Let me put it to you as straight as I can. The city is surrounded, you know that. Save these men, Captain, and I promise your safety after the Russians win the war."

The captain nodded. "The name is Eisenbein, Karl Eisenbein."

Wallenberg jotted the name down. "You won't regret this, Eisenbein."

***

Meanwhile Libik waited impatiently. He cracked his knuckles. It had been over twenty minutes. He ought to leave and let the legation know. No, he decided, he'd wait a few more minutes. No sooner had he finished that thought when Anger and Wallenberg came out the main entrance. Libik's jaw dropped. Hundreds of men and women followed them out of SS headquarters. He rolled down his window, as Anger approached. "How…?"

Anger put up his hand. "Never mind that for now, just follow us. We are going to walk these people back to the safe house. It's only two blocks away."

Libik kept the car down to a slow crawl as he watched a march to safety and life—over three hundred people led by two unarmed Swedish diplomats. It was very different from the marches he'd become used to.

Buda, Majestic Hotel, Eichmann's Office, the Same Day

Eichmann, at his desk, eyed Hungarian Interior Minister Gábor Vajna, waiting for his reaction. "I want all the Jews in the

International Ghetto moved to the Central Ghetto. Then we can annihilate them all at once. Right now, they are too spread out."

Vajna smiled. "I will issue the necessary orders to round them up and decree that any Jew found concealed outside the Central Ghetto will be summarily executed. Is that sufficient?"

Eichmann nodded. "The members of the Judenrat are no longer of any use to me. They shall be executed."

"You want my men to do it?" Vajna offered.

Eichmann shook his head and smiled icily. "No, Minister. This is one project I want to supervise personally." After Vajna left, Eichmann phoned General August Schmidthuber, commander of the German Budapest garrison, to arrange a meeting.

Buda, Wehrmacht Headquarters, an Hour Later

When he heard Eichmann's demand, General Schmidthuber exploded. "You think I have nothing else to do but kill Jews, Colonel? I have to defend Budapest, just in case you've forgotten."

While the general paced, Eichmann calmly sat watching him. "You have no choice. Those are the Führer's orders."

General Schmidthuber flopped heavily into his chair. "Just like the Führer's orders to hold this godforsaken place to the last man? What a waste of resources and lives!"

Eichmann leaned forward, his eyes narrowed and he tightened his hand, the one with the death's head ring, into a fist. "General…"

Schmidthuber put up his hand. "Save your Gestapo looks, gestures and spiel for someone else, colonel. It's a little late in the game to worry about you pencil-pushing bastards being awarded Iron Crosses for killing millions of unarmed civilians. Besides, if you arrest me, who'll defend of this place. You?"

"Are you saying you refuse to follow orders?" Eichmann rasped.

"No, Colonel, I am still a soldier and I will do as ordered. I just get really angry receiving my orders through the likes of you. I will kill your Jews with men I could have used to defend this worthless place. I follow even stupid orders, Colonel, and this is among the stupidest. Now, if you don't mind, I have work to do."

Eichmann stood. "One more thing, General. Your orders are also to find and kill Raoul Wallenberg."

"You want me to do some more of your dirty work? I'm a soldier, not an assassin."

"Orders of the *Reichsführer*." He handed the general a one-page order. He did not tell the general that he, Eichmann, had forged the order. Without looking, the general dropped it on his "crazy orders" pile.

CHAPTER 19

Buda, Swedish Legation, December 27, 1944

Minister Danielsson assembled his diplomats. To their great joy, Berg and other missing diplomats surfaced, having escaped the clutches of the Arrow Cross. The gathering talked excitedly about the escape until Danielsson quieted them. "We have important decisions to make, so let's have your attention. I have been in contact with our foreign minister for instructions. He left it up to me to decide whether we leave Budapest."

Wallenberg shook his head. "There's no way I'm leaving." Anger and Berg echoed his declaration.

Danielsson nodded. "That's what I thought you'd say, so I advised the foreign minister that most of us would be staying. Any one of you who feels otherwise is, of course, free to leave."

Danielsson looked around. No one stirred. "Second item: The Hungarian Foreign Ministry has invited the entire legation staff to a boar hunting party in western Hungary with the prime minister." His audience snickered. He put up his hands. "I know, but you haven't heard the best part. We've been told to dress warmly because it's cold. Isn't their motherly concern touching? Vajna said a bus will pick us up here tomorrow morning."

Anger snorted. "Does he think we're that gullible? One minute he's threatening us, the next he's trying to entertain us royally. It's a ruse to get us out of Budapest."

Danielsson nodded. "Obviously, so I told Vajna that only Anger, Berg and Ekmark would go. Wallenberg and the others, and I, would stay in Budapest."

Anger shook his head. "Thanks a lot, Minister."

"Let me finish," Danielsson snapped. "That called his bluff. Vajna called me back an hour later, canceling the hunt. He said the proximity of the Russians made the outing too dangerous."

Berg spoke up. "At Minister Danielsson's request, I just checked with Pál Szálai. He sniffed around—the real destination of the 'hunt' was Szombathely."

"The bastard," growled Wallenberg.

"True," replied Danielsson. "But nevertheless, we can't keep thumbing our noses at the Arrow Cross government. They want us to relocate to Szombathely. I'm afraid I'll have to give them something. I'm going to tell Vajna that we'll send one representative to Szombathely."

Berg's eyes met Danielsson's. "We should have recognized their government. It would have helped our efforts to protect the Jews."

Danielsson didn't flinch at the criticism. "As you know, I never agreed with you on that issue. On moral grounds, I don't like recognizing rogue governments like the Arrow Cross."

"What we should do in a theoretical moral vacuum, and what we do as a matter of practical strategy to save lives, may be very different," Wallenberg interjected.

"Look," Danielsson grumped, "even though I didn't agree, I understood all your positions and did try. I sent several telegrams to Stockholm urging some sort of recognition to make our continued rescue work possible, hoping to save face all around. But now, the argument's moot. Our foreign ministry just won't do it."

Wallenberg spread his arms and shook his head. "Then perhaps it will protest the latest Vajna outrage. He told me I'd better take my Jews out of Budapest or I'll find them floating in the Danube."

"I'll deliver a note on my own authority," Danielsson promised, "not that it will do much good." Looking at no one in particular, he asked, "Have we located Greta Bauer and the other secretary yet?"

"I asked the Red Cross to search the Central Ghetto," Wallenberg replied. "I am pleased to report that they have been found and taken to a safe place." The diplomats applauded, then stood up to leave.

Anger raised up his hand. "Before you leave, listen for a moment. Avoid all Arrow Cross encounters until the Soviets get here. We must take Vajna's threats seriously. Find yourselves places to stay at night other than your own homes."

"I'll see what Szálai can do for us," Wallenberg volunteered.

Pest, Pál Szálai's Office, the Same Day

"Pál," Wallenberg said, "we need help. I fear for the lives of my associates."

Szálai smiled. "I'm glad you consider me a friend." He handed Wallenberg a sheet of paper. "Here's a list of safe night places for your diplomats and staff. I will assign a guard to each of these sites during the nighttime hours. As for you, two of my veteran policemen will be available to escort you whenever you wish."

Wallenberg ran a hand through his thinning hair. "You've been a loyal and helpful ally. I am going to make good on that promise to take you to Sweden after the liberation. I'll get you an audience with King Gustav himself."

Szálai nodded. "This has been a terrible year for both of us. I've been a strong supporter of the Nyilas Party, I admit it. In my defense, I really thought Hungary needed the Arrow Cross. But when I saw the brutality…" He bowed his head, shuffling some papers on his desk.

Wallenberg waited for Szálai to complete his sentence. Then he cleared his throat. "I have another favor to ask of you."

Szálai looked up. Wallenberg thought a moment, shifting in his chair. He finally spoke. "The Jews trapped in the Central Ghetto need protection from the marauding bands of Arrow Cross entering the ghetto. Can you provide guards?"

Szálai frowned. "That'll take a lot of policemen. I can get them, but I don't have the money to pay them."

"I anticipated that," said Wallenberg, opening his briefcase. "This should help." He handed Szálai a bundle of *pengös*.

Szálai hefted the roll. "That's enough for the time being."

Wallenberg stroked his chin. "Your Arrow Cross government is bent on destroying the Jews, so I tried appealing to the Wehrmacht, but the Germans have turned a deaf ear. Their only concern right now is the Soviets."

Szálai snickered. "Not quite their only concern, if Colonel Eichmann has his way. I've heard that Vajna and Eichmann have been meeting daily. They're planning to enlist the German army in their murderous scheme. My police can handle the Arrow Cross thugs in the Central Ghetto. But Wehrmacht…?" He shook his head.

Wallenberg spread his arms. "Damn, the Soviets are so close. Their artillery now reaches into the city proper. Maybe, just maybe, we'll be lucky."

Szálai looked at his visitor sympathetically. "I wouldn't rely on wishful thinking."

"You're right, of course, but I have a few more ideas, so we'll just see."

"You must be careful. Vajna has ordered your assassination. It's not even safe for you to be meeting with me."

After a moment's thought, Szálai said, "There's a Christian friend of mine, Károly Szabo, who's fiercely anti-Arrow Cross, but they don't know it. He can circulate freely throughout the city. He's willing to act as a messenger between us." As Wallenberg's forehead creased, Szálai smiled. "No need to worry. I would trust Szabo with my life."

Wallenberg nodded.

The telephone rang. Szálai answered. He frowned, hung up and leaped out of his chair, grabbing his greatcoat. "That was Lars Berg. An Arrow Cross raid of the Swedish Legation annex at 20 Revai Street is underway. Come on, I'll take a squad of policemen."

***

Despite the artillery barrage falling on the city, police cars raced through the streets of Pest, sirens blaring. Pulling up to the Revai Street house, one corner of which had been destroyed by a shell hit, Wallenberg jumped out of the lead car and pushed through the door to the courtyard. Eighty inhabitants of the building, legation employees and their families, were lined up against a wall. A familiar sight to him by now. The green-uniformed Arrow Cross guards shouted anti-Semitic obscenities at them while two Arrow Cross leaned over a light machine gun. One adjusted the tripod and took aim, the other inserted the ammunition belt.

Whispers of "Wallenberg is here!" could be heard.

Wallenberg stepped in front of the machine gun. "I am a Swedish diplomat and these people are my legation's employees."

The gunner looked up at Wallenberg. "Then you can join them."

A voice boomed out behind them, "Not likely."

Pál Szálai, machine pistol cradled in his arms, took aim at the machine gun triggerman. Behind him, armed Budapest police filled the courtyard.

The gunner looked up at Szálai, shrugged, and began to disassemble the machine gun. Other Arrow Cross men slipped out of the courtyard, one by one, disappearing into the street. One bent down to pick up the bundle of rings and jewelry they had taken off the Jews. A swift kick from Szálai sent the man sprawling. "Just get the hell out of here before I shoot your balls off." The man scrambled to his feet and limped out of the building. A middle-aged woman stepped away from the wall, walked up to the Swedish diplomat and hugged him.

Buda, Office of Proconsul Veesenmayer, December 29, 1944

Anger waited in the proconsul's office while Veesenmayer read Wallenberg's memorandum detailing the imprisonment of seventy thousand Jews in the Central Ghetto, the conditions of starvation there and the inhumanity of moving Jews from the International Ghetto and safe houses to the already impossibly crowded Central Ghetto. Anger had convinced Wallenberg, with a price on his head, not to attend this meeting.

Veesenmayer put down the memo and looked at Anger. "So, what's your point, *Herr Legationsekretär?*"

"It should be obvious, Sir. Since you, as the highest German authority in Budapest, have the power to stop these brutal acts, it is you who will bear full responsibility for them if they continue."

Veesenmayer eyed Anger, unmoved. "I don't think so. Sweden has made its bed and now you Swedes must lie in it. You and the other neutrals have not lived up to your promises to recognize the Arrow Cross government. They, and we, therefore, are not bound by any prior agreements with the neutrals. But for your meddling, the Jews would all have been deported and there would be no 'brutal' conditions in Budapest." He shrugged. "Sweden has no one to blame but itself."

Anger glared at the proconsul, "Just drop the euphemisms, why don't you? Everyone knows what 'deporting' means. It won't be long before you and your superiors will answer for your crimes." He stood up, grabbed his overcoat and left.

Veesenmayer shouted at Anger's retreating back. "Tell Herr Wallenberg he'd do himself a favor hiding in some cellar instead of risking his neck for a bunch of dirty Jews." Anger heard the laughter as he slammed the door behind him.

Wallenberg is here!

Pest, Cellar of a Safe house, the Same Day

Wallenberg looked over his chief lieutenants in Section C. "Pass the word around to all the Jews in the International Ghetto that the safe houses are no longer immune. Jews should try to find shelter with trustworthy Gentiles, churches or convents. More important—they have to stop making the roundups easy for the SS and Arrow Cross. They must remove all identification that labels them Jews. That means no yellow stars, no prayer shawl fringes showing, and no skullcaps. We can create chaos and havoc with the Nazi extermination program simply by not cooperating with their murderous plans."

Hugo Wohl objected. "Some of the older Jews will resist. They're petrified of not following Gestapo orders."

Wallenberg slammed the palm of his hand on the wooden table and raised his voice. "Damn it, you tell them that if I see a yellow star, I will shoot the wearer myself. Get it through their heads that a yellow star is a death sentence. Their only salvation is defying the Germans!"

Wohl nodded.

"All Section C employees will move to the main legation building in Buda. And tell any member of the *Judenrat* you can locate to remain in hiding. Under no circumstances, and I mean none, are they to meet with Eichmann. I just received word from Szálai that the colonel personally plans to murder them. Is that clear?"

Wohl nodded again.

Pest, Offices of the *Judenrat*, Sip Street, and Buda, the Offices of Eichmann and of General Schmidthuber, Late Evening

Eichmann, who had been drinking heavily, entered the *Judenrat* with two of his SS henchmen armed with machine pistols. He walked unsteadily toward the frightened janitor, Jacob Takacs, and leaned over the short man. Takacs could smell the heavy odor of whiskey on the colonel's breath.

"Where are they?" Eichmann screamed, his words slurring.

Takacs backed away a step. "Who, Sir?"

"The council members, you idiot. They were supposed to be at my office at nine o'clock this evening. It's now eleven."

Takacs bowed his head. "I-I'm sorry, Sir. They probably thought the meeting was for nine tomorrow morning. A misunderstanding, I'm sure."

"Get them here immediately!"

"But I don't know where they are, Sir, I'm just the janitor here. I take care of…"

"Oh, shut up and listen, you old Jew. You tell them that they'd better be at my office at nine in the morning or they'll face the most horrible consequences. Is that clear?"

Takacs nodded vigorously.

Eichmann looked at one of the SS bodyguards and gestured toward Takacs. The bodyguard stepped forward and smashed the janitor on the temple. Then he did it again. The old man collapsed, bleeding profusely.

Eichmann bent over close to the assaulted man's ear. "That's so you'll remember." The bodyguard leaned over Takacs, raising the butt of his pistol again. Eichmann grabbed his arm. "That's enough, I don't want you to kill him. We can do that tomorrow, after he delivers the message."

***

On Eichmann's return to his office in Buda, an aide gave him a written message from General Schmidthuber—the Soviets were in the eastern suburbs of the city. Major Krumey entered the office. "I saw the message from the general. What are your plans, Sir?"

"To get the hell out of here. I suggest you do the same. Have the office staff remain and burn all the files."

"But Colonel, the escape corridor may be closed at any time. They'll be trapped here."

Eichmann shrugged. "They are Gestapo and that's their duty. After they burn the files they can join the Waffen SS and help defend the city."

"But as Gestapo, the local populace and Jews will be out to slaughter them," protested Krumey.

Eichmann smiled. "We'll take care of the Jews. As for the rest of the populace, the staff will simply have to defend themselves for the glory of the fatherland."

Wallenberg is here!

Eichmann gathered up his papers and swept out of the office and to the street to a waiting staff car. "Drive past General Schmidthuber's headquarters."

***

The middle-aged general looked much older than his years. He glanced up and as Eichmann entered his office. "Now what, Colonel?" he sighed. "I don't have time for your games."

"Have you found Wallenberg?"

"Is that all you care about? Did anyone ever tell you that you have a one-track mind? If we find him, I will do as the *Reichsführer* ordered, but I'm not going to devote a lot of soldiers needed to defend the city to search for him."

Eichmann leaned on the desk. "What are your plans for annihilating the ghetto?"

"It will be handled. I will be glad to turn over the responsibility to you, Colonel, if you want. You are staying with us until the last man falls, aren't you?" he asked sarcastically.

Eichmann glared at Schmidthuber. "That's your job, General. Mine is internal security and I am needed elsewhere."

"Spoken like a true, heroic Aryan Gestapo officer, avoiding any confrontation if the enemy can fight back."

Eichmann curled his lip, gave a smart *Heil* Hitler, and left. The general did not bother returning the salute.

Eichmann climbed into his staff car and poured himself a brandy. "To Vienna," he ordered.

CHAPTER 20

Budapest, January 3, 1945

The new year saw an Arrow Cross gone wild. Anti-Jewish incidents occurred daily all over the city. Frustrated Arrow Cross men, unable to find significant numbers of Jews because they had removed their yellow stars and melted into the general population, began raiding hospitals and orphanages, killing doctors, nurses, the ill and children. They caught and shot three members of the *Judenrat*.

Forty Arrow Cross gunmen attacked a safe house on Vadász Street, where hundreds of Zionist youths were forging papers and hundreds of others, deserters from the labor battalions, hid from the war. Only the armed intervention of Szálai's police saved them. In yet another Arrow Cross raid on the Swedish Legation itself, the Arrow Cross rounded up Section C workers and marched them through the streets. On the way the guards argued among themselves whose turn it was to brave the bitter cold to take the Jews down to the Danube to be shot. The police, this time led by the go-between, Károly Szabo, burst on this scene and freed the captive workers.

Between the Allied bombing and the Soviet artillery, much of the city was reduced to rubble. This state of affairs, plus the increasing hostilities toward Jews, prompted Anger, Berg and Danielsson to plead with Wallenberg to stay out of Pest and remain in the relative safety of Buda. He refused, insisting on being near his Jews.

Buda, Office of the Foreign Minister, January 6, and January 8, 1945

Foreign Minister Vajna looked at the high official of the Budapest Police through hooded eyes. "Let me understand this. That Jew-Swede is proposing to meet with me? For what purpose?"

Szálai shrugged. "The message I received was that he has something you desperately need; he wants to trade."

Wallenberg is here!

You've been kissing that Wallenberg's ass. Don't think I don't know," snorted Vajna. "Playing on both sides of the fence may get you killed."

Szálai leaned forward. "All I'm interested in is maintaining a shred of law and order in this city. God knows this place is a jungle thanks to the scum that the Arrow Cross military has recruited. If kissing Wallenberg's ass will save lives, so be it. I am sorry if you take offense to my objection to the thugs killing of unarmed women and children. You know I have always been a loyal supporter of the Arrow Cross, but these depravities cross the line. Nevertheless, I shall remain at my post."

Vajna looked down at his hands. "If you're finished justifying your treachery, suppose you tell me how we can set up a meeting."

Wallenberg had been right after all, Szálai thought. Vajna's curiosity had been piqued. "Wallenberg needs a safe conduct guarantee and the meeting should be in Pest."

Vajna nodded. "Against my better judgment, I grant the safe conduct. We will meet at three this afternoon in the Town Hall cellar. We'd probably end up there anyway with all the bombs and shells raining down on us."

Pest, The Town Hall, Later that Day

Wallenberg showed up at the Town Hall precisely at three o'clock. A Hungarian gendarme led Wallenberg into the cellar. A table had been set up and Vajna sat behind it. He said, smiling coldly, "Well, Herr Wallenberg, things are not going so well for you and your Jews, eh?"

"No worse than for you and your German masters, Minister, with the Soviets closing in on all sides. I know there is little food available to feed your men."

"Enough of this banter," Vajna snapped. "What do you propose?"

"A simple tit for tat, Minister. Order your Arrow Cross men to cease all raids on our safe houses and attacks on Jews and I will supply food to the Arrow Cross. If they resume their attacks, I will stop the shipments."

Vajna frowned. "You must also tell us where your food supply is stored. We will protect it for both our sakes."

"I don't think so, Minister," Wallenberg replied crisply. "This deal is the only one I can offer. You stop the attacks and I supply the food. It's that simple."

"I could have you killed where you sit."

"I know, but then you'd never get the food your men need for the forthcoming battle."

Vajna shrugged. "Very well, I agree, but I must know quantities."

Wallenberg rose. "Fine, when my people tell me tomorrow that the attacks have ceased, I will truck in enough food to feed one thousand men. Every other day, so long as there are no attacks on the Jews, we will ship in like amounts."

***

The truce lasted for two days and one truckload of food. Then, on Saturday, January 8, the Arrow Cross marched five thousand Jews from safe houses to the Central Ghetto. Wallenberg met again with Vajna.

Vajna didn't waste any time. "All the Jews in the International Ghetto must move to the Central Ghetto, now."

Wallenberg glared at Vajna. "So much for your word. The Arrow Cross will get no more food from me."

Vajna stood and banged on the table. "Listen to me, Jew-attaché. Any Jew who hides or resists being transferred to the Central Ghetto will be found floating face down in the Danube. Do I make myself clear?"

"Perfectly. And let me make myself clear. I will see that you pay for any murders."

Vajna laughed. "Empty words, Herr Wallenberg, empty words. When we get all your Jews sealed in the Central Ghetto, they will, in due time, be cut down by the machine guns of the Arrow Cross and the Waffen SS. Chew on that, Herr Wallenberg!"

Pest, a Cellar, January 8, 1945

Vajna worked hard to make good on his threat to herd every Jew into the Central Ghetto. The Jews, however, had disappeared into the churches, convents and homes of sympathetic Gentiles. Those who ventured into the street did so with no visible signs of their

Jewishness. The Arrow Cross, under orders to liquidate Jews and Wallenberg, roamed the streets like packs of hungry wolves, rounding up anyone they found and raiding homes at random. Meanwhile, half of Pest had become the latest battleground of World War II, with German and Hungarian troops fighting the advancing Soviets, street-by-street, house-by-house. Most citizens huddled in their cellars for the duration. The Gentiles awaited an uncertain fate at "liberation" by Soviet troops. The Jews, of course, felt differently. Anyone who released them from the terror of the SS and the Arrow Cross they would welcome with open arms.

In the midst of this turmoil, the photographer Tom Veres located Wallenberg in one of the Pest cellars. "Raoul, come quickly. The Arrow Cross raided the home of a Swiss family on Väröszmarty Square. They were hiding my parents," he wailed.

"When?"

"Two or three hours ago," Veres cried.

"I'm sorry, Tom, it's too late. Your parents must have been in the group of over a hundred people marched down to the Danube. By the time we could get there, they all had been shot."

Veres collapsed into a chair, holding his head in his hands, convulsed with sobs. Wallenberg sank to one knee and wrapped his arms around Veres, who wept on the Swede's shoulder.

***

Wallenberg spent most of his time hiding in various cellars in Pest. In one such refuge he penned a letter to his mother in time for inclusion in the diplomatic pouch scheduled to go out that day.

> Once again, all you'll get from me are a few lines written in haste. The situation is risky and tense, my workload almost superhuman. Thugs are roaming around the city, beating, torturing, and shooting people. Among my staff alone there have been forty cases of kidnapping and beatings. On the whole we are in good spirits, however, enjoying the fight.... We can hear the gunfire of the approaching Russians here day and night.... Greetings, tender and heartfelt kisses to you and the whole family. Lots of kisses to Nina and the little girl.

Wallenberg also used the time in the cellars to draft a postwar program of recovery for the Jews and for Hungary. He planned to enlist the aid of the Soviets. After all, hadn't the Swedes looked out for Soviet interests in Hungary? Hadn't Soviet prisoners of war been placed under the protection of Berg's Section B? Hadn't wounded Soviet troops been treated at a hospital managed jointly by Swedes and Hungarians?

After Budapest's liberation, Wallenberg planned to see the Soviet commander for the purpose of initiating his program to bring families together; distribute food and medical supplies; set up emergency hospitals to deal with epidemics, disease and malnutrition; construct housing; render economic assistance; provide employment and to return looted business and personal assets to the victims. His priorities, however, were to supply the Central Ghetto, where starvation and disease were most acute, and reunite children with their parents. He called his program the Wallenberg Institution for Support and Reconstruction.

He instructed his chief accountant, Rezsö Müller, and other economists and accountants from the Section C staff, to draw up detailed plans while he went to see the Soviet commander after the city was secured. All the energy he put into saving Jews now would be channeled to the reconstruction of Hungary.

But, as Wallenberg soon discovered, he wasn't yet finished saving Jews, not by a long shot.

Buda, Royal Hotel, January 11, 1945

Pál Szálai headed for a breakfast meeting at the Royal Hotel. The street surrounding the hotel and the hotel lobby itself were filled with German troops and Arrow Cross soldiers. Szálai spotted a friend from the Arrow Cross militia.

"Andor, what's going on?"

"We've been put on alert. The Germans have asked us to help destroy the ghetto. We're waiting to be briefed."

Szálai turned around and rushed out of the hotel.

Wallenberg is here!

Pest, Hazai Bank, January 11, 1945

Wallenberg, Veres, some Section C employees and several Jewish families had found temporary refuge in the vicinity of the International Ghetto in the vault of the Hazai Bank. Finding Langfelder, his missing driver, in the vault delighted Wallenberg.

A few minutes after his arrival, a breathless Károly Szabo burst into the vault, interrupting Wallenberg's discussion of his reconstruction program with members of Section C. Szabo leaned against the wall, pausing to catch his breath.

"...going to kill the Jews in the Central Ghetto."

Wallenberg grabbed his arm. "Slow down, who's going to kill the Jews?"

"The Wehrmacht and the Arrow Cross. They're assembling the troops as we speak. It may already be too late. Szálai awaits your instructions."

Wallenberg slumped in his chair, his sleep-deprived mind trying to focus on the new crisis. Suddenly he leaped up. "I must see General Schmidthuber. He's the only one who can stop it."

Szabo shook his head. "No, Szálai said you mustn't go out. The Germans and Arrow Cross have orders to shoot you on sight. You must tell me what you want Szálai to do."

Wallenberg sat down again, opened his briefcase and took out a sheet of Royal Swedish Legation stationery embossed with the blue and yellow crowns. He scribbled a note. "Here, get this message to General Schmidthuber, and hurry."

Szabo pocketed the note and rushed out of the bank.

Buda, Wehrmacht Headquarters of General Schmidthuber, a Few Minutes Later

General Schmidthuber took off his reading glasses and rubbed his temples. He was tired of looking at maps showing the advances of the Soviet troops, tired of taking orders from a raving maniac and tired of seeing his troops being slaughtered trying to hold godforsaken Budapest. He contemplated his next military move, not that he had many options remaining. An orderly interrupted his thoughts.

"Sir, Hungarian Police officer Pál Szálai is here requesting to see you. He says it is of utmost importance."

General Schmidthuber waved away his orderly. "I don't have time for the Hungarians. Send him away."

Szálai burst past the startled orderly. "I'm sorry, General, but this is of critical concern to you personally. It won't take but a minute." He handed the general Wallenberg's note.

Schmidthuber, annoyed but at the same time, curious, put his reading glasses back on and tore open the envelope. He unfolded the single sheet of Swedish Legation notepaper and read the handwritten message:

> General Schmidthuber:
>
> I implore you. Stop the slaughter of innocents in the Central Ghetto. You are a soldier in the proud tradition of the Prussian military, not a mass murderer of civilians.
>
> If the mass execution of the Jews is carried out, I will see to it personally, that the War Crimes Tribunal charges you with murder and genocide. You will be hanged.
>
> If you desist, then I promise to mount a most vigorous defense on your behalf for acquittal or leniency.
>
> Raoul Wallenberg
> 11 January 1945

The general put down the note and looked over his glasses at Szálai. He smiled ever so slightly. "I see our Herr Wallenberg is alive and well. With the Russians breathing down my neck, is this supposed to frighten me?"

"No, Herr General, it's supposed to present you with other options and support."

The general nodded. "That will be all."

After Szálai left, Schmidthuber picked up the note and re-read it. Putting it down, he closed his eyes, squeezing them with his thumb and forefinger. He knew the Third Reich was finished. Wallenberg was perceptive, going for the general's soft underbelly by saying what the general feared but had dared not think about—his own future. "To hell with him, to hell with them," he muttered. Then he called for his orderly.

"Ring up Colonel Posner right away."

The regular city phone service no longer functioned so the orderly cranked up the field telephone and got the commander of the Budapest garrison on the line.

"Colonel, please come over to my headquarters right now—and bring Minister Vajna and the Arrow Cross commander, Vilmos Lucska, with you. They're in the staging area at the Royal Hotel."

***

Some twenty minutes later, Schmidthuber motioned Colonel Kurt Posner, Commander Lucska and Minister Vajna to sit down. Lucska spoke up. "All our men are in place. We are ready to strike the Jews down in the Central Ghetto." He seemed to be fishing for a compliment.

"Stand your men down," the general demanded. "There will be no massacre. The pogrom's been canceled."

Lucska shot to his feet. "What? Why?"

"Because I have ordered it."

They waited for more, but it was clear that the general was not disposed to further explanation. Lucska shook his head. "That's impossible, we are all prepared to fulfill our destiny. We cannot stop now."

Vajna put up his hand. "I also must protest this last minute weakening of resolve. I agree with Commander Lucska. We will proceed with or without the Germans."

The general looked at Colonel Posner, Waffen SS.

The colonel also stood, ramrod straight, and clicked his heels. "General, in case you've forgotten, we are under the orders of the *Reichsführer*. Only he can rescind them."

The General glowered. "I have no written orders from the *Reichsführer* to that effect, only the word of that coward who abandoned us, Colonel Eichmann. The only written order the Colonel gave me concerned Wallenberg. Do you have a copy of written orders to annihilate the Central Ghetto?"

"No, Herr General, but nevertheless my SS sworn oath is to carry out the Final Solution. I must carry out those orders, as transmitted by Colonel Eichmann."

Now the general rose behind his desk. His face flushed, he drew his pistol and pointed it at Posner's chest. "That, Colonel, is insubordination. Consider yourself under military arrest." Turning to Vajna, he advised, "Minister, I suggest you place your commander under military arrest, as well."

"I will do no such thing! We are not cowards."

"Do you consider killing unarmed civilians acts of bravery, Minister?"

Vajna stood up. "I refuse to discuss this with you any further." He turned toward the door.

"Hold it," the General thundered. They stopped. "Hear me clearly, Minister Vajna, Commander Lucska. Attempt to disobey my orders and I will crush you with all the troops at my command. I hold both of you personally responsible for any harm to the Jews in the ghetto. Or, should I have all of you shot right now and save myself the trouble later?" Glaring at his Hungarian visitors, he snapped, "Now get out." Then he placed Colonel Posner under arrest.

After contemplating his next move Schmidthuber called in his orderly again. "Get General Erich von dem Bach-Zelewsky on the field telephone." A few minutes later, the orderly handed him the telephone.

"General? Schmidthuber here. Prepare to pull all our forces out of Budapest through the western corridor while we still can. Get the word to all the field commanders. My men are not going to be cannon fodder any longer."

He hung up. "To hell with the Führer," Schmidthuber muttered.

CHAPTER 21

Budapest, January 12, 1945

As darkness fell, Wallenberg bade farewell to those with whom he'd shared the shelter of the bank vault for the last three days. His co-workers urged him to stay—it was too dangerous to take to the streets. Mortar rounds, machine gun fire, exploding grenades and the roar of tanks added to the cacophony outside the vault.

"I must keep moving," he insisted. Too many people know where I am. I will only endanger all of you and myself if I stay here."

Wallenberg climbed the stairs to the street level and stuck his head out the front door. He could hear guns firing in the distance, but the area in front of the bank now appeared to be quiet. He stepped into the darkened street, his frozen breath floating beside him in the bone-chilling cold. With the failure of city power, the streetlights were out. A black sedan, its headlights off and brake lights disconnected, gave him a start when it pulled up to the curb next to him. It was Langfelder. Wallenberg jumped in. "I'm going to Benczur Street, to International Red Cross headquarters. It's not far from here."

Langfelder nodded. He had become an expert in the art of driving in Budapest's war-ravaged streets. He drove the sedan with his window open, despite the intense cold. In the darkness, his ears were more reliable than his eyes. Suddenly he braked.

"What is it?" Wallenberg asked.

Langfelder put his forefinger to his lips for quiet. "There! Did you hear it?"

Wallenberg strained to listen, a task made more difficult because he wasn't sure what he was listening for.

Langfelder shifted into reverse and backed slowly down the street to the intersection behind them. He jammed the steering wheel to the left and gunned the engine. As the car leaped forward and swerved into the cross street, Wallenberg caught a brief glimpse of a huge tank just rounding the corner they'd been heading for.

"Whose is it?"

"Russian, probably, but it doesn't matter. They'll fire first and ask questions later."

Ahead about five blocks, red streaks of tracer fire arched across the night sky. Langfelder turned sharply at the next intersection abandoning yet another street.

The normally three-minute trip took a nerve-wracking fifteen minutes. Langfelder reached Benczur Street, easing the sedan into the safety of the enclosed courtyard. Wallenberg turned to him. "Vilmos, I want you to stay here with me until the Russians arrive. It's no use getting yourself killed trying to drive these streets. Besides, I'll need you at a moment's notice, when the opportunity presents itself, to drive me to the Soviet commanding general."

Langfelder nodded.

The ground shook as a shell landed nearby. They climbed out of the car and ran into the building to the comparative safety of the cellar, where George Wilhelm, head of the International Red Cross in Budapest, greeted them.

"They're looking for me," the grim-faced Wallenberg said.

Wilhelm patted him on the back. "Here, you'll be safe from the Arrow Cross. They haven't bothered us. And with the war in the streets, there is nothing more you can do."

While fierce fighting raged outside, Wallenberg spent three days underneath International Red Cross headquarters recovering his strength with food and sleep and working on his report to restore the economy of the city, return the assets and businesses of the Jews and set up emergency teams to tackle the dangers of starvation and disease facing the Central Ghetto.

During these days, he also had some time to contemplate his own future. First he needed a place to live in Stockholm. In one of his last letters, he had asked his mother to look for an apartment for him in a certain neighborhood. Then, he needed a job. Going back into the food export business didn't interest him. Pursue a career in architecture? He'd have to be licensed in Sweden after a period of apprenticeship. That wasn't appealing either. He could go to cousins Jacob and Marcus, hat in hand, for a position somewhere in the vast Wallenberg business empire, but they had never been receptive to that idea. Better not to think about that now.

Wallenberg is here!

Buda, Swiss Legation, January 12, 1945

Per Anger had taken refuge in the Swiss Legation. From Gellért Hill, he could see the fighting down in Pest. The Soviets were pressing close to the Danube on the Pest side. Then he heard shells whistling overhead. A large explosion rattled the windows and set the plates and glasses sailing to their shattered demise. Anger went into the street to reconnoiter. He threw himself on the ground as a Soviet fighter plane suddenly roared overhead, strafing everything in its path with heavy-caliber cannon gunfire.

The Swiss envoy, Charles Lutz, grabbed Anger's arm. "Come, they're zeroing in on this area. We must get to the cellar right away."

As another fighter swooped in, the two men dove into the dark basement, electricity having been knocked out long ago. Anger tripped over a squealing piglet. The basement, in this time of food shortage, now doubled as a pigsty. He found himself a place to sit. Closing his eyes, he realized just how tired he was before drifting into a light sleep. He awoke with a start when an explosion shook the basement. Someone yelled, "Each of you, keep your mouth open if you don't want burst eardrums!"

The next one was closer. The concussion from the burst lifted Anger off his chair. Grunting, squealing pigs darted frantically about the room. The legation must have taken a direct hit. The rattle of small-arms fire eventually replaced the explosions of artillery shells. The Soviet infantry had reached Buda.

Two hours later, relative quiet had returned. The sounds of battle were still there but muffled and farther off. Lutz and Anger emerged from the shelter. Anger had been right—the legation had sustained a direct hit. The room above the entrance to the basement was gone.

Buda, Swedish Legation and Soviet Headquarters, the Same Day

While Danielsson, Anger and other diplomats took shelter in cellars throughout Buda, Berg and several members of Section C elected to remain in the Swedish Legation, or what was left of it. They sat in the basement during the street fighting and the shelling. It was well that they did, because shortly thereafter several direct hits severely damaged the building. When the firing appeared to have died down, they ventured cautiously out of the basement and began inspecting the damage. They retreated to a room that appeared still intact when a Soviet advance patrol found them.

Soviet soldiers herded Berg and the others into the main reception hall where they waited while other soldiers searched the building for Germans. Half an hour later, a Soviet military truck pulled to the front steps. Several soldiers leaped out of the back, rushed into the building and started carrying out paintings, silver and almost anything movable.

Berg pushed past the surprised guard to confront the looting soldiers carrying out legation assets. "This is a legation, Swedish territory," he protested. "We are nonbelligerents and I demand that you stop the pillaging our property and return what you have already taken." The soldiers seemed not to understand Hungarian or German. Their response was to push Berg aside roughly. One soldier put his rifle under Berg's nose and motioned him back into the room with the others. More soldiers followed, demanding that Berg and the others surrender all the valuables on their persons. Berg was nonplused. Although he hadn't expected to be greeted with open arms by the Soviets, he certainly hadn't expected this hostile treatment.

"Who's the person in charge here?" a Soviet Army captain shouted. Berg stepped forward.

"Open the safe."

Berg shook his head. "This is a diplomatic mission. You are forbidden to violate Swedish sovereignty."

The Soviet officer understood German, but unlike the Germans, he was not impressed with Berg's authoritative tone. The captain waited a few moments. Berg simply stood there, defiant, his arms folded across his chest. The captain shrugged and motioned to his sergeant. Several soldiers trotted in, set dynamite charges and blew the safe. They cleaned it out, taking the diplomatic papers and all the money, securities, jewelry and other valuables, including those left for safekeeping by Swedish citizens and Hungarian Jews.

Berg shoved under the nose of the captain, his diplomatic passport and papers showing that the legation represented Soviet interests in Budapest. The officer shook his head. "These are not valid. They're not in Russian. I refuse to accept them."

Berg thought ruefully how he had urged the Foreign Ministry to issue duplicate documents in Russian for just such an eventuality, but the bureaucrats had ignored his request.

Wallenberg is here!

"Very well, then take me to your commanding officer—unless you are willing to accept personal responsibility for this serious diplomatic incident."

The captain paused to think it over and then spoke in Russian to his sergeant.

"Go with the sergeant," the captain ordered.

A military vehicle drove them into Pest and pulled up to one of the relatively undamaged buildings. Already, a Soviet flag hung limply from one of its windows. The sergeant led Berg into a small room and shut the door, leaving him alone.

Ten minutes later, a man in a poorly tailored civilian suit entered and identified himself only as NKVD, the Soviet secret police. He didn't give a name. The agent eyed Berg for a minute, saying nothing, so Berg spoke first, in Hungarian. He had a feeling German would not be well received by this Soviet agent.

"I'm a Swedish diplomat…"

"I know who you are," the man snapped, holding up Berg's passport.

"Then you must also know that I asked to see the commander of your forces. The looting of the Swedish Legation must cease and everything must be returned."

The NKVD officer rubbed his chin, studying Berg. "I also know what you are. You're a German spy. And you don't fool me. You can go back to speaking German as you did at the legation, I understand the language."

Berg shook his head. "That's insane, I'm a Swede, not a German."

The officer smiled. "I know, but your legation, using a diplomatic cover, is really a German espionage nest, and you and that other Swede, Wallenberg, are the leaders of the spy ring."

"Those are crazy and unfounded accusations."

The NKVD officer smiled. "Are they, now? We know that Wallenberg is being financed by the American OSS and Roosevelt and that you were assisting Wallenberg."

"That's ridiculous. Wallenberg was sent to Budapest to save the Jews from the Nazis."

"I'm surprised at such a transparent cover story. No one in his right mind would seriously risk his life to save Jews."

Berg glared at the officer. "Perhaps saving unarmed innocent civilians is a concept foreign to the Soviets, but it is a tradition Sweden values and pursues."

The Soviet agent shook his head. "As a representative of a country that has delivered iron ore to Germany, thereby helping it prosecute the war, you have no standing to object and would do well not to complain so much." He spread his arms and smiled. "But look, I do not wish to argue with you. You are under investigation for spying activity. Admit that the legation represented American and British intelligence interests and perhaps we may release you."

"Hear this clearly, whatever your name is. We did not and do not represent American and British interests, and even if we did, it would not have been for the purpose of spying. I am a Swedish diplomat and until you have the decency to accord my position the respect it deserves, I will say no more."

Berg stared impassively into space. The NKVD agent contemplated Berg for a while and then left the room.

A half-hour later, another man, dressed in better-fitting civilian clothes, opened the door and motioned to Berg to follow him. Berg just sat there.

"Come, come, Secretary Berg. Stop being petulant. I am taking you to see General Tjernysjov, as you requested." The man was undoubtedly another NKVD agent. Berg rose and followed him out of the room.

The man turned to look at Berg and smiled. "By the way, you'll be happy to know that we found your Minister Danielsson and a Margareta Bauer in a house in Buda. They are safe and unharmed and have been returned to the legation."

***

A five-minute ride in a Soviet military vehicle left Berg at the headquarters of the Soviet general. An orderly immediately escorted him into the general's makeshift office. The general, a small, balding man in his fifties, smiled and offered Berg his hand.

Unlike the Soviets whom Berg had previously encountered, General Tjernysjov was respectful and polite. Nevertheless he remained firm.

"I'm sorry, Secretary Berg, but I cannot possibly stop what you call looting while my soldiers are still engaged in a fight to the death in Buda. When the city is secure, I would be pleased to talk again with you. Now, if you'll excuse me, I have important work to do. One of my men will drive you back to your legation."

Budapest, January 13, 1945

The Soviet soldiers fought, pillaged and raped their way through Budapest. Debrecen, in eastern Hungary, became the headquarters of Soviet Field Marshal Rodion Malinovsky. From there, the Supreme Soviet Military Authority for the area announced that a new Hungarian Communist government had been set up, also in Debrecen. Leading politicians in the prior Hungarian capitalist governments were hunted down and arrested. The Cold War, it seemed, had already begun, though neither Wallenberg nor most of the Western World, knew it yet. It would soon become an accepted fact, but too late for Wallenberg.

Pest, International Red Cross Headquarters, Benczur Street, January 13, 1945

From the cellar they could hear the rat-tat-tat of small-arms fire, much more intense in the last hour, and an occasional heavier explosion, probably a mortar or artillery round. The battle had arrived on Benczur Street. George Wilhelm, with reassuring words, comforting thoughts and an occasional pat on the back, circulated among the frightened people filling every corner of the cramped shelter.

Wallenberg's fear of the bombardments hadn't lessened, but his obsession with reaching Soviet military headquarters as soon as possible overrode the great personal risks. Several times, on the verge of leaving the cellar to try to make contact with the Soviet troops, he had changed his mind when the explosions and gunfire erupted nearby. He fidgeted like a racehorse at the starting gate. Dr. Ernö Pëto of the now defunct *Judenrat*, who offered to accompany Wallenberg to see the Soviets, tried to keep the Swedish diplomat calm.

Suddenly the door to the cellar flew open violently. Wallenberg stiffened at the sudden intrusion. Soviet soldiers stood framed in the door opening, their weapons trained on the frightened, huddled figures within. Satisfied that this group presented no threat, the soldiers lowered their weapons and climbed down the stairs.

Wallenberg greeted the first soldier in Russian. "This is the headquarters of the International Red Cross. Most of these people are Red Cross workers." Surprised at hearing his own language, the soldier glanced over to the group.

"I am a Swedish diplomat," announced Wallenberg, pulling out his diplomatic passport. The document was not in Russian. The soldier waved it away.

"Look. See the crowns? That's the seal of the government of Sweden. We are friends, not enemies of the Soviets. As an official of my government, I request to see the commanding general, Field Marshal Malinovsky."

The soldier's eyes widened at the mention of Malinovsky's name. That, and Wallenberg's passable Russian, gave the soldier pause.

"Come with me," he muttered. They mounted the steps to the courtyard, where the soldier spoke to his superior officer. After an animated conversation, only snatches of which Wallenberg could catch, the officer approached Wallenberg.

"You understand Russian?" the officer asked in a belligerent tone.

"Yes. I must see the commanding general on a matter of utmost urgency."

The officer's eyes narrowed. "We are fighting for our lives on these damn streets, digging out Germans and Hungarians, house by house, and you have a matter of 'utmost urgency?'" He emitted a harsh laugh.

Wallenberg glared back. "Swedish diplomats have been representing Russian interests in Budapest and in many countries throughout the world. It would not sit well with Foreign Minister Molotov if you ignored an official Swedish request, which this is. All I ask of you is to let me see your superior."

The officer rubbed his nose with his forefinger. "Go back into the house. There is still fighting going on around here. Later, I will consider your request."

It was the best Wallenberg could do for now, so he pushed no further. He returned to the cellar to wait.

During the next two hours, the explosions became muffled, sounding like distant rolls of thunder, as the battle moved on. Wallenberg realized he hadn't heard any small-arms fire for a while.

He began to wonder if the Soviet officer had forgotten about him or, more likely, just didn't give a damn. He was contemplating venturing outside again when a short, stocky Soviet Army officer, bounded down the steps of the cellar.

"Comrade Wallenberg?"

Wallenberg nodded and stepped forward. The officer stuck out his hand. He had a too powerful handshake, but Wallenberg suppressed the wince.

"Major Dimitri Demchinkov, at your service. Please follow me, if you would."

Wallenberg signaled Langfelder and Pëto to fall in behind him. The major frowned. Wallenberg smiled. "Don't worry, this is my driver, Vilmos Langfelder and my assistant, Dr. Pëto."

The major smiled. "Of course. Do you have a car here?"

Wallenberg nodded. "In the courtyard, if it's still in one piece."

The car still sat undamaged where it had been parked, and the major instructed Langfelder to follow his vehicle to Soviet headquarters on Erzsébet Királynö.

Buda, a Cellar, January 14 to 17, 1944

With the damage to the Swiss Legation on January 13, Anger moved the next day to the cellar of a friendly neighbor. He joined others, who, for days, had been holed up below ground without gas, electricity or water.

Despite the sporadic gunfire, every morning Anger and some others ventured out into the street with pails to collect snow, which they boiled on a wood-burning stove to make tea, thin soup and some water for washing. On the second morning, Anger found a dead German horse lying on the sidewalk in front of the house. He gathered a group from the cellar to make a foray. Brandishing knives, they braved the fighting to cut up the carcass. The owner of the house, a woman who claimed to be a baroness, prepared a dish of Hungarian horse goulash. Anger couldn't recall enjoying a meal more.

Pest, Swedish Legation Annex Office, January 17, 1945

Wallenberg had been gone for three days. There had been no word from him since he left Red Cross building for the Soviet headquarters. Accountant Rezsö Müller fretted. He had been working long hours, preparing the numbers for Wallenberg's proposal for the reconstruction of Hungary and emergency assistance to the Central Ghetto inhabitants. Müller checked with the legation. All the diplomats and employees had been accounted for except Wallenberg and Langfelder. Anger told him that Minister Danielsson would initiate inquiries. Müller worried that Wallenberg might have been caught up in the fighting and been wounded or killed.

He needn't have worried. At midday, Wallenberg came bounding into the Tátra Street offices followed by Dr. Ernö Pëto. Brimming with enthusiasm, Wallenberg announced, "The Soviets have given me permission to see Field Marshal Malinovsky at his headquarters in Debrecen. I am to leave within the hour."

Müller frowned. "Is that smart, Raoul? The Arrow Cross is still determined to kill you and sporadic fighting continues in and around Budapest. Wait a more few days, at least."

"Now is not the time for timidity," replied Wallenberg with annoyance. "Every day that goes by means death by starvation for hundreds. Besides, I am under the protection of Major Demchinkov here." He swept his arm towards the major. The major smiled.

Müller shrugged. "I still think you should wait. It's too dangerous."

Wallenberg laughed. "Rezsö, you're a born worrier. I appreciate your concern, but I'll be safe. After surviving for the past six months, what can possibly happen to me now?"

Major Demchinkov paced impatiently around the office. "We must leave soon," he scolded. "I want to get there before dark."

Wallenberg nodded. He pulled Müller into an empty room. "Keep working on my relief plan. Here, hold this until I get back, it will get our project started." He handed Müller a large roll of currency.

Returning to the large office, Wallenberg announced to the assembled group, "I'll be back in seven days, ten on the outside. You can be sure of that. I will meet with the Russians in charge and the new Hungarian government to get our project moving. Meanwhile, I want all of you, under Rezsö, to keep the operation rolling along."

Müller tried once again. "Let me check with Minister Danielsson, before you go."

Wallenberg grabbed Müller's arm and led him to the window. He pointed to the Soviet motorcycles and military vehicle. "You see? I have an escort." Wallenberg lowered his voice, smiling. "To tell you

Wallenberg is here!

the truth though, I'm not sure if I'm going as their guest or their prisoner." Müller started to say something, but Wallenberg, followed by Langfelder, was already out the door.

***

A blast of cold air hit Wallenberg's face, making him wince. His frozen breath hung suspended above him for an instant before drifting away. The sun was out, but the temperature, still below freezing, had more of a bite because of the breeze. He looked at the Soviet motorcyclists and marveled how they could survive a winter so exposed, especially in battlefield conditions. Had they ridden all the way from Moscow on those things?

Those fleeting, disjointed thoughts were enough to take his mind off important things—like negotiating the slick sidewalk. His heel came down on a patch of ice and first one leg, then the other took on lives of their own, flying out from under him and landing him flat on his back. He lay still for a few seconds, his mind and muscles trying to assess the damage, if any.

"Are you all right?" Wallenberg looked up at an elderly gentleman, a yellow star still stitched to his overcoat, who was bending over him with a look of concern. He extended a hand, which Wallenberg took, careful not to drag the old man down.

Slowly he got to his feet, grimacing in pain, and thanked the old man. Wallenberg then noticed another elderly man behind him, also with a yellow star on his coat. Now Langfelder, who had gone on ahead to the car, came running back.

"Where did you just come from?" Wallenberg asked the elderly gentleman, though he was certain he knew the answer.

"The Central Ghetto. The gates were opened by the Soviets and we just walked out."

Wallenberg smiled and patted the old man on the back. He gave the man a start when he grabbed the yellow star sewn on the coat and tore it off with great flourish. "You don't need that now—or ever again!"

The other elderly man, watching, smiled and ripped off his yellow star. He dropped it into the frozen-over gutter. A gust of wind lifted and floated it to the sky, riding the air currents like a gull. All three watched the patch of yellow, mesmerized.

The honk of a horn by Major Demchinkov broke the spell, and Wallenberg moved toward his car. Notwithstanding his fall, which left him with some dull aches, he felt in a wonderful mood. He turned to look for Dr. Pëto but not seeing him, simply shrugged.

Langfelder opened the door for him. Wallenberg nodded toward the two elderly Jews. "See? My mission hasn't been in vain."

Though he was smiling, Langfelder could also see the tears in Wallenberg's eyes.

Dr. Pëto rushed out of the building and up to Wallenberg. "I know I promised to go with you, but my parents are in Buda and I just heard there's still some fighting going on there and…"

Wallenberg squeezed Pëto's arm. "Don't concern yourself, you're doing the right thing. I'm perfectly safe and I'll come back with the help the people need." They embraced. "God speed, Raoul," Pëto whispered softly.

Wallenberg nodded and climbed into the back of the Swedish staff car.

***

From the second floor window, Rezsö Müller watched the motorcycles roar to life and Wallenberg and his Soviet escort start down the street, turn the corner, and disappear. Neither Müller, Dr. Pëto nor any of Wallenberg's colleagues at the Swedish Legation ever saw him again.

Wallenberg is here!

EPILOGUE

Of the nearly 825,000 Jews in Hungary in 1941, just over 140,000 were left at the end of the war, nearly two thirds of them, and four fifths of the children, perished. Of the 120,000 Jews who survived in Budapest, many, if not most of them owed their lives to the heroic efforts of Raoul Wallenberg, Per Anger, Lars Berg and other neutral diplomats.

***

Adolph Eichmann elected to go into hiding and later escaped to Argentina, but was tracked down by Israeli agents who secretly transported him to Israel in May 1960. There, after a long trial, in which Colonel Kurt Becher testified against him by deposition in Germany, the Israelis, in May 1962, hanged him. Major Dieter Wisliceny was taken prisoner by the Western Allies and after testifying before the International Military Tribunal in Nuremberg, was extradited to Czechoslovakia where he was tried by the Czechs in Bratislava and executed in February 1948 for complicity in mass murder. Colonel Kurt Becher prospered in business ventures in postwar Germany. The fates of General Heinrich Müller and Major Hermann Krumey are unknown.

Baron Gábor Kemény was turned over to the Communist Hungarian government where he was tried, along with Szálasi and other members of the Arrow Cross hierarchy, and sentenced to death by hanging and executed in 1946. The baroness, who gave birth to a son three weeks after leaving Hungary, did not return to Budapest from her journey to Switzerland. She never saw her husband again. She learned of his execution from a BBC radio report.

Heinrich Himmler committed suicide in May 1945, during the Nuremberg trials, by swallowing a poison vial concealed in his mouth. Hitler, it is believed, committed suicide in a bunker in Berlin. Rudolph Höss was tried and executed by a Polish military tribunal. Czech agents assassinated General Reinhard Heydrich in June 1942.

Proconsul Edmund Veesenmayer was sentenced to twenty years in prison for war crimes and released in 1951 on the intervention of the U.S. High Commissioner in Germany.

All the diplomats in the Swedish Legation in Budapest were incarcerated by the Soviets and eventually released, arriving in Stockholm in April 1945. All, that is, except Raoul Wallenberg.

***

This is an historical novel. Had this been a work of pure fiction, I would have ended it by giving Wallenberg a hero's welcome in Stockholm, Budapest, Washington and throughout the world. That is the ending Raoul Wallenberg so richly deserved. The facts, unfortunately, are far different—a tragedy resulting from the Soviet's paranoia and outrageous conduct and Swedish government's indifference or timidity, or both.

On the way to Debrecen, the Soviet NVKD stopped the Wallenberg convoy and replaced the military escort. NVKD agents took Wallenberg and Langfelder to Bucharest. From Romania, they were flown to Moscow and incarcerated in Lubianka Prison. Long before Winston Churchill coined the term, the Iron Curtain had descended swiftly and decisively behind the courageous Swede.

We know from the NKVD questioning of Lars Berg and others of Wallenberg's coworkers that the Soviets believed Raoul Wallenberg was a spy for the Americans, that he was funded by the Joint Distribution Committee, an organization the Soviets accused of being an international spy ring and that he was their agent in Hungary. German prisoners, who shared a cell with Wallenberg in Lubianka Prison, reported on their release that Wallenberg told them the Soviets had accused him of being a spy for America and Britain.

Where was the Swedish Foreign Ministry when people of other nationalities in Soviet prisons were released in exchange for apprehended Soviet agents? Among those released were Swiss, Vatican and Red Cross officials, and yes, even the hated enemy, the Germans, such as Gustav Richter (Eichmann's representative in Bucharest), Otto Sheur (who served on the Eastern Front), and a host of other Nazis, but not Wallenberg. Why not?

Several theories have been advanced why the Soviets did not release Wallenberg. Stalin, a known anti-Semite and a well-documented paranoiac, was certain that a group of Jewish doctors had almost succeeded in poisoning him and that they had been funded by the Joint Distribution Committee in the United States, the same group that funded the WRC rescue operation led by Wallenberg. Also, Stalin, as soon as Hungary was overrun, installed a Communist puppet government. He did not need a hero like Wallenberg upsetting things as the diplomat had done with the Nazis. Soviet insecurity further manifested itself when Soviet troops reportedly removed, in the dark of night, a commemorative statue of Wallenberg erected in Budapest's St. Stephen's Park.

For his part, Wallenberg probably fueled Soviet suspicions by acknowledging that he worked for Roosevelt. Given his lack of awareness that the Cold War had started before the hot war ended, it undoubtedly seemed reasonable to him to impress his captors that he was no spy. To Stalin's suspicious mind, his openness, of course, had the very opposite effect.

At first, early in the occupation of Hungary, the Soviets let it be known that Wallenberg was in their protective custody. Later, through Deputy Foreign Minister André Vishinski, they claimed that Wallenberg was "unknown to us."

It wasn't until 1957 that Deputy Foreign Minister André Gromyko conceded that Wallenberg had been held in Lubianka Prison but claimed he'd died there of a heart attack in 1947. In other words, Gromyko tacitly admitted that the Soviets had lied for ten years about not knowing Wallenberg. Therefore, why believe their statements in 1957 about his supposed death? There was no way to find out the truth. The Soviet officers who had taken Wallenberg into custody had conveniently disappeared, and the state security chief at that time, Viktor Abakumov, who had been responsible for Wallenberg's incarceration, had been executed in 1955.

Wallenberg's unselfish purpose was certainly alien to the Soviet Communist government and the bureaucrats who served its interests. His proposals for the reconstruction of Hungary and assistance for the Jews would have struck them as a typical cover for espionage. After all, Hungary was not his country and the Jewish faith was not his religion. At that time, for the Soviets, working for the Americans was far more threatening and unforgivable than working for the Germans. Consistency not being a particular virtue of the Soviet leaders, they alternately accused him, at various times, of being a spy for Germany and for the United States!

Yet that alone would not explain why he disappeared permanently into the bowels of the Soviet prison system. After all, real spies, those who did actual damage to the Soviet Union, such as Francis Gary Powers, were exchanged for Russians, without problem.

Another contributing factor was the indifference of the Swedish government. The Swedes, neighbors of the colossus to the east, apparently felt it more important to keep on good terms with the Soviets than to upset them by trying to obtain Wallenberg's release. Perhaps the Swedes thought that if they didn't make waves the Soviets would eventually release him. After all, even the Nazi murderers of the Third Reich had had some respect for diplomatic immunity.

Swedish envoy in Moscow, Staffan Söderblom, more impressed with Stalin than with his own countryman, met with the Soviet leader to inquire about Wallenberg. In his most obsequious manner, Söderblom *volunteered* his own belief that Stalin was *correct*, that Wallenberg had been killed in Budapest in 1945. This freely offered view gave the dictator an open invitation simply to confirm that view and consign Wallenberg to oblivion. If Wallenberg had faced up to the Nazis as Söderblom did to Stalin, there would have been no Jews left in Hungary.

Many opportunities presented themselves to the Swedes to exert pressure on the Soviets. In 1946, Sweden had provided significant trade credits to the Soviets, almost a billion dollars, without obtaining anything in return. The American ambassador to Moscow, Averell Harriman, offered to the Swedish Foreign Ministry, his assistance and the good offices and the prestige of the United States, to intercede on behalf of Wallenberg. The Swedes declined, and not even politely. Too bad, for even if the Soviets could have resisted diplomatic pressure from small Sweden, it would have been far more difficult for them to resist pressure from the United States.

The weak-kneed Swedish Foreign Minister Östen Undén sacrificed Wallenberg on the altar of pristine neutrality. Yet the Swiss, who maintain their neutrality just as scrupulously, acted forcefully when, like Wallenberg, Harald Feller of the Swiss Legation in Budapest was interned in Lubianka by the Soviets. The Swiss, however, did not hesitate or vacillate. They seized several Soviet diplomats in Berne and would not release them until the Soviets coughed up Feller. Why could Sweden not have exchanged the many Soviet citizens it had captured and accused of spying, for Wallenberg? Per Anger, who had been assigned by the government to a committee investigating the Wallenberg case, confronted the Swedish prime minister and foreign minister with that very question. The answer: the Swedish government does not do such things. Anger resigned in frustration.

There have been many reports of sightings of Wallenberg in the Moscow prisons and later, in a Gulag. In the 1960s, a prominent Soviet physician first confirmed that Wallenberg was alive and then, apparently under the furious wrath of Premier Khrushchev, retracted his statement. There is certainly enough anecdotal evidence, much of it extensively researched and detailed in books such as Danny Smith's *Wallenberg: Lost Hero*, Harvey Rosenfeld's *Raoul Wallenberg*, and Per Anger's *With Raoul Wallenberg in Budapest*, that leaves little doubt that Wallenberg had survived well after his alleged death and had been swallowed up by the Soviet prison system.

In the 1980s, the onset of the economic and political restructuring of *perestroika* and the new "Russian openness" of *glasnost* and later, the decline of the Communist Party in the Soviet Union, brought a flurry of diplomatic and private activity on Wallenberg's behalf but still, with no results.

The confluence of bad timing, bad luck and an indifferent Swedish government, it seemed, fostered this outrageous result. It gave new meaning to that tired cliché, no good deed goes unpunished.

Wallenberg had acted at the behest of the American War Refugee Board. He had gone willingly where no American could go, into the maw of the Nazi killing machine in Budapest and, with some of his brave colleagues, had faced down the brutes. Independent of whatever Sweden does or does not do, I believe that the United States should show the same moral courage it expected from Wallenberg and demand that the Russians provide an accurate and honest account of his fate.

And what of Vilmos Langfelder, the brave Hungarian Jew who continually risked his life to protect and transport Wallenberg in his mission to save Jews? Nobody, it seems, took up his cause. Not Sweden—he wasn't a Swede; not Hungary—the Soviet puppet regime wouldn't put itself out on the limb for one of its Jewish citizens, much less one associated with Wallenberg.

Some have suggested that the enormous adverse publicity that would accompany the revelation of the facts about Wallenberg and Langfelder keeps the truth hidden within the bowels of the Kremlin. Yet Russian leaders today are not those of the 1950s, 1960s, or even the 1970s. They have not assumed the mantle of responsibility for the earlier Soviet excesses and crimes. These new leaders have gradually revealed the atrocities Stalin committed against his own citizens and those of the other Soviet republics—and have survived. They have laid bare the great purges—and have survived. They have stripped away the hidden oppression of the NKVD and KGB—and have survived. Surely, they could stand the embarrassment of the truth about Raoul Wallenberg. The Russians owe that to Wallenberg, his family, the people he saved, and the world.

BIBLIOGRAPHY

Adachi, Agnes. *Child of the Winds*. Chicago: Adams Press, 1989.

Anger, Per. *With Raoul Wallenberg in Budapest*. Washington, DC: Holocaust Publications, 1996.

Arendt, Hannah. *Eichmann in Jerusalem, A Report on the Banality of Evil*. New York: Penguin, 1995.

Berg, Lars, *The Book that Disappeared: What Happened in Budapest*. New York: Vantage Press, 1990.

Berk, Eta Fuchs. *Chosen, A Holocaust memoir. As told to Gilbert Allardyce*. Fredericton, NB, Canada: Goose Lane, 1992.

Berk, Stephen M., Ph.D. *The Holocaust*. Schenectady, NY: Union College, 1992. (Audiocassette of lecture.)

Bierman, John. *The Righteous Gentile*. New York: Viking, 1981.

Breitman, Richard. *The Architect of Genocide, Himmler and the Final Solution*. Hanover, NH: Brandeis University Press, 1991.

Chartock, Roselle and Jack Spencer, eds. *Can It Happen Again?* New York: Black Dog & Leventhal, 1995.

Crankshaw, Edward. *Gestapo, Instrument of Tyranny*. New York: Da Capo, 1994.

Davidowicz, Lucy S. *The War Against the Jews*. New York: Bantam books, 1975.

Fleming, Gerald. *Hitler and the Final Solution*. Berkeley: University of California Press, 1984.

Fowler, E.W.W. *Nazi Regalia*. Edison, NJ: Chartwell Books, 1996.

Friedlander, Saul. *Reflections of Nazism: An Essay of Kitsch & Death*. New York: Harper & Row, 1984.

Goldman, Guido. *The German Political System*. New York: Random House, 1974.

Haffner, Sebastian. *The Meaning of Hitler,* trans. Ewald Osers. Cambridge, MA: Harvard University Press, 1979.

Handler, Andrew. *A Man for all Connections-Raoul Wallenberg and the Hungarian State Apparatus, 1944-1945*. Westport, CN: Praeiger, 1996

Hausner, Gideon. *Justice in Jerusalem.* New York: Harper & Row, 1966.

Hitler, Adolf. *Hitler's Table Talk: 1941-1944,* comp. Martin Borman, trans. Norman Cameron and R.H. Stevens. Bungay, Suffolk, U.K.: Richard Clay & Co., 1953.

——. *Mein Kampf,* trans. Ralph Manheim. Boston: Houghton Mifflin Company, 1962.

Höhne, Heinz. The *Order of the Death's Head,* trans. Richard Barry. New York: Coward-McCann, 1970.

Holliday, Laurel. *Children in the Holocaust and World War II: Their Secret Diaries.* New York: Washington Square Press, 1995.

Höss, Rudolph. *Death Dealer.* New York: Da Capo Press, 1996.

Lang, Jochen von and Claus Sibyll, eds. *Eichmann Interrogated: Transcripts from the Archives of the Israeli Police.* New York: Farrar, Strauss & Giroux, 1983.

Lawliss, Charles. *And God Cried, the Holocaust Remembered.* New York: JG Press, 1994.

Lester, Elenore. *Wallenberg, the Man in the Iron Web.* Englewood Cliffs, NJ: Prentice-Hall, 1982

Lévai, Jenö. *Eichmann in Hungary.* New York: Howard Fartig, 1987.

Levy, Alan. *The Wiesenthal File.* Grand Rapids, MI: William B. Eerdmans, 1993.

Lewin, Ronald. *Hitler's Mistakes.* New York: William Morrow & Co., 1984.

Lumsden, Robin. *SS Regalia.* Edison, NJ: Chartwell Books, 1996.

Malkin, Peter and Harry Stern. *Eichmann in My Hands.* New York: Warner Books, 1990.

Marton, Kati. *Wallenberg: Missing Hero.* New York: Random House, 1982.

Nicholson, Michael and David Winner. *Raoul Wallenberg.* Milwaukee: Gareth Stevens, 1989.

Niewyk, Donald, ed. *The Holocaust, Problems and Perspectives of Interpretation.* Lexington, MA: D. Heath & Co., 1992.

Remak, Joachim. *The Nazi Years.* Englewood Cliffs, NJ: Prentice-Hall, 1969.

Reynolds, Quentin. *The Minister of Death.* New York: Viking Press, 1960.

Rosenfeld, Harvey. *Raoul Wallenberg*. New York: Holmes & Meier, 1995.

Shirer, William A. *The Rise and Fall of the Third Reich: A History of Nazi Germany*. New York: Ballantine Books, 1960.

Skoglund, Elizabeth R. *A Quiet Courage: Per Anger, Wallenberg's Co-liberator of Hungarian Jews*. Grand Rapids, MI: Baker Books, 1997.

Smith, Danny. *Wallenberg: Lost Hero*. Springfield, IL: Templegate, 1986.

Stafford, Lillian E. *Raoul Wallenberg Remembered*. Ann Arbor, MI: Michigan Alumnus, May 1985.

Suhl, Yuri, ed. *They Fought Back*. New York: Schocken Books, 1967.

The Swedish Institute. *Raoul Wallenberg*, trans. Victor Kayfetz. Uppsala, Sweden: Ord & Form, 1988.

Toland, John. *Adolf Hitler*. New York: Doubleday, 1976.

Vogt, Hannah. *The Burden of Guilt*, trans. Herbert Strauss. New York: Oxford University Press, 1964.

Wallenberg, Raoul. *Letters and Dispatches*. New York: Arcade, 1995.

Walton-Kerr, Philip St. C. *Gestapo, the History of the German Secret Service*. London: Robert Hale, Ltd., 1939.

Williamson, Gordon. *The SS: Hitler's Instrument of Terror*. Osceola, WI: Motor Books International, 1994.

Wistrich, Robert S. *Who's Who in Nazi Germany*. New York: Routledge, 1995.

Wyman, David S. *Abandonment of the Jews*. New York: Partheon Books, 1984.

Yahl, Leni. *The Holocaust, The Fate of European Jewry*. New York: Oxford Press, 1990.

About the Author

Carl Steinhouse is a retired lawyer and former federal prosecutor for the United States Department of Justice, and thereafter in private practice specializing in class actions, white-collar crime, RICO civil and criminal trials, and criminal and civil antitrust investigations and litigation. He served in the U.S. Army Counterintelligence Corps, with a tour of duty overseas during the Korean War.

He had been active in the National Committee on Soviet Jewry, making several trips to the Soviet Union and to Jerusalem and Helsinki on fact-finding missions. A board member of the Cleveland Anti-Defamation League until 1999, he remains active in ADL matters, including monitoring activities of hate groups.

He is happily married and lives in Naples, Florida, where he does his writing.

Printed in the United States
22538LVS00003B/196